A Guide to Amazing Sandwiches

MAX'S
WORLD OF
SANDWICHES

Max Halley & Ben Benton

Hardie Grant

BOOKS

This book belongs to:

_____ Magali _____

The bacon in my BLT,
the wind in my willows,
the love of my life

PART ONE
SANDWICHES

40 of the most delicious sandwiches ever

PART TWO
COMPONENTS

Loads and loads of brilliant things to help you
make your own mega sarnies

PART ONE: SANDWICHES

**REALLY
EASY**

19

**A BIT LESS
EASY**

49

PART TWO: COMPONENTS

BREADS

137

**MEAT
& FISH**

145

VEGETABLES

185

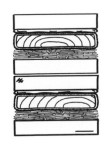

A BIT OF EFFORT

79

LABOUR OF LOVE

103

TAKE A DAY OFF WORK

123

SOFT & CRUNCHY

205

CONDIMENTS & SAUCES

217

PICKLES

251

FOREWORD
BY NED HALLEY
(MAX'S DAD)

Max has taste. I'm not claiming he's fail-safe in matters of the arts or fashion (definitely not fashion), but I'm convinced he's the cat's pyjamas (as his mum would say) in the best sense: the field of flavour. He knows where flavour comes from, and he also knows how to exploit, and explain, its infinite variations.

As a child, he showed early signs. He was omnivorous from the off. Tried anything, ate (nearly) everything. He entertained us by identifying all the ingredients in our cooking (and, in the food shopping), all simply by taste. It was spooky.

We lived (still do) in rural Somerset, where the great annual farming event is the Royal Bath & West Show. It's competitive. Prizes for local produce and, one year, a blind-tasting contest. Max, still a lad but with holiday experience in a pub kitchen, applied.

All the others were chefs and food business professionals, and he still won. The problem round was a tasting of cheeses. Max had (still has) a horror of cheese. On the day he couldn't eat the mystery varieties. But from appearance, texture and smell, he placed the lot: cow, sheep, goat, pasteurised or not, aged or not, and so on.

Local media were amazed. He started appearing on BBC Radio Somerset as a quirky young food expert and soon acquired a following. He now appears regularly across the national media and is a familiar face at food events throughout the country and further afield.

Max's Sandwich Shop in London, award-winning and widely-renowned, marks its tenth anniversary in 2024. Max has put the sandwich on the map and has championed his concise formula for deliciousness – hot, cold, sweet, sour, crunchy, soft – into a veritable culinary mantra.

The secret is simple. Max has a phenomenal palate. To this priceless gift he adds showmanship and an enduring mission to bring joy to all lovers of great food – between two slices of bread or otherwise. In this spectacular book, he brings it all together with animation and lucidity. As a proud father, it is my privilege to commend it to you.

"There are flowers everywhere, for those who wish to see them."

Henri Matisse

Dearest Lovely Everyone,

Of the many salient questions of our time, four currently preoccupy me: is Avi Loeb right and with the discovery of Oumuamua, our solar system has now been visited by something genuinely extra-terrestrial? Will the world as we know it be improved or destroyed by AI, and whose AI will it be? What will the new world order be, now the era of the dominance of the West is over? And, the big one: is a hotdog a sandwich?

I get more DMs than you could shake a 30-foot stick at shouting 'A HOTDOG ISN'T A SANDWICH YOU MORON!' In this mad world, filled with horror, terror, injustice, joy and magic, it blows my tiny mind how cross people get about the existential nature of a sausage sandwich. To clear things up, the answer to the hotdog conundrum is the same as to 'Triangles, rectangles or squares?': Who cares?

Something that does matter, which this book takes very seriously, is deliciousness. Deliciousness isn't a Pollyanna musing or a pointless quibble, it is fundamental, palpable and accessible to everyone. You don't need to have been brought up like this, know about that or have driven an open-top car down the f***ing Amalfi coast to know when something's delicious. We've all had that moment, after taking a bite or a sip of something: BAM! Deliciousness!

Defining a sandwich is more problematic. If you want specifics, I guess it's mostly some kind of bready/fillingy arrangement, but not always. Tricky.

Utilising that fluidity, this book plays fast and loose with the definition of one. There are burgers, hotdogs, bao, kebabs, wraps and all manner of sarnie-esque things. I'm only kind of sorry if that upsets you, because seriously, we might have been visited by aliens!

When cooking from this book, if there's anything you don't like, change it, drop it, do it completely differently, I don't mind, and neither should you.

Like the badass he was, Matisse invented a completely new art-form in his seventies with those massive, beautiful cut-paper pictures. Right to the end, his unwillingness to stop creating and his lack of prosaic, linear ideals about how and what things are or how they should be done, should provide much inspiration to cooks and sandwichers everywhere. When it comes to making your lunch, there's no need to be preoccupied with what things are or aren't, but with what they can and could be. Think of all the opportunities for deliciousness, loitering in the cupboards or lurking in the refrigerator. Dig them out and slap them between two bits of bread with carefree abandon. And please, always remember: anything can go in a sandwich – it might just need throwing in the deep-fat fryer or blending up and mixing into mayonnaise first.

So, with a favourite condiment in hand, some crushed crisps at the ready and a spirit of bready/fillingy adventure nipping at your heels, get yourself a drink, turn the page and let's sandwich the sh*t out of it.

Big love, Max

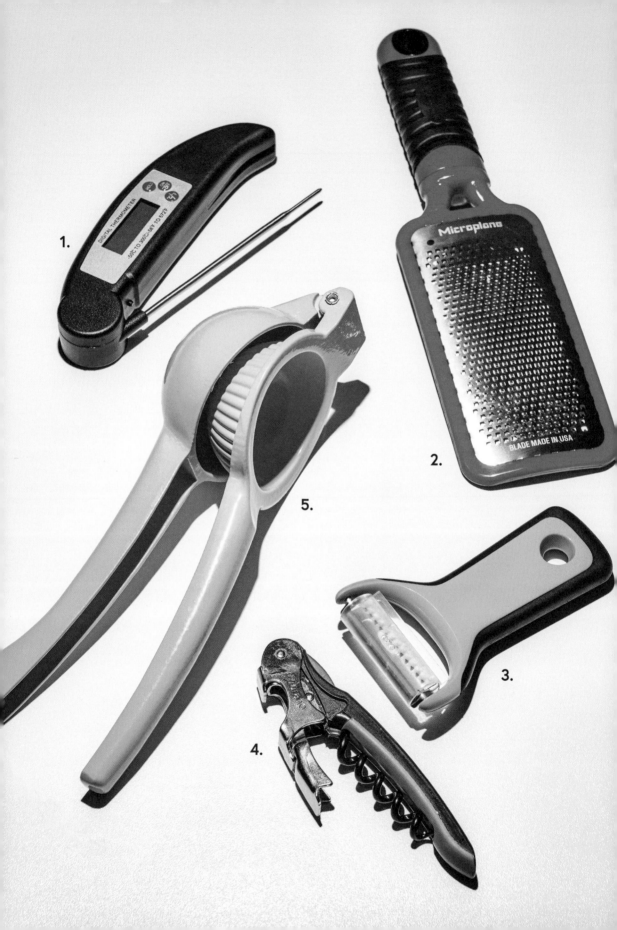

1.

2. Microplane

BLADE MADE IN USA

3.

4.

5.

EQUIPMENT YOU SHOULD INVEST IN

Temperature Probe
Fig. 1.

Imagine if every chicken you roasted, steak you cooked, fish you fried, prawn (shrimp) you barbecued, or custard you attempted was PERFECT...

Microplane
Fig. 2.

Garlic, ginger, chillies, Parmesan, chocolate, nuts, lemon zest, nutmeg and about a million other things, EASY to get thin and tiny all of a sudden...

Oxo Good Grips Julienne Peeler
Fig. 3.

Please buy one, they're brilliant! This one's for julienne/ little sticks, but ALL peelers should be this 'Y' shape. Welcome to the speed peeler team!

Waiter's Friend
Fig. 4.

These are the best corkscrews, end of. And must have either a two-piece or double-jointed metal arm bit. There's a tiny blade for cutting the bottle's foil off nice and neat too!

Citrus Squeezer
Fig. 5.

When life brings you lemons, SQUEEZE THEM LIKE A PRO.

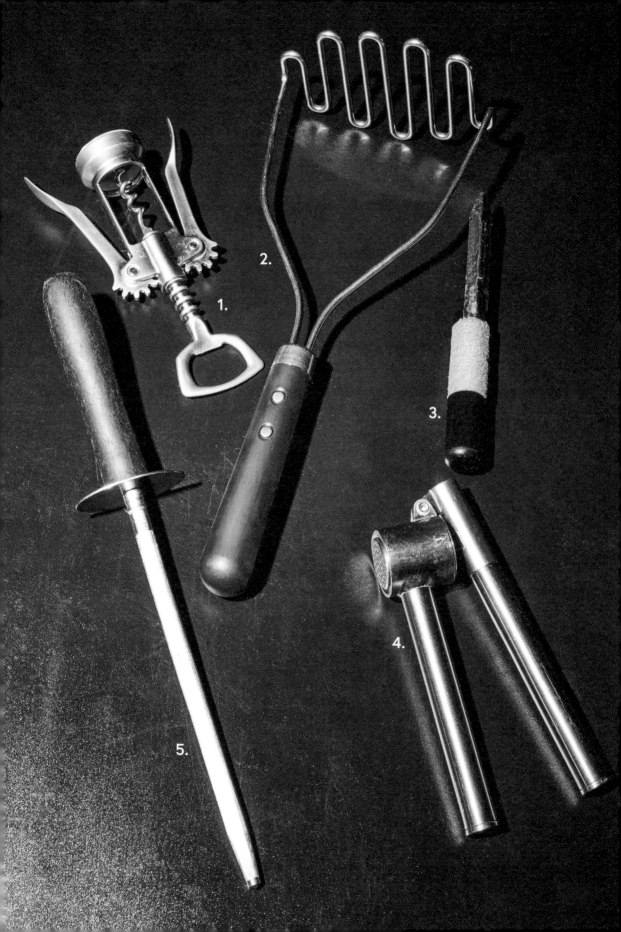

EQUIPMENT THAT YOU SHOULD CHUCK OUT

Winged Corkscrew
Fig. 1.

Always makes you look like you've got the shakes. And you always have to re-screw it in. Rubbish. Get a waiter's friend (see previous page).

Squiggly Masher
Fig. 2.

Chuck it! Get one that forces the potato through little holes and makes your mash more mashy.

Straight Peeler
Fig. 3.

Useless! Everything takes ages, gives you the wrist version of tennis elbow and peels in a horrible way, more akin to grating the skin off something. Peelers should be a 'Y' shape (see previous page).

Garlic Crusher
Fig. 4.

No one ever said 'now turn your garlic into liquid AND bits AND leave half of it in the crusher'. Use a microplane; MILES better (see previous page).

Steel
Fig. 5.

Did that ever successfully sharpen your knife? Technically for KEEPING a knife sharp, not sharpening it. Get a two-stage one that grinds as you pull the knife through.

PART ONE
SANDWICHES

A BRUSCHETTA/PANZANELLA SANDWICH

This is a flavour scud missile of a sandwich. Thankfully though, when the bomb drops, all that comes out is tonnes and tonnes of juice.

This is too much mix for sure, have some on toast tomorrow.

1 crispy, baguette-ish roll, or baguette
(about 15 cm/6 in long)

400 g (14 oz) big, fat, ripe beefsteak, Marmande-type
tomatoes, cores removed and chopped into small chunks

50 g (1¾ oz) onion, grated, in the sink, into a sieve,
on the coarse side of a grater and left to drain
for 30 minutes

50 g (1¾ oz) onion, cut into tiny chunks

2 large garlic cloves, finely grated, sprinkled with
salt and crushed to a moosh with the side of
a big knife on your chopping board

7 g (⅛ oz) salt

20 ml (1½ tablespoons) really good extra virgin olive oil

30 ml (2 tablespoons) lemon juice

7 g (⅛ oz) caster (superfine) sugar

8 basil leaves

The secret of this is to let the mix sit for at least 1 hour after it is made and stir it regularly throughout that time. It is important to let the salt and sugar work their magic, and for everything else to get to know each other. So, bang everything into the bowl apart from the bread and basil and let's pull that rabbit out of the hat.

Once the mixture has sat for at least 1 hour, cut your bread in half lengthways, but not all the way through. Pick out the soft bread from inside, break it up into bits and chuck it into the bruschetta mix. Stir everything about. Tear in the basil.

Spoon the tomato/bread mix into the hollowed out bread, top and bottom, bring the thing together, get a plate, 50 napkins and go, go, go.

This goes down extremely well on a hot summer day with a bottle of that rosé you like and someone you like even more than the rosé, as long as you don't breathe on each other and don't mind being COVERED in juice.

TINKERINGS

Two bottles of rosé?

A PRAWN COCKTAIL SANDWICH

This sarnie, while nothing clever or particularly original, is an amalgamation of simple ideas had, things read and eaten, tried and stolen from all over the place over many years and here they are.

In 2020 I got my dream job and wrote a book for Walkers about crisps sandwiches (check their website). One of the sarnies HAD to involve prawn cocktail crisps and we will be doing that again today.

Richard Corrigan and Simon Hopkinson put brandy in their Marie Rose cocktail sauce, so I do too, but it is of course completely optional. When I was making this I felt the sarnie wanted some pops of acidity beyond the malt vinegar and lemon, so I put a load of pickled cockles from a jar in and absolutely loved it. If it's a bit much for you, just leave them out.

The best prawn cocktail (of sorts) I've ever had was at a lunch cooked by Pierre Koffmann and it had avocado mousse in it. I have neither the time nor the inclination to learn how to make avocado mousse, so there's some sliced in here, quietly bringing its pleasing smoothness to the proceedings.

The last thing to discuss is the bread. Tricky. Some (Heston Blumenthal included) love the softness provided by sliced white bread and say that the lettuce provides crunch enough. Personally, I think it's an abomination to say that lettuce is crunchy. Crisps are crunchy, lettuce is for freshness. I do however agree about the bread, so I've gone for a nice sliced white here. You could hollow out a baguette and skip the crisps if you want to, but I dunno… Sometimes, when the filling of a sandwich is very soft, like egg mayonnaise or prawn cocktail, the softer the bread the better. If the bread is really crunchy, the softer fillings have a tendency to evacuate the sandwich when you bite into it.

---

50 g (1¾ oz) mayonnaise (Hellmann's, Duke's or Kewpie)

25 g (1 oz) tomato ketchup (Heinz or you're in trouble)

Splashes of Tabasco sauce, Worcestershire sauce and malt vinegar, to taste

1 teaspoon brandy or cognac (if there's some lying about, but don't worry if there isn't)

50 g (1¾ oz) frozen, mini North Atlantic prawns (shrimp), defrosted

50 g (1¾ oz) frozen, considerably bigger prawns (shrimp) of similar provenance, defrosted

1 heaped tablespoon pickled cockles from a jar (optional – but really nice)

25 g (1 oz/1¾ tablespoons) extremely soft salted butter

2 slices of nice, fresh, soft, squidgy white bread

2.5-cm (1-in) long piece of cucumber, cut at both ends

Handful of really finely shredded iceberg lettuce

1 teaspoon finely chopped fresh tarragon

Juice of ½ lemon

½ avocado

½ pack of prawn cocktail crisps, crushed

Salt and pepper

Put the mayonnaise and ketchup in a bowl and mix thoroughly. That now needs seasoning, which is very personal, so I'm not giving quantities. Schploof in some malt vinegar, Tabasco and Worcestershire sauce and stir everything together. Try it. Is it delicious? Could it be a little sharper? More vinegar. Spicier? More Tabasco. Richer and rounder? More Worcestershire sauce. Once it's delicious, stir in the booze if you're using it, keep mixing, and bang the seafood in.

Spread the soft butter on both slices of bread with a spoon. Spoons are always better than knives for spreading soft things in sandwiches!

Stand the cucumber straight up on your chopping board. Cut it into about six slices all the way down, discard the first and last slices which will be mostly peel. Lay the remaining slices back on top of each other and cut them into long strips like fat, floppy noodles. Cut those, across, into loads of little cubes and mix them up with the shredded lettuce and chopped tarragon and dress with the lemon juice.

→

Take the avocado, separate the flesh from the skin and cut it into long, thin slices from tip to toe and lay them neatly over the buttered bottom slice of bread.

Heap the prawn cocktail mixture generously on top of the avocado and use a spoon to flatten the heap into an even layer. Put the lemony salad on that. Sprinkle the crushed crisps all over the buttered top slice of bread and press them in gently with your hand. Put the crisped lid on, cut the thing in half gently and fill your boots.

TINKERINGS

You could try salad cream instead of mayo and see what you think? Really, it's just mustardy-vinegary-mayonnaise, whatever anyone says. You could go super fancy and put lobster meat, posher prawns (shrimp), white crab meat, crayfish and all kinds of things to add some glamour. You could put horseradish (fresh or jarred) in the Marie Rose. You could add cream cheese to the sauce to make it thicker and creamier. Chopped, pickled jalapeños might be nice. In *Is This a Cookbook?* Heston Blumenthal says that 'you could make a double quantity of Marie Rose sauce, put half in the salad and have the rest on the side, to dip your sandwich into', which is an excellent idea. He does however, also put vanilla bean paste in the Marie Rose. Knock yourself out.

A SUPERMARKET SANDWICH

This is more a method than a recipe. Like many of the world's most fun people, it is unhealthy, irresponsible and probably best only seen one day a year. I suggest that day be the one when you are so hungover, even Domino's is a no-go – mine's a large Vegi Supreme with extra ham, jalapeños and a stuffed crust by the way. If you're going to the supermarket to buy all the stuff below, get a pack of Snickers Ice Creams, Drumsticks and/or Fruit Pastilles Lollies too.

Enough beige, frozen, mostly breaded supermarket treats of your choice to cover a large baking tray:
onion rings, chicken dippers, fish fingers (fish sticks), turkey dinosaurs, spring rolls, waffles, breaded prawns (shrimp), potato smilies, etc etc
1 huge slug of your favourite hot sauce
(I like Encona for this)
1 decent size bowl of mayonnaise
(I like Hellmann's)

Lots of little schploofs of malt vinegar
(it had better be Sarson's)
1 brand-new, unopened loaf of Hovis-type bread
1 large lump of soft, nice butter on a little plate (I like Kerrygold or that bougie Président stuff) (optional)
A few wedges of lemon for squeezing (optional)

When you get back from the supermarket, put the ice creams in the freezer and preheat the oven to 10°C (50°F) hotter than it says you should on the beige food's bags – we want these puppies crisp.

Get something feelgood and comforting on the TV: *Road Trip, Varsity Blues, Blade, Almost Famous* or *The Vicar of Dibley* for all I care and pause it after the opening credits.

Sling the hot sauce into the mayo with a few schploofs of the vinegar, mix until combined and put the bowl on the table in front of the TV. Put a pile of paper towels, the still unopened bread, the bottle of malt vinegar, extra hot sauce just in case and the butter plate and a spreading knife there too.

Put the frozen goodies (not the ice creams) on a baking tray and slam them in the oven. Set a timer for half their cooking time, go upstairs and put your pyjamas on. Wear a dressing gown if you've got one. Wear your slippers if you have them or cosy socks if you don't.

When the timer goes off, use two spoons to turn every item in the oven over and put them back in. Set another timer for the second half of the cooking.

Make a cup of strong milky tea.

Choose your favourite plate. When the timer goes off, switch the oven off, take the tray out and put the plate in the oven for a minute to warm up. Dump everything onto the plate and go and sit down, taking the tea with you.

Sprinkle everything on the plate with malt vinegar. Take a few paper towels for greasy fingers, put them on your lap and open the bread. Press play. Put three or four items at a time across the middle of a piece of bread, fold it over and dunk it into the spicy mayo. Eat and repeat, until you no longer can. Go and get an ice cream. Lie back down.

Fall asleep. Go to bed when you wake up there at 4 a.m.

TINKERINGS
If you're feeling cheffy, butter the bread and swap the vinegar for wedges of lemon. Yes, you can have ketchup, you can have anything you want.

AN OPEN SANDWICH

I'm sorry, but this can't be in this book.
It isn't a sandwich.
It's stuff on bread, or occasionally toast.

JAMBON BEURRE, AKA LE PARISIEN

I'll fess up now, this sandwich is in the first sandwich book, but it's just so great
I wanted to go at it again! Hope you don't mind. The Jambon Beurre is a Parisian classic.
Traditionally made with just three ingredients: baguette, butter and (cooked) ham.
It is either a welcome reminder of the truth in those 'simple things' clichés, or a culinary
travesty akin to claiming that making popcorn is cooking.

Despite the proliferation of protestations from digitally confident people about the
'purity' of this sandwich and how little it should ever be messed with, Paris's vendors offer
countless variations on the theme. I've had ones with cheese, mustard, mayonnaise, onions,
cured Parma-type ham and quite frankly cornichons are always welcome at the party.
Three Michelin-starred French chef Daniel Boulud puts grated Comté, cornichons and fresh,
grated horseradish in his, so let's face it, the floodgates are open.

At home when sticking to the classic contents, which I mostly do, I've found a very thin
baguette makes all the difference as it makes the most of the crunch while keeping the
bread-to-filling ratio in favour of the butter and ham.

---

1 nice long bit (20 cm/8 in) of the thinnest and best
  baguette you can find
2 heaped tablespoons really good salted butter,
  softened
A heap of the best cooked ham you can buy
  (or have made, page 156), thinly sliced

Small handful of (ideally Maille Extra Fine) cornichons
  and a few of the onions from the jar if they're about,
  cut in half lengthways (optional)
Salt

Cut the baguette in half lengthways, but not all the way through, and crack it open.

Cover every millimetre of the inside of the baguette with butter (top and bottom)
and scatter it lightly with salt.

Pile in the ham with a spirit of generosity and if using, scatter the cornichons and dinky
onion halves about the place, close the trap door and get busy!

TINKERINGS

In Ambrose Heath's *Pig Curing and Cooking* (1952) he suggests a few sandwiches with the Jambon Beurre's
ingredients that couldn't be more different. The first is made by putting a mixture of cooked ham and butter
through a mincer. This meaty moosh is put between two slices of bread (mustard may be added), the whole
sandwich is then dipped in a mix of salt, milk and egg, then fried until a 'delicate brown'. He also suggests smearing
mashed potato on both sides of a slice of ham and putting that in a sandwich before dipping it in egg, then into
breadcrumbs and frying that. Who says we've progressed?

A LEFTOVER DAUPHINOISE TOASTED CROISSANT
AND/OR
A LEFTOVER LASAGNA TOASTED CROISSANT

My obsession with stuffing croissants with things with melty, gooey potential, crushing them in my toastie machine and grilling the hell out of them has been going on for nearly ten years now. Quite frankly, Parma ham in an untoasted croissant is a great breakfast and I don't know why more people don't do it.

1 croissant
50 g (1¾ oz) grated supermarket mozzarella
1 slab of leftover Dauphinoise (page 192)
   or lasagna

Some condiments of your choice (optional)
Drizzle of honey

Get the toastie machine on to heat up.

Cut the croissant all down one side and open it up like a book. Sprinkle half the mozzarella on the bottom. Slap the slice of leftover dauphinoise or lasagna on top of that and put the other half of the cheese on top.

Consider condiments. The lasagna doesn't need anything barring maybe hot sauce or maybe some 'Nduja if you're that way inclined. The dauphinoise however, loves mustard (Dijon particularly) and anything truffle-y (oil/mayo/paste, etc). If you're gonna do either, smear or drizzle whatever it is all over the inside top of the croissant before closing the thing up.

Depending on the depth of the trays in your machine, and the size of the croissants you've used, you might need to cut the croissant in half and put the two halves in separately to get the lid closed. If you've used little croissants, they'll probably fit quite neatly into each triangle toastie tray. Stuff will probably run out a bit, but it's worth it. Sit back and wait for the magic to happen. When you get the croissant out of the machine and have let it cool a little, drizzle with honey before devouring.

TINKERINGS

It was making the lasagna version of this at home, the morning after having lasagna for dinner, that I got the idea for the Sandwich Shop Lasagna Sandwich (page 127), which doesn't have lasagna in it but tastes like EXACTLY LIKE LASAGNA. Five lasagnas in one sentence – this is practically Dickens.

THE IN-A-RUSH-FOR-A-TRAIN-BECAUSE I-GOT-UP-LATE SUPERMARKET ROTISSERIE CHICKEN SANDWICH

One trip to the supermarket, one massive sandwich. I've been doing this for decades and it has always brought me great joy, got me funny looks on the train and made me the biggest boss in the carriage to some, and disgusting to others. Welcome to the club. Sandwich.

I understand the provenance of these chickens is questionable, but occassionally, needs must.

Before I get inside the supermarket, I psyche myself up, and remember the order I need to do everything in, so I can work with maximum efficiency. I'm already stressed because there's a train to catch, I'm doubtless hungover and I haven't had breakfast.

I sail in through the doors of the supermarket and grab a basket. A quick 'hello' to the person working the cigarette counter and I ask 'where's the free disposable cutlery please?' I get myself some if they're available or find out what aisle they're in.

You know where I am now, I'm in the fruit and veg! I grab a bag of shredded iceberg lettuce from the weird refrigerator/shelf thing, with a little shame but complete acceptance in my heart. Next, a tub of coleslaw and I'll try to spot the coriander (cilantro). I never get posh coleslaw, always the cheap one, much better. I grab the coriander.

Like a lion looking for gazelles, I scope the room for crisps, which are sometimes here. If they are, I'm taking Salt and Vinegar or Prawn Cocktail, depending on my mood. Sometimes the hot rotisserie chickens are in this bit too, in that funny cupboard and, if they are, I get myself one, and always a whole one.

Next, the condiment aisle for hot sauce (Tabasco or Encona) and a jar of jalapeños. I know. I'm a baller. Very occasionally I might get some pickle slices, sweet ones like Mrs Elswood, but not this time.

Now, to the bakery. I grab a half baguette because I'm a big, greedy man. Would I recommend you get the same? No, I'd recommend you do whatever you think is responsible...

If the hot, cooked chickens are by the butcher section not near the front, as they sometimes are nowadays, I pick a nice plump-looking one, cooked as recently as possible for maximum succulence, procure myself the cutlery if necessary, grab a small pack of wet wipes or tissues and head to the self-service area to pay.

Sadly I take a bag, because I don't carry a tote and without a bag this just wouldn't be possible. Beep, beep, beep at the till and I dash for the train.

On the train, I go as far down as possible, hoping for an empty carriage so I'm not so embarrassed by what I am about to do. I do not sit at a table seat, oh no, too exposed. I get the baguette out and rip a line all the way down it with my finger or a plastic knife. Then, spoon and a fork in hand, I shred the whole chicken, inside its bag, like the waiter or waitress does with your crispy duck at a Chinese restaurant. I use the cutlery like tongs and start shovelling the meat into the baguette, followed by some jalapeños, the coleslaw, lashings of hot sauce, some cursory lettuce and the coriander ripped up a bit. I look up, proud, but shy. No one has seen me. I take another bite, it tastes even better than the first, and my hangover slips by as quickly as Woking.

TINKERINGS

Did I or did I not buy a bag of Tangfastics and a cold Coca Cola? You decide.

A BLACK PUDDING AND CRISP OMELETTE SANDWICH

Where would we be without eggs? Scratch that, where would be without crisps? I have a great love of cheap tortilla sandwiches from Spanish petrol stations, especially when they have garlic mayo in them. This led me to making Spanish tortilla-type and classic French-type omelettes for breakfast sandwiches at home and I've never looked back. I read that El Bulli (very fancy and now closed, best restaurant in the world-type-place, run by chef Ferran Adrià) used to have crisp omelettes for staff lunch. I kept that in my omelette arsenal, and now often have this tortilla/classic omelette hybrid sandwich for breakfast or lunch. Life's a dreamboat!

---

1 normal sausage-sized Spanish morcilla or an equivalent amount of firm, English-type black pudding, skin removed

3 free-range eggs

2 tablespoons extra virgin olive oil

2 tablespoons garlic mayo (page 220)

1 mini baguette (or 15-cm (6-in) length of normal baguette), split lengthways but not all the way through

25 g (1 oz) ready salted crisps (chips) of your choice (but they have to be actual potato crisps, like Kettle Chips or Walkers/Lays, nothing made from reconstituted potato will do the job), given a little crush in the bag

Salt and pepper

If you have morcilla, at room temperature, cut down the sausage with a knife and empty it out of its skin into a big bowl (discard the skin), crack the eggs into the bowl, add salt and pepper and whisk, whisk, whisk the whole lot up together with a big balloon whisk until it's all foamy.

If you have English-type, firmer black pudding, or the Spanish stuff from Burgos with the rice in it, fry in a hot pan in some veg oil until browned and with a bit of a crust. Using a spoon, break it up into little bits and keep frying for 30 seconds or so. Empty the pan onto a plate with a few paper towels on it and let the bits cool down a little. Crack the eggs into a bowl and whisk, whisk, whisk with a balloon whisk until they are foamy.

Whack the crisps into your beaten eggs (now's the time to put the fried black pudding in if you did that rather than morcilla) and gently stir everything about. Let it sit for 2 full minutes.

Put a non-stick frying pan (skillet) on a medium heat with 1 tablespoon of olive oil in it. Once hot, tip the contents of your egg bowl into the pan and gently stir it around, moving from the outside to the middle and shaking the pan to flatten the thing out. Once the bottom layer of egg has set (about 30 seconds/1 minute depending on how hot you've got it), run a spatula round the edge of the pan to loosen the omelette. Give the pan a little shake to check the thing is slipping around as a whole (if it isn't, let it cook a bit more) and slide it out of the pan on to a big, flat plate, just larger than your frying pan. Put a second, similar plate on top, upside down, and flip the thing over. Put the second tablespoon of oil into the pan and let that get hot, then slide the omelette off plate two back into the frying pan and cook for another 45 seconds(-ish). Some runniness inside is delicious and not to be sniffed at.

In that time, quickly smear the mayo all over the inside of your baguette. Tilt the frying pan and using your spatula, starting at the highest side of the pan, roll the omelette over itself (messily) into a loose tube and straight into the baguette. Gracias, Ferran.

TINKERINGS

You could drop the black pudding completely and just do the crisps (chips). And you could use mayo without garlic. And you could definitely add some hot sauce. And all the other components of a fried breakfast.

TRIANGLES?

SQUARES?

RECTANGLES?

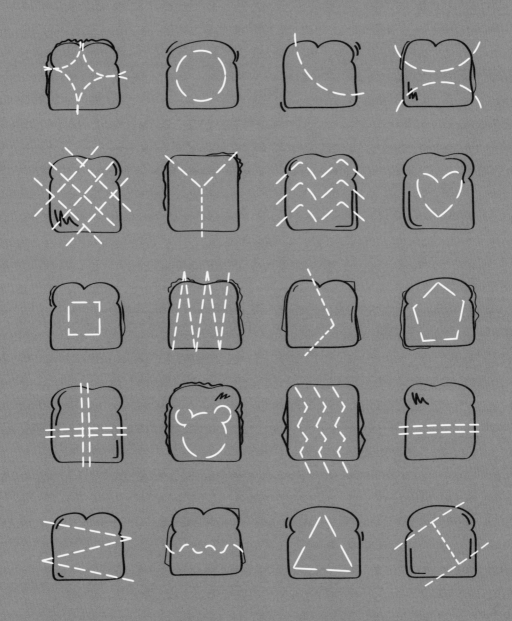

WHO CARES!

PAN BAGNAT

Meaning 'bathed bread', the Pan Bagnat is fundamentally a Salade Niçoise sandwich and some of Nice's finest work. Made right, it is every bit as good as its more famous cousin and one of the only sandwiches in the world that gets better and better for at least 12 hours after you make it. This sarnie superpower, brought about by squishing and lashings of vinaigrette, sits it proudly at Zeus' right hand in the picnic pantheon. #picniclikeaboss

Whether it's in a kid's lunchbox, sunning yourself in Nice, stood in the biting February wind on Skegness seafront or chugging round the Greek islands on your own private boat, this puppy's a 10/10 banger.

Traditionally just olive oil and lemon juice are used for the vinaigrette, but I prefer it mustardy in this instance, so that's what you're gonna get.

---

1 big crusty roll (plenty of crust is a must)

8 small, black/browny/purply olives with stones (ideally Empeltre, Arbequina or Niçoise types)

1 x 150 g (5½ oz) ish (undrained weight) tin of posh tuna in oil (Ortiz is great), drained (you will need some of the oil for the dressing)

2 or 3 big, fat slices of ripe tomato (depends how big they are)

½ small onion, sliced about 1 mm (too thin to convert to a fraction of an inch!) thick and soaked in cold water for 5 minutes, then well drained

8 slices of cucumber

⅓ red (bell) pepper, deseeded and sliced

6 anchovy fillets in oil (Cantabrian if possible), cut in half lengthways (save the oil for the dressing)

1 heaped teaspoon capers (if salted, soaked in water for 10 minutes, then drained)

1 x 9-minute hard-boiled egg (some people like runnier, I think it's creepy), sliced (page 211)

4 Little Gem lettuce leaves (not the really dark green, outside ones)

For the vinaigrette:

½ garlic clove, grated

1 teaspoon Dijon mustard

2 tablespoons tuna tin oil

1 tablespoon anchovy tin oil

1 tablespoon extra virgin olive oil

2 tablespoons lemon juice

Whisk up all the vinaigrette ingredients.

Cut the bread completely in half.

Push the stones out of the olives and discard them – the olives'll break up loads but that doesn't matter.

Put 2 tablespoons of vinaigrette on both the inside top and bottom of your bread and let it soak in for 2 minutes.

Put all the tuna on the bottom of the bread in an even layer with 1 tablespoon of vinaigrette drizzled evenly over it. Then the tomatoes, onions , cucumber and red pepper. Dot the olives, anchovies and capers about next and finish with the egg slices and a final tablespoon of vinaigrette. Last thing is the lettuce leaves. Put the lid on, give it a bit of a squish and wrap the whole thing tightly in three layers of cling film (plastic wrap).

Now you need to press this overnight. You can do this in the refrigerator if you worry about that kind of thing, at home I do it in a cool room somewhere, and don't worry too much about it. I'd recommend you do it in the refrigerator though, obviously.

Take a wooden chopping board and start pressing down onto the sandwich until it has significantly flattened, by about 40-50% probably. Now find a weight to keep it there (about 2 kg/4½ lb per sandwich, roughly). Balance is key, as the weight can easily fall off and the pressing will fail. In an ideal world you'll be making four of these and you can put one sandwich beneath each corner of the board, then stack things on top pretty willy-nilly. This, along with a cling-filmed brick or two, is what your granny's cast-iron skillet was made for.

You could try it with two boiled eggs to redress the balance and change the vibe a bit. Some might put basil in. Aspirational restaurants that do a Salade Niçoise always seem to do it with tuna steak instead of tinned and with boquerones (those white, pickled anchovies) rather than the salted ones and you could most certainly do that here too. If you happen to have it, there's a recipe in my first book (page 191) for confit tuna which would be great in here. I'm also sure if you slam 'confit tuna' into Google or ask the chatbot about it or whatever, you can find someone much less handsome to show you how to do it.

This sandwich can also be made MASSIVE by cutting the top off and hollowing out a whole loaf of bread, filling it with vast quantities of the things listed here, popping the lid back on, wrapping it in many layers of cling film, pressing it overnight beneath something genuinely heavy (at least 10 kg/24 lb) and eating it the next day, sliced like a massive cake!

SCALLOP AND BACON BUN

Brought to my attention by Holly Chaves, never mind Marco Pierre White's leek and lobster terrine, THIS is the ultimate meeting of the land and the sea. There's also a good chance it is the greatest breakfast sandwich of all time.

Made famous at the Billingsgate Cafe this is, as far as I can tell, the only good thing about getting up at 5 a.m. to buy some fish.

My favourite bacon is smoked streaky and normally it's all I go near, but here, I think it has to be unsmoked back bacon as you'd have in the caff at the fish market.

The only change I've made to the caff's sarnie is the mayonnaise. Feel free to leave it out, but I won't goddammit, I just won't.

At least 4 scallops (the biggest, best ones
   you can find, roes attached)
3 slices of unsmoked back bacon
Glug of extra virgin olive oil
1 crusty roll

1 heaped tablespoon mayonnaise
1 tablespoon butter (soft is good)
Hot sauce, lemon juice or malt vinegar,
   or a touch of all three (optional)
Salt

Put the scallops on paper towels and press more paper towels on top, so that they're nice and dry.

I have written before about cooking bacon (*Max's Sandwich Book*, BLT recipe) but that's in the context of smoked streaky, so I won't bore you again.

Get a pan (non-stick if possible) on a medium heat and get it hot.. Put the bacon in and, flipping it regularly, cook it until it's a little browned and the fat has begun to render but it is no way near crisp (2–3 minutes total, maybe less). Take it out of the pan. Crisp bacon is for crumbling into salads, not putting in sandwiches, unless you're going to blend it up and mix it into mayonnaise OBVS (page 220).

Leave the pan on the heat, increase the heat to high, put a good glug of olive oil in and get it really hot.

Remove the paper towels from the top of your scallops and sprinkle them with salt.

Put them salted-side down, clockwise, in a circle in the pan, starting at midday. Don't move them. Season what was the bottom, and is now the top, with salt and let them sit and sizzle for 2 minutes, still without moving them. After 2 minutes, flip them over in the order they went in the pan and leave them there, on the heat, for 1 minute. Take the pan off the heat, throw the bacon back in to warm up again and do not move the scallops.

Slather the inside top half of the roll in the mayonnaise and the bottom in butter. Put the bacon on the butter and the scallops on top of that. Decide if you're having hot sauce, lemon juice, malt vinegar or the whole triumvirate. Feel free to have nothing else at all, apart from a cup of tea the colour of He-Man.

TINKERINGS
I've probably sinned enough with the mayo, hot sauce and other ungodly delights.

A HOT CROSS BUN WITH
SALTED CARAMEL ICE CREAM

The problem with ice-cream sandwiches not in choux buns tends to be that the ice cream slips out the sides. Many of the cookie-clad ice-cream sandwiches I've had end up with me holding two cookies in one hand and WHOOSH, my ice cream heading for the pavement. Not here my friends: 'Make it like a Maritozzi!' That's what we said. No, we didn't, Ben said it, while I frantically Googled Maritozzi.

You could leave out the crumbs here if you like, but I wouldn't, they are fun and delicious and add a whole new dimension, and they look like Grape-Nuts, which is cool.

---

1 hot cross bun (whatever your favourite is – I like them all, but not so much when they have additions of chocolate and things), plus an extra ½ a bun
1 tablespoon caster (superfine) or light brown sugar

A squeeze of pomegranate molasses or REALLY old balsamic vinegar (see trick on page 241)
1 huge scoop of salted caramel ice cream

Preheat the oven to 140°C (275°F). Didn't see that coming in an ice-cream sandwich, did you?

Toast the hell out of the extra half a hot cross bun in the toaster, let it go cold and blitz it to little chunks in a food processor. Put those on a baking tray and sprinkle all over with the sugar, mix it all up and bang the tray in the oven. Every 10 minutes get the tray out and push all the crumbs round with a spatula. Do this for about 20–30 minutes, then tip the crumbs onto a piece of greaseproof paper, scraping everything off the tray with the spatula. Let them go cold and pop them back in the food processor for another quick whizz until they're mostly the size of really big breadcrumbs. They should be super crunchy and delicious, not burned.

Take the fresh, whole hot cross bun and cut a slit most of the way into it along one of the sides. You're making a pocket in it. Open that up as best you can and squish the insides a bit with your finger. Drizzle the pomegranate molasses or old balsamic inside.

Take a tablespoon of ice cream at a time, roll it in your cold, hot-cross bun crumbs, pressing some into it, then spoon the ice cream inside the bun. Keep going like this until you can't get any more ice cream in. Pop this on the shelf of your freezer for 10 minutes to firm everything back up a bit. Get it out and squeeze and mould the bread (carefully, without crushing it or driving the ice cream out somewhere). Last thing is to roll the exposed ice cream on the front in more of the crumbs and get stuck in.

TINKERINGS

If you wanna push the boat out, buy some REALLY old balsamic vinegar. I bought a 12-year-old one from souschef.co.uk that was insanely expensive, and I'm embarrassed to say, it's absolutely amazing. The stuff's like bloody treacle, sweet and sour, it's as good on steak as it is on ice cream, and I thought only pomegranate molasses could do that. There is a sneaky trick from the 1990s to get balsamic a bit like this, for much less money on page 241.

You could try different buns, you could try different ice creams, you could try different buns AND different ice creams… Cinnamon ice cream would be AMAZING! As long as it looks a bit like a Maritozzi (ask the chatbot) it doesn't really matter and now we all know what one is, Ben'll let us do anything we like.

A BIT LESS

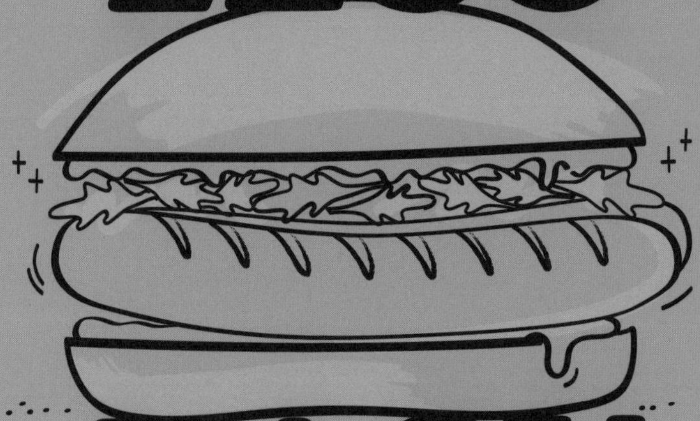

EASY

A CELERIAC TONNATO SANDWICH

I love celeriac, and I love tonnato sauce. I would never have thought of putting the two together, but luckily for me one of England's best cooks, Paul Merrony (of Newell French Bistro in Sherborne, Dorset) did it for me. One of the starters at his and his wife Tracey Peterson's wonderful restaurant is slices of (cooked) celeriac with a tonnato dressing. So simple, so delicious. People are funny about tonnato, which is traditionally a dish of cold poached veal, with a tuna dressing. Sounds weird, wait until you try it!

MAKES 2 – MAKE A FRIEND'S DAY

1 small celeriac (celery root) (way too much, but you want leftovers)

6 tablespoons extra virgin olive oil

2 large free-range eggs

1 x 100-g (3½-oz) (drained weight) tin of cheap tuna (in oil or water – whatever you've got), drained

Juice of ½ lemon

6 tablespoons mayo (I like Hellman's)

4 slices of nice, soft white bread

8 anchovy fillets, cut in half lengthways, tin oil kept (get the Cantabrian ones, if possible)

1 heaped tablespoon capers, drained (if salted, soaked in water for 10 minutes, then drained)

The leaves from a few sprigs of fresh oregano/marjoram

2 handfuls of crushed ready salted crisps

Salt and pepper

Preheat the oven to 180°C (350°F).

Cut the top and bottom off the celeriac and peel it with a vegetable peeler. Lay a big sheet of foil in front of you, put the celeriac in the middle, pour 2 tablespoons of the olive oil all over it and rub it in everywhere. Wash your hands, sprinkle salt all over the greased root, wrap it up in the foil with a scrunch at the top, so it's easy to undo later, pop it on a baking tray and bang it in the oven for 1½ hours. Once the time is up, take it out, undo the scrunch, open it up, watching for steam, and push a skewer into it from the top heading all the way to the bottom. If there is any resistance in the middle at all, it isn't cooked through. So re-scrunch it and back in the oven it goes. Once it is completely soft all the way through, it is done. When just so, take it out, keep it scrunched up and set it aside.

While the root is cooking, boil the eggs for 9 minutes (page 211), then run under the cold tap (faucet) until you can handle them. Peel and slice them into rounds, nice and thin.

Make the tonnato sauce. Put the tuna in a Pyrex jug (heatproof pitcher) or the cylindrical pot thing your stick blender came with. Add the remaining olive oil, a tablespoon of anchovy tin oil, a big grinding of black pepper, a pinch of salt and the lemon juice. Blend until smooth. Weird I know. Wait though.

Mix the blended tuna into the mayonnaise. Congratulations! You have just made a blagger's version of tonnato sauce and slipped seamlessly into the upper echelons of Italy's gastronomic scene. Give the sauce a taste. Does it need more lemon or more salt? If you think so, bang some in. Get your celeriac out of the foil, put it on its side and cut whole slices off it about 7 mm (¼ in) thick. Two per sandwich I'd say. Lay them separately on a plate and douse them with the tonnato sauce. Be bold.

Put the saucy celeriac on the bottom bits of bread and slather the top bits of bread with more sauce. Lay the slices of boiled egg all over the celeriac. Put the slithers of anchovy everywhere in some checkerboard-type pattern and dash the capers about. Sprinkle the oregano/marjoram leaves about the place. Don't they smell lovely?!

Sprinkle the saucy tops with the crushed-up crisps, put the lids on and get straight in there. There's celeriac and sauce left, isn't there? Keep reading.

→

Instead of making a sandwich with this (or indeed as well as), you can lay celeriac slices on a big serving plate, dress liberally with the sauce, put the anchovy fillets, egg slices and capers on in some kind of attractive pattern, sprinkle the oregano on, and email The Newell to say thank you to Paul and Tracey for giving you one of the great, surprisingly doable, dinner party starters that no one saw coming. Serve it with good toasted bread and you're on the way to Michelin stars.

You can make this sauce whenever you like as a great way to transform leftover roast meat into another, rather glamorous meal. It literally goes with anything. Tweet me or X me, or whatever.

AN ODE TO ADANA HOTDOG

Named after a city in Southern Turkey, an Adana is my favourite kebab. Minced, spiced, fatty lamb wrapped around a big flat skewer, grilled over coals and garnished with delicious sauces and loads of onions, it's enough to make you believe in magic and a welcome reminder of all a sandwich/kebab can be.

Is a hotdog a sandwich? Oh whatever... My dear friend Owen Barratt (he of the Birthday Wrapwich on page 86) and I throw these hotdog parties at places because Owen makes amazing sausages and I do the other bits well. At some of those parties, we make this hotdog. Owen makes special lamb sausages, bound with the things you'd get in an adana: onion, red (bell) pepper, pul biber, cumin, salt and pepper. I've done it here with a nice merguez, because telling you to make sausages might be a step too far.

One of the secrets to a great hotdog is steaming the bun! It's really worth it. Just make sure to cut it before steaming. They go really soft and become an even better, less intrusive vehicle for the sausage and the other goodies than when they are warmed up in a conventional oven or used straight out the pack. Whether you have a proper steamer, one of those bamboo things or a colander or sieve on top of a saucepan of boiling water, pop the buns in for 30-ish seconds until they're real soft and away you go.

This hotdog came about via a sarnie shop sandwich called An Ode to Adana that was in turn based directly on the best adana that I ever had, which was somewhere in Istanbul. Sadly, due to being at a wedding, imbibing with enthusiasm and accidentally getting on the wrong boat across the Bosphorus, that is all the information I can give you.

I lived on Green Lanes (Grand Parade) in North London for many years and if you're ever in London you MUST head up there for lunch and/or dinner. To get your hands on the exact kebab I so love, go to Gökyüzü (26–28 Grand Parade) when they're not too busy, and order 'one large Adana please, in a wrap, but in pide bread [pronounced pead-eh], not lavash, with onions, sumac, parsley, pomegranate molasses, cacik [ja-jik] and chilli sauce. Thank you.' Welcome to the fam.

To make recreating this easier at home, you could arguably buy tzatziki in the supermarket to use instead of the cacik and you could use a favourite store-bought hot sauce. But, if you wanna go for it, which I hope you do, recipes for cacik and an appropriate chilli sauce are given in the back, and it is DEFINITELY worth it!

---

1 huge merguez sausage or 2 small ones

1 heaped tablespoon Cacik (page 239)

1 hotdog bun, a nice posh one if you live near a good bakery, or a supermarket one, ideally steamed (see intro)

2 heaped tablespoons of Istanbul Onions (page 187)

1 tablespoon Chilli Sauce (page 244)

This sausage wants grilling and blistering and browning quite heavily (on a barbecue, or under your cooker's grill). Alternatively, cook it in a pan with a bit of oil, but do so hotter and quicker than you normally would a sausage.

Smear the cacik all over the inside of the bun and pop the banger in. Heap the onions generously on top of the sausage, zigzag hot sauce on as best you can, ready a large stack of napkins and congratulate yourself, you're having one of the great lunches.

TINKERINGS

Over my dead body. I'll forgive asking for garlic sauce instead of cacik, but that's it.

THE SABICH

This dreamy staple of the Israeli street food scene has origins as hotly contested as the Choripan (page 71). I'm gonna steer clear of that though and just say how delicious I think it is. Making the amba is the most laborious part and like pretty much everything else in this, it's all doable in advance. As long as you keep the cooked aubergine slices warm (in a baking tray with foil on it?! In a low oven?) and have someone on pitta toasting duty, you could knock loads of these out for a tonne of people and satisfy a crowd. And the amba bears a distinct resemblance to piccalilli, which brings me great personal joy.

Extra virgin olive oil, for frying

2 big, thick (1–1.5 cm/½-⅝ in) round slices of aubergine (eggplant)

1 best-quality pitta bread you can find

2 tablespoons hummus (page 201) or your favourite store-bought one

2 tablespoons tahini (I like Al Yaman and please remember, whatever tahini you have, to always stir the hell out of the jar first)

1 big gherkin, sliced into rounds

1 x 10 minute hard-boiled egg (page 211), sliced into rounds

3 tablespoons amba (page 237)

2 heaped tablespoons Israeli Salad (page 201)

Salt

Get a frying pan on with a good lot of olive oil in it (about 2 mm/¹⁄₁₆ in deep) and get it medium-hot. Fry the aubergine slices in the oil for 3-5 minutes, until they are golden and soft with zero rawness left in them. (Cooked = golden/oily/squidgy/floppy; Raw = pale/dry/firm/not floppy.) Once cooked, put them on a plate, on some paper towels and give them a good sprinkle of salt.

Pop the pitta in the toaster and get it nice and hot. If it's round, crack it open and if it's oval, cut it in half and build as two halves. Smear hummus all over the insides of the bread.

Flop two bits of warm aubergine in (or flop one in each half), and drizzle them with tahini. Arrange the gherkin slices in a layer everywhere and the same with the boiled egg. Smear/drizzle amba everywhere, bundle in the salad getting it right to the bottom and you're done! Mazel tov!

TINKERINGS

I keep thinking how nice some chopped up guindillas (those green pickled chillies) would be in here, but it doesn't want much messing with, I don't think. My friend Itamar (of Honey & Co fame) makes his with fried eggs, which is definitely a good idea! I made one recently with a poached egg in there once, which I'm not convinced was worth the effort and I have occasionally added a spoonful of thick, full-fat yoghurt which has been nice, but similarly I'm not 100% convinced.

GARLIC BREAD/A SPRING ONION SANDWICH

At the tender age of 41, I hope to be only halfway through a life-long love affair with garlic bread. A few years ago, after a long and loyal relationship, the penny dropped and I realised that my beloved frozen supermarket garlic breads were not only lacking in butter, garlic and parsley, but in joy and deliciousness generally.

I came up with this as a replacement, which is fundamentally a spring onion (scallion) sandwich and as much as I love it served classically with lasagna, or pasta and tomato sauce, it's also great with steak, alongside a Sunday roast or dunked in Heinz Tomato Soup.

Despite my best efforts, it's hard to get away with serving a sandwich as a side dish. Somehow though, this gets away with it. My friend Jamie Green says it's the best garlic bread in the world and requests it whenever he comes to stay, and who am I to argue?

½ big bunch of parsley (flat or curly),
250 g (9 oz/2¼ sticks) salted butter, cut into chunks
4-finger pinch of salt
8 big, fat garlic cloves, peeled
Juice of ½ a lemon

1 fresh, squeaky bunch of spring onions (scallions), any floppy bits removed
1 big supermarket ciabatta from a packet or the bakery section

First, preheat the oven to 200°C (400°F).

Pop the parsley (stalks and all), butter, salt, garlic and the lemon juice in a food processor and whizz it until a relatively uniform green colour. You could also hand-chop everything and mash it with a fork, but still grate the garlic and smoosh it together with the salt on a chopping board with the side of your biggest knife or the back of a spoon, into a purée.

Discard the top 5 mm (¼ in) and rooty bottoms of the spring onions and thinly slice the entire lot (white and green) into rounds. Give them a jumble to mix up green and white.

Cut the ciabatta in half completely and slather the inside top and bottom with **all** the butter, from edge to edge, leaving no bread unbuttered.

Sprinkle all the spring onions evenly over the bottom half of the bread, put the lid on and give it a gentle squish. Wrap the whole caboodle tightly in two layers of kitchen foil, round and round, and pop it straight on to the oven shelf, the right way up. Every 5 minutes (for a total cooking time of 15 minutes), turn the bread over (i.e. twice), so that all the butter doesn't soak into only one half.

On a big chopping board, remove the foil and cut the garlic bread into thick slices. Gaze lovingly into its green eyes and be thankful you did this and chucked out those crap ones you've had in the freezer for three years.

TINKERINGS

Depending on what I am having it with, I've been known to switch the parsley for coriander (cilantro) or basil, add hot sauce to the butter, roast the garlic first and sling in spices like cumin, caraway, turmeric or fennel seeds. The possibilities are pleasingly endless, and invariably delicious. *Bon voyage mes amis.*

BOCADILLO DE CALAMARES

A squid sandwich? YES! I'm always saying I'm going to visit my friend Jonno in Madrid and when I finally do, the second I'm off the plane I'm gonna get one of the city's signature sarnies down me. 'Madrid's not even that close to the sea, though' blah, blah, blah, it is what it is.

The squid in the photo is soaked in milk, then tossed in cornflour, then fried, which is how it should be done. You could, arguably, try this with frozen, breaded calamari rings... but I don't want to know about it.

In Madrid these sarnies are served simply: bread, fried squid, mayo, lemon. Years ago, someone made me one with Morunos mayo (page 235) and it was delicious, but for your first time, just go with this one.

10–20-ish fried squid rings and pieces
   (including tentacles if you're lucky),
   depending on size (page 181)

1 heaped tablespoon Garlic Mayo (page 220)
1 crusty little baguette
1 lemon wedge, for squeezing

Once you've fried all the squid and made the garlic mayo (don't worry, it's only garlic grated and mixed into Hellmann's), you're ready to assemble.

Cut down the length of the bread but not all the way through. Slather the inside top and bottom with the mayo. Ram in as much squid as you can, squeeze the lemon over it and get it down you quicker than I'll be off the plane in Madrid.

TINKERINGS

You could make this with grilled squid, LOADS of chopped red chillies in olive oil and some rocket (arugula) like they serve squid at the River Café, but quite frankly, that'd be a completely different sandwich.

A HAM AND CELERIAC RÉMOULADE SANDWICH

Celeriac rémoulade is just posh coleslaw really.

The ham in this could be bought from a shop, cooked yourself or procured from just about anywhere. My mum always cooks a ham at Christmas, as many do, and to celebrate I often make celeriac remoulade. On Boxing Day, washed down with a Michelada or two, me and the fam have ham sandwiches all day, whenever we like, potentially without stopping. Please buy yourself a julienne peeler (I like the Oxo Good Grips one)! They make things like rémoulade simple to do and we don't have to have a long, boring chat about mandolines and their dangers.

The dipped edges of this are a nifty technique that add a splash of colour and a touch of glamour to a high-tea type sarnie. I always knew mayonnaise could do anything, and this certainly proves it! I've stolen the idea from the *Chez Panisse Vegetables* book where Alice Waters uses the technique to make James Beard's favourite spring onion sandwiches a bit more interesting. No mean feat.

---

2 nice, thick slices of good white bread
Lashings of butter
Heap of cooked ham, cut thin, or thick if that's
   what you prefer (I like it thin) (page 156)
2 heaped tablespoons Celeriac Rémoulade (page 200)

1 teaspoon mayo
1 tablespoon very finely chopped flat leaf parsley
   or chives (whatever you prefer) (you might need
   more herbs; be prepared)

Butter the bottom of your bread with a heavy hand and pile on the ham in a nice even layer. Pile on the rémoulade. Lid on, bit of a squish, trim the crusts off and cut the sarnie in half with a serrated knife, back and forth, back and forth, being careful not to squidge the bread. Spread all round the open, now crustless edges of the sandwich with mayo. Sprinkle the chopped parsley onto a little plate or something and dunk the mayo'd edges into it. Sit down, feet up, TV on, enjoy yourself. Have a glass of wine, or two; it's Boxing Day.

TINKERINGS

Gosh, the things you could do here! All the world's herbs are available to you for this method depending on what you come up with as fillings. Now I think about it, you could do it with crushed-up crisps too!!

Chopped-up ham and some celeriac rémoulade is an absolute banger of a baked potato topping too! You could easily replace the rémoulade with store-bought coleslaw and give yourself less to do on such a busy day doing nothing, which is the best kind of busy to be on a day when you want to do nothing.

I'm not quite sure why I'm telling you this, but my mum used to make my sister and I cucumber sandwiches when we were kids. She peeled the cucumber, used loads of butter and always put Marmite in, too. Legend.

A tale of two toasties...

Thomas Edison (seriously) invented The Edicraft Sandwich Grill in the late 1920s but it didn't sell and was discontinued in 1934. The idea lay dormant, a sleeping giant, until 1949 when Dr Earnest Smithers, an Australian national hero, patented a thing called the Jaffle Iron. It was similar to Edison's invention but, crucially, it crimped the edges of the sandwich as it toasted. The game changed, minds were blown and the true toastie was born. In 1974 Breville released a similar machine, and brought the crimped toastie we all know and love to the UK and everywhere that isn't Australia.

One of my earliest sandwich memories is the delicious (cooked) ham and Branston Pickle toasties my school friend Michael Walker's mum Janet used to make us when we were little. Michael and I lost touch decades ago but I fondly remember getting attacked by a vicious cockerel (not a euphemism), smoking rolled-up newspaper under the bridge together, his Dad's Jag and kind, quiet manner, his sister Alison, and of course, lovely Janet and those toastie-catered Top Gun reruns.

Were Edison alive today he would doubtless agree that with the sandwich overleaf, his idea for a hot sandwich machine has really reached a zenith.

A TUNA MELT TOASTIE

The idea for this hot little pocket of heaven came to me while eating an allegedly great tuna melt in Elephant and Castle. While eating it, I thought to myself, 'God, I wish this was a toastie and not all floppy.' I had also recently watched Kenji López-Alt (food vlogger, writer and sandwich enthusiast) on YouTube or somewhere making himself a nice tuna melt for lunch, which gave me the idea for this one. And that my friends, is how semi-plagiaristic magic happens hahahaha. This'll make too much filling. Have another one.

1 not-posh tin of tuna (unless you fancy one), in water or oil, emptied into one side of a large sieve (strainer) and drained in the sink for at least 10 minutes
¼ onion, cut into tiny chunks, soaked in cold water for 5 minutes, drained in the sieve (strainer)
5–6 pickled jalapeño slices, cut into little chunks, drained in the sieve
½ big gherkin, grated and put in another bit of that sieve
1 heaped teaspoon tinned sweetcorn (full sugar), drained in the sieve

¼ celery stalk, cut lengthways into 3–4 pieces, then into little chunks
Splash (½ tablespoon) of malt vinegar
4 tablespoons Hellmann's mayo (or homemade, page 220)
3 tablespoons your best extra virgin olive oil
2 slices of Hovis-type, supermarket white bread
75 g (2½ oz) grated supermarket mozzarella
Salt and pepper

Put the drained tuna in a bowl with the onion, jalapeños, grated gherkin, sweetcorn, celery, malt vinegar, a big pinch of salt, a few grinds of black pepper and 3 tablespoons of the mayo. Mix everything together with a fork and, once combined, a tablespoon at a time, mix your tastiest olive oil into the tuna mix. Be sure to completely combine each spoonful of oil before adding the next, or Kenji López-Alt (whose little trick this is) will be very cross indeed, I should imagine.

Spread the remaining tablespoon of mayo on one side of both the slices of bread and put one of them mayo-side down on the work surface in front of you. Sprinkle half the mozzarella on it. Put some tuna mix on top of that and spread it evenly all over the sandwich, leaving a little gap round the edges. If you can, echo the shape of the toastie's pockets, with less in the middle, if you know what I mean, but no worries if you don't.

Put the rest of the cheese on top and put the other piece of bread on, mayo'd side up.

I've said it before and I'll say it again, mayo works better on the outside of toasties than butter. It's made of oil and egg, making it brown beautifully, crisp well and taste fantastic.

Using a spatula, or your hands, put the sandwich in the machine, shut the lid and wait until it's hot as hell and a delectable colour.

TINKERINGS

There are millions of things you could add or exchange in this sandwich. If you happened to have pickled celery instead of raw... Different veggies (no tomatoes though, remember they go hotter than the sun in a toastie), salad cream instead of mayo, no sweetcorn, spring onions (scallions), horseradish, different pickled things, different cheeses, butter on the outside if you must, one of the many hot sauces of the world, take a punt, toastie the hell out of it...

A CHORIZO ROLL

Many of my fondest memories of getting started in the food business are from when I worked for Brindisa, Britain's greatest Spanish food importer. As well as a great shop, Brindisa have something at Borough Market that dreams are made of... a sausage stand! They sell sandwiches similar to this, but without the mayo or lemon.

When there's a break in the rain, get some mates round and light the barbecue for this one. The chorizos love the flames and you can grill (broil) the insides of the buns really easily, which makes a surprisingly big difference to the toasty smokiness of the thing.

You can of course grill the sausages in the kitchen, if you're not happy at the coals, or if it's January, or breakfast-time or something. The only real clincher is not to overcook them. Chorizos don't work like a British banger which likes low and slow cooking – these puppies like it HOT for as short a time as possible. Once they're no longer raw (and hopefully blistered a bit), they're done, cook them no more than that – don't let all that oil out.

In the summer, I often throw a barbecue party at the roastery of my dear friends Allpress Coffee, and we nearly always make this sandwich because it is SO DAMN GOOD and you can knock 'em out for loads of people without too much bother.

2 fresh cooking chorizos (spicy or not, up to you), cut in half, not all the way through and opened up (I refer to this as burger-vanning but I think butterflying is probably the proper name)
1 soft, floury white bap

1 heaped tablespoon Garlic Mayo (page 220)
1 roasted red (piquillo) pepper from a jar, cut down one side and opened up (or page 203)
Handful of rocket (arugula)
1 wedge of lemon, for squeezing

Light the barbecue or fire up your cooker's grill (broiler). Barbecue or grill (broil) the sausages and toast the insides of the bun. Garlic mayo the top and bottom of the bun. Sausages on the bottom, pepper on top of them, rocket on, squeeze the lemon in and put the lid on.

TINKERINGS

This sandwich demands you have a beer, unless you're having it for breakfast, in which case have half a beer.

You could grill (broil) some squid or prawns (shrimp) and put them in the sandwich too?! Cumin mayo (some ground and some seeds) would also be lovely. A fried egg would be nice. A hash brown or two? Watercress might make a nice alternative to the rocket, but really, what's the point?

CHORIPAN

The original rights to this sandwich are hotly contested, but at their hottest between Argentina and Uruguay. That aside, this may be simple, but hot damn is it good and another gift to barbecuing. These are often served at the beginning of a barbecue in both the claimant nations because the sausages cook quickly and don't mind a high heat. You could grill (broil) them in your kitchen or cook them in a pan too, but maybe save this one for the summer and do it right.

1 huge, fat length of fresh cooking chorizo (sweet or spicy), or 3 normal-sausage size, fresh cooking chorizos
15-cm (6-in) piece of baguette, slightly depending on how big your sausage/sausages is/are

1 tablespoon olive oil
1 garlic clove, peeled
Lashings of Chimichurri (page 231)

Once the barbecue is lit and ready for grilling (broiling), get the sausages on. Once they're cooked (they won't need long), with some nice colour on them, put them on a plate to rest for a moment.

Cut down the length of your baguette but not all the way through. Open it up like a book and drizzle the olive oil all over the inside of the bread and pop it, inside down, on the barbecue. Toast the inside and get some colour on it. Take it off, let it cool and crisp for a moment, then rub the garlic clove all over the toasted surface. Bang your sausages in and drizzle any juice they've given off in there too. Slather chimichurri **liberally** all over the place and ride 'em cowboy!

TINKERINGS

What harm could it do to put some mayonnaise in?

OLLIE REYNOLDS' JAMIE THICCSTON PANUOZZO AKA THE BEST DELI SANDWICH IN THE WORLD

When I eat or drink the best example of something I've ever had, I always know immediately. The best steak, the best olive, the best pint of lager, it could be anything – but the second I pop it in, something goes BAM and I just know without hesitation: that's the most delicious one of those I have ever had.

The first time I went to Pizza Loco in Leeds, something went BAM. Excited to see it on the menu, I ordered a classic and one of my favourites: Salsiccia e Friarielli (if there's a sausage on the menu...). The pizza came and I could tell immediately it looked good, but when I had a bite – BAM – I knew. 'That's it,' I said, flabbergasted, 'that's the best pizza I've ever eaten.'

Then I said something I regret about Naples.

When my friend Woffy and I were leaving, Ollie (the owner) gave us each something he described as 'a little treat for later'. We put them in our bags, went out drinking and forgot about them completely. In the morning we woke up in a panic, late for a train and had to dash to Edinburgh.

On arrival, we checked into a hotel and went to our rooms. I unpacked my bag, came across Ollie's package, unwrapped it, took a bite and BAM – it was the best deli sandwich I had ever eaten.

Thankfully Ollie and I had swapped numbers the night before (don't lose touch with anyone who makes pizza that good) and I called him to ask what I was eating. 'Just eating it now?' he asked laughing. 'Then it's a 16-hour old, unwisely unrefrigerated, Jamie Thiccston panuozzo.'

I didn't know what a panuozzo was, but I knew how delicious Jamie Thiccston was. At Pizza Loco, you can get one every day they're open, so if you live in Leeds you need to get down there pronto tonto.

And if you live somewhere else, you need to get to Leeds just as quickly. They do pizzas at night, and panuozzi during the day – panuozzi (plural) being sandwiches made in rolls/balls/buns of pizza dough that you cut mostly in half, open up like a book and fill with goodies.

Here, with Ollie's permission of course, is the recipe for the Pizza Loco Jamie Thiccston, so you can make one for yourself. I've done it in a supermarket ciabatta so it's easier to do. Never forget, a supermarket mini ciabatta run under the tap (faucet) and re-baked in a hot oven on a greaseproof paper-lined baking tray, and turned a few times until as crisp as the moment it was made, is really good sandwich bread. Sorry Ollie.

You should be able to get most of these things in one trip to a good deli. And make sure to ask for those meats THIN. @pizzaloco

---

1 mini supermarket ciabatta re-baked (see above)

100 g (3½ oz) thinly sliced finocchiona (fennel salami)

100 g (3½ oz) wafer thin mortadella

125 g (4½ oz) burrata

50 g (1¾ oz) Lemon Basil Aioli (page 222)

4 slices of gherkin (Ollie specifies Mrs Elswood Sandwich Gherkins)

Zest of ¼ unwaxed lemon

25 g (1 oz) escarole or romaine lettuce

½ roasted, skinned red (bell) pepper (page 203, or look for a jar of Spanish piquillo peppers and use one of those)

A drizzle of excellent extra virgin olive oil

A drizzle of excellent balsamic vinegar

Maldon salt and freshly ground black pepper

Take the finocchiona, mortadella and burrata out of the refrigerator 30 minutes before you want to make the sandwich.

Preheat the oven to 180°C (350°F). Get the ciabatta, wet it and bake it as discussed in the intro.

Slice your bread, leaving a 'spine' and open it up like a book. Decide which side is top, and which side is bottom, then slather both with all the aioli.

Lay the gherkin slices on the bottom and pile the finocchiona on top. Ollie is very specific that you do not lay the meat slices flat, but ruffle them up, scrunch them a bit, and stick them all in like that. (As we might not have done very well in the photo.)

Plonk the burrata on top, in the middle of the layer of meat, tear it open and pull it in opposite directions across the sandwich, right to the ends. Season the burrata and its innards with the lemon zest, a sprinkle of salt and a grinding of black pepper. Lay the whole salad leaves on this. Thus far everything has gone on the bottom section.

Lay your red pepper on the top section. Ruffle your mortadella slices on top of it, as you did the finocchiona on the pickles. Drizzle both the sections with the olive oil and vinegar.

Then Ollie says: 'Stare at it for a moment and carefully fold it over and lightly press down before grabbing the biggest, sharpest knife you've got, and then cut it in half. And for the love of God, saw lightly and let the knife do the work. Do not press down hard or you risk losing everything.'

He follows this up with: 'Reveal the cross-section to yourself, and using a tissue, wipe away any tears of joy from your eyes before walloping down the first half and pondering the second's existence.'

What he doesn't recommend, at any point, is to stuff it in a bag next to some pairs of pants and take it on a train to Edinburgh and eat it 16 hours later.

TINKERINGS

I'm sure you could try messaging Ollie @pizzaloco and ask him for his dough recipe, if you're that way inclined and he is inclined to give it to you.

THE BALIK EKMEK

Many years ago I went to Istanbul, and it was just extraordinary. I had been living on Green Lanes in London for a while and was unexpectedly familiar with many of the dishes I'd eat in the city. One of the great surprises was this roadside fish sandwich, and a pudding with chicken in it that I never saw coming. Down by the Bosporus there were carts with little barbecues on. From the roadside, men fished with rods, into the sea (it is not really a river, but the meeting of two seas) and when they caught something (mostly mackerel, I think), the fish would be given to one of the men at the barbecue carts, who'd whip the fillets off, grill 'em and give them to you in a sandwich. Magic! As so often with magic, some might argue there was an element of trickery and many of the fish actually came from the fish market, but what did/do I know?

When I was little, my parents used to take my darling sister Lydia (best sister in the world) and I mackerel fishing in a tiny boat round the bay at Beer (near Lyme Regis) in Dorset. They'd chug wine from Duralex glasses and smoke fags, my dad driving or manning the tiller or whatever it is, and my sister and me fishing with lines. We never left empty handed/bucketed and when we got home my dad would light the barbecue and we'd grill our catch. Heavenly. We never thought to do this though.

2 mackerel fillets, barbecued, grilled (broiled) or fried

1 small, crusty baguette about 15 cm (6 in) long

1 tablespoon extra virgin olive oil

Handful of chopped salad (equal amounts of parsley, onion, tomato, red (bell) pepper and cucumber), licked with more olive oil, a squeeze of lemon juice and a heavy sprinkling of sumac

Sprinkling of pul biber (Aleppo pepper/red pepper flakes) or, at a push, chilli (hot pepper) flakes

1 teaspoon pomegranate molasses or posh thick balsamic vinegar (see page 241 for a tricksy cheat)

Cooking mackerel fillets with crisp, burnished skin and perfect, soft oily flesh is simple as long as two things are done right. First, the fish must be dry. When the slippery little beggars come out the paper they're wrapped in (or the supermarket packaging) they'll be a bit slimy. Give them a rinse under the cold tap (faucet), lay them skin side up on some paper towels and pat them dry with more paper towels. Once dry, leave them as they are, with nothing on the skin but the air. Do this a good while before cooking. At the very least, before you light the BBQ or heat up the grill (broiler).

Secondly, get your cooking device HOT – be that the grill bars on your barbecue, a griddle pan or a frying pan (skillet). It needs to be hot, but not out of control hot. If it's a frying pan, razz it on full heat for about 2 minutes, a griddle pan for about 4, but then reduce the heat to just above medium before the fish goes in. For a barbecue you want those coals as red hot embers and it should be difficult to hold your hand above them for any longer than a few seconds.

In both cases, you now want to lightly oil the skin of your fish and place it skin side down, into the cooking arena. DO NOT MOVE IT. Leave it where it settles. It will let you know when it can be turned. The fish will lift itself from the pan or grill bars, watch it start round the edges. Move it too soon and the skin will stick.

As a general rule, cook the fish fillets for 80% of their cooking time on the skin. This will be about 2–3 minutes for fillets; for a whole fish maybe 4–6 depending on its size. Once the fish releases happily from the bars/pan and is dark and dangerous, flip it, give it a minute or so on the flesh side (or for a whole fish give it another 4–6 minutes and that's it, you're done). 'Fish fish fish, fish fish.'

→ **75**

Open the baguette up and drizzle olive oil all over the insides. Pop the bread on, or under the grill (broiler), until nicely toasted. Put the salad in first, the fish fillets on top, sprinkle with the pul biber, drizzle with the pomegranate molasses or balsamic and you're off.

TINKERINGS

One of the delights of this is its utter simplicity. Just get the freshest fish you can and practise cooking the stuff. Once you've nailed that, you won't need to tinker, you'll be happy as Larry eating a nice fish sandwich.

A BIT OF

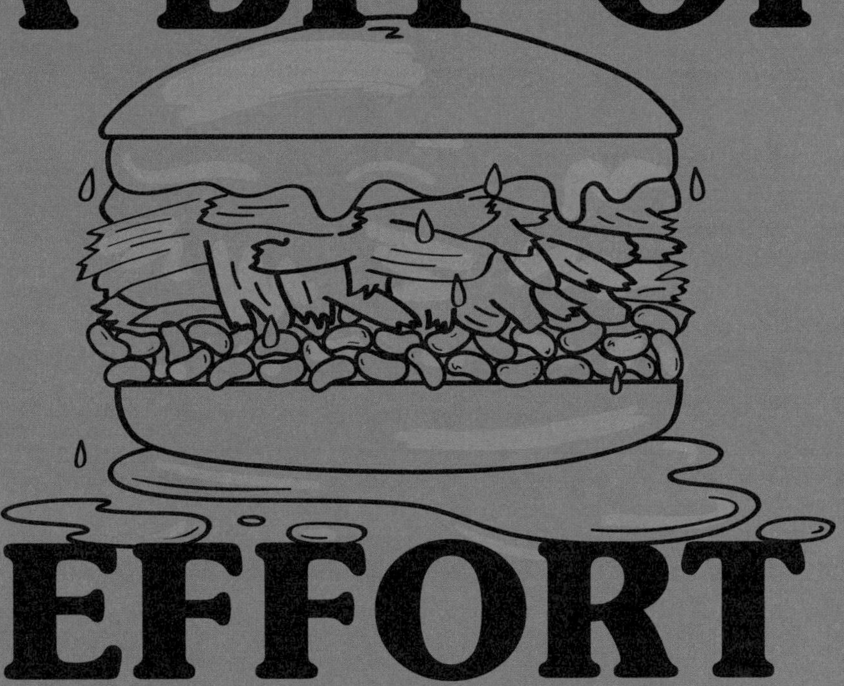

EFFORT

I came up with this little ripper for the legends at The Hippodrome Casino in Leicester Square, and jolly good it is too. Coronation Chicken meets Fried Chicken?! Yes chef.

In the UK, for me, there is only one King of Fried Chicken (KFC), and that is Carl Clarke. Every time I have eaten at the exemplary Chick 'n' Sours the chicken sandwiches have blown my tiny mind. It's also the only restaurant I know of that will deep-fry you an entire chicken for Sunday lunch.

In his mad book *The Whole Chicken*, Carl tells us that he puts MSG along with salt in his buttermilk brine, so I put MSG along with salt in my buttermilk brine and hopefully you will too. When Carl says jump, reach for the powder.

Much as I'd like to palm the chicken element of this sandwich off as my own, I can't, because it's not mine, it's Carl's and it's THE BEST.

If you want to make this easier, make the easy bits, then buy some chicken Kyivs instead of frying the chicken and whack one of them (cooked, obvs) in instead. Watch out for that boiling butter though, and mind that t-shirt.

---

1 brioche or burger bun, cut in half

3 generous tablespoons Coronation Chicken Sauce (page 237)

Small handful of Bombay mix (finer London Mix is better if you can get it – the CoFresh brand is excellent)

1 x Carl Clarke's fried boneless chicken thigh (page 174) (or a chicken Kyiv bought or made (page 175), see intro)

1 heaped tablespoon Lime-pickled Onions (page 261)

Sprinkling of nigella seeds (if you've got them)

1 heaped tablespoon shredded iceberg lettuce mixed up with a regular tablespoon of finely chopped coriander (cilantro) and mint

---

Slather the inside top and bottom of the bun in the Coronation Chicken Sauce and sprinkle the London/Bombay mix all over the top.

Put the fried thigh (or Kyiv) on the bottom and cover it in the pickled onions.

Sprinkle the nigella seeds (if using) all over those, then the lettuce and herb mix, put the lid on and you're done.

TINKERINGS

A load of pickled jalapeños in the salad mix might be nice? The whole thing works well with a piece of battered fish (page 182) too. Or as a veggie breakfast alternative, you could even just use a couple of mashed 7-minute boiled eggs (page 211) to give you a CRAZY kedgeree-type concoction hahaha.

A STEAK TARTARE SANDWICH

Is a burger a sandwich? Is it stuff between two bits of bread?

I used to have a girlfriend who lived down the road from one of London's (the world's?) greatest restaurants: Otto's French Restaurant.

We often went to have steak tartare there because it's just so damn good! She could only ever eat half, so we'd take hers home and the next day, devil that I am, I'd fry it in a patty and have it as a burger for my lunch. Half travesty, half brilliant.

At Otto's they, and if you are lucky, the man himself, will mix your steak tartare at the table in a wonderful piece of restaurant theatre. I cannot recommend it enough. They'll also squash you a whole duck, lobster or pigeon, but I'll let you find out about that for yourself.

Have a read of the fried egg chat on page 212. These soft, floppy fried eggs are just so, so good in the right sandwiches. And don't worry, you don't need to make shoestring fries like we do at the Sarnie Shop (unless you want to, of course, page 214). The internet sells these wonderful Portuguese crisps called Dalimar Potato Sticks (Batata-Palha) which you can use instead. Some supermarkets sell their own brand potato sticks, but they're often made of reconstituted potato and are consequently very dry and tend to be too thick anyway. As I say in the recipe, you can always just crush up some ready salted crisps.

---

1 x 150-g (5½-oz) steak tartare patty, the same diameter as your bun and about 2.5 cm (1 in) thick (page 167)

1 Harry Mackintosh's Slow-Fried Egg (page 212)

Vegetable oil, for frying

1 floury bap or any nice bread roll, cut in half

1 teaspoon Dijon mustard (I like French's mustard too), mixed with a touch of mayonnaise to make it easier to spread

1 tablespoon Tarragon Mayonnaise (page 224)

Handful of Shoestring Fries (page 214), Dalimar Potato Sticks or crushed ready salted crisps

---

Make the tartare into a nice, tight patty in your hands. Make a ball first, then shape into a puck and squeeze it all together relatively tightly. Slap the puck a bit on both sides to get the air out. Do this 2 hours before you want to cook because it needs to sit in the refrigerator for that long first. This will make it less likely to fall apart and make sure it's really cold, so you have more time to get it crisp and crusty on the outside without overcooking it as a whole.

Put your Slow-Fried Egg on; it'll take 15–20 minutes (page 212). If you have neither the time, nor the inclination to bother with a slow-fried egg, just fry yourself one however you normally do it, but do it while the burger is resting.

Now to the cooking. Take the patty straight from the refrigerator and into one side of a super-hot frying pan (skillet) with a good splash of veg oil in it – it should be literally smoking hot when the patty goes in. Fry the inside top and bottom of the bun in the pan with the patty until toasted. Squish the patty down gently with the spatula and flip it (really carefully) only once so a nice crust and some colour can build up – about 2 minutes. Give it another little squish and cook it for the same time as the first side, pushing it back together a bit if necessary. Don't move it about or touch it at all. Because it isn't minced, as burgers normally are, it will fall apart if you try to move it about. You could cook it inside a metal pastry ring if you've got one.

Spread the mustard mayo on the bottom of the bun. Remember you eat tartare raw, so don't overcook it. Using your spatula, carefully pick it up and put it straight on the bottom of the bun.

Spread the tarragon mayo on the inside top of the bun, then sprinkle the shoestring fries/crisps all over it.

Egg on top of the burger. Lid on. GO, GO, GO.

TINKERINGS

Don't worry too much if the patty does fall apart a bit, as my friend Dan from Seattle's exemplary Mean Sandwich well knows: a steak tartare sandwich is still a lovely thing.

A few cursory lettuce leaves (romaine or baby gem) might be nice. Some chopped raw onion would be great. Different flavour crisps are worth a go. You could use veal, or if you're really bougie, fresh Ibérico pork for the tartare, instead of beef. You could melt cheese on the burger?! Try it with different mayonnaises, hot sauce or different mustards. You could add ketchup to the sandwich, it's in the tartare anyway. Put caviar in there if you want (the cheap, refrigerated lumpfish roe from the supermarket would be perfect). I've always liked nigella seeds in steak tartare, but I'm weird and really, how much do you want to mess with steak tartare?

A PICKLED PRAWN BÁNH MÌ WITH
BROWN BUTTER MAYONNAISE

In Delia Smith's 1993 magnum opus *Delia's Summer Collection* she has a recipe for pickled prawns (shrimp) that is a bit like a ceviche. I came across it while flicking through the cookbook in a charity shop and was reminded of a recipe I'd seen in Gabrielle Hamilton's *Prune* cookbook, which has led me to this. Gabrielle's recipe for pickled shrimp is very laborious, so the one in this book is a bit less complicated.

The little baguettes they use for Bánh Mì in Vietnam are tough to buy anywhere else, so I'd suggest trying to hunt down the crunchiest baguette-type bread you can, but not stressing about it too much.

Bánh Mì are often made with the wonderful combination of roast meat AND pâté, so I've stuck to that idea, but gone fishy. Madness!

---

1 very crunchy little baguette

1 heaped tablespoon homemade Cod's Roe (ooh la la) (page 224) or store-bought taramasalata

1 heaped tablespoon Brown Butter Mayo (page 226)

150 g (5½ oz) Pickled Prawns (shrimp – page 147)

Handful of pickled carrots and daikon/mooli (page 257)

½ long, hopefully not TOO hot red chilli, thinly sliced on a diagonal, seeds and all

A few splashes of Maggi Sauce and fish sauce

4 sprigs each of coriander, parsley and mint, leaves picked and mixed

1 tablespoon peanuts with skins on, roughly crushed

Cut the baguette in half lengthways but not all the way through. Smear the cod's roe all over every millimetre of the top and the same with the mayo on the bottom.

Put the pickled prawns in, in an even-ish layer, all over the bottom, followed by the pickles, then the sliced chilli and shoot a few schploofs of Maggi Sauce and fish sauce in there, all about the place.

Next, put the herbs in and finally, sprinkle the nuts on.

Sit back, take a bite, and remember this: It's the taste of happiness – as long as you like prawns, taramasalata, the potential for a big mouthful of chilli and provided you don't have a nut allergy.

TINKERINGS

Yes, you can put sriracha in if you have to.

OWEN BARRATT'S BIRTHDAY TUNNBRÖDSRULLE
AKA THE BIRTHDAY WRAPWICH

This one sounds like I made it up because the fillings are unexpected companions, but I swear it's a classic! My friend Owen made me one of these round his house on his birthday once, grilling the sausages, and warming the flatbreads, on a little barbecue in the garden – it is also eaten in Sweden in a hotdog bun sometimes. You could grill (broil) the sausages in your kitchen if you don't fancy lighting the BBQ, or fry 'em or boil them if that's your vibe. But don't do it in the kettle, your tea will taste like lapsang souchong for six months and no one you live with will be able to figure out why. Sorry guys.

2 hotdog sausages of your choosing

3 heaped tablespoons mashed potato
 (warmed up a bit) (page 118)

1 piadina-type, rough flatbread (that's what
 Owen used) or a flatbread you've made (page 142)
 or a hotdog bun if you prefer

1 tablespoon Honey Mustard (page 229), or any
 mustard you like

2 medium pickled onions from a jar that you like, finely sliced

1 tablespoon store-bought crispy onions (you know the ones)

3 heaped tablespoons Dilly Prawn Mayo, which is:
 3 heaped tablespoons defrosted, little,
  North Atlantic prawns
 1 teaspoon horseradish sauce from a jar
 1 tablespoon chopped fresh dill
 1 heaped tablespoon mayonnaise
 1 tablespoon ketchup
 Salt and pepper

Get your sausages hot in the manner you have chosen (mine are barbecued or boiled), and warm up the mash.

Mix all the ingredients for the Dilly Prawn Mayo together in a little bowl.

Flatbreads are all better warm – whether they are folded in half and popped in the toaster, given a moment in the oven or brushed with butter and grilled (broiled) a bit – do what you will.

If you're hotdog bun-ing, steam the bun, it's worth it. And make sure to cut it before steaming. They go really soft and become an even better, less intrusive vehicle for the sausage and the other goodies than when they are warmed up in a conventional oven. If you have a steamer or one of those bamboo things or a metal thing that goes on top of a saucepan of boiling water, just pop the buns in for 30 seconds until they're real soft and away you go.

Lay your warm flatbread (or hotdog bun) on a plate or chopping board and spread your mash all over one half (or down the middle of the bun).

If your mustard is in a bowl and will need spreading, spread it all over the potato, if it's in a squeezy bottle, hold off a minute. Hotdogs in, right down the middle of the mash (if you're using a hotdog bun, you might only have room for one sausage). Dilly Prawn Mayo all over the sausages. If your mustard is in a squeezy bottle, zigzag it all over now. Sprinkle the pickled and crispy onions everywhere, roll it up and enjoy. Some people say a flatbread sandwich isn't a sandwich, they say it's a wrapwich. I say life's too short to worry and why ruin your day getting cross, when you could just be happy and scoff down that lovely wrapwich you just made?!

TINKERINGS

One of the most famous places in Sweden for less traditionally Swedish, more global/American type-hotdogs is Günter's Korvar in Stockholm. The bread they use blurs the lines between hotdog and sandwich, which I like very much... There's loads of different bangers (duck ones even!) and loads and loads of fillings available. The possibilities for tinkering are endless, as they are with hotdog/sausage sandwiches generally. In the context of this sandwich, you might be able to try a few different types of banger without upsetting anyone with anything to do tomorrow. Fried, Sloppy Onions (page 186) instead of pickled onions is common in Sweden. Could I use a kielbasa here instead of a frankfurter I hear you asking?! Deffo, but they might want steaming or boiling to soften up a bit.

86

A CHICKEN SCHNITZEL SANDWICH, GONE THE FULL HOLSTEIN

I'm sorry to Italy, Germany, Austria, Argentina or anyone else who claims the schnitzel (escalope/Milanese/Milanesa, etc), but I think chicken makes the best one. It stays the softest inside. Sure, pork, veal or whatever are all great and there's recipes on pages 178–179, but really, for me, it's chicken every time.

After a night getting one tied on at the Sandwich Shop or somewhere, I'm doing one of two things in the morning: staying in my jimjams and getting Sausage and Egg McMuffins delivered or getting dressed and heading to the caff at the end of my road for a breaded meat sandwich. Caffs often have breaded meats for sarnies and pleasingly, they're nearly always chicken.

I mostly have mine between two pieces of white bread with melted mozzarella, lettuce, mayonnaise and Tabasco.

There are many ways to skin a cat though, and to cook a schnitzel, but this (page 176) is the classic way and infinitely superior to the microwave method seemingly favoured by the caffs I frequent. Rather than recreating the shifty sandwich I have on a hangover, this is the one I make for my mum and she just LOVES it. The cooking method involves litres of oil, which is always nice, and is the best way to get a real rigorousness to the breadcrumb layer and the classically desired separation between crust and meat.

Most schnitzelly [sic] places I've been to, offer a Holstein upgrade, and you should never turn that down, so I've gone all in here, which makes it the perfect time for one of Harry Mackintosh's Slow Fried Eggs (page 212).

---

1 cooked chicken schnitzel (page 176), faintly in the shape of the bread you have chosen
1 x Harry Mackintosh's Slow-Fried Egg (page 212)
1 teaspoon mustard (Dijon will do but a slightly coarser, slightly browner, less yellow one would be perfect here)
1 tablespoon mayonnaise (I like Hellmann's)
2 slices of nice, soft white bread of your choice
25 g (1 oz) butter

Juice of ¼ lemon
1 tablespoon capers, drained (if salted, soaked in water for 10 minutes and drained)
4 anchovy fillets, cut in half lengthways (get the Cantabrian ones if possible)
Handful of sauerkraut from a jar, left in a sieve (strainer) for 10 minutes to drain (I like Krakus)
½ teaspoon caraway seeds

When your breaded meat is cooked and resting and while your slow fried egg finishes cooking (which bear in mind for timings, etc, takes about 15 minutes), it's time to move on to the garnish.

Mix the mustard and mayonnaise together and spread them edge to edge over the top slice of bread.

Put a small saucepan on a medium heat, get it hot and bang the butter in it. Swill it about as it melts and foams. When the foam subsides, keep it on the heat and swill it about some more. Soon the butter will begin to darken and, once it's just lighter than the colour of Grandma's sherry, bang the lemon juice in and shake and swirl the pan, keeping it on the heat. Once the butter and lemon juice have combined, add the capers and the anchovies, shake, shake, shake again for 10 seconds and take it off the heat.

Put the schnitzel on the bottom of the bread. Then the sauerkraut in an even layer all over the meat and sprinkle the caraway seeds on. Tip the whole contents of the butter pan all over the sauerkraut and pop the egg on top (unlike the photo). Put the lid on the sandwich, pop that yolk, decide if you're gonna cut the thing in half, and cock the hammer, it's time for action!

TINKERINGS

You might think my statement about chicken a complete scandal. If you do, please accept my apologies and do everything just the same with a nice bit of veal, pork or kangaroo, whatever you feel is right.

If you'd like to delve further into the schnitzel cooking world, I recommend having a look at Meredith Erickson's excellent *Alpine Cooking*, and/or *The German Cookbook* by Alfons Schuhbeck.

TWO TORTAS AHOGADAS

These my friends, are one hot mess and two hot winners. Allegedly invented when someone dropped a sandwich in a bucket of salsa and thought it was nice, tortas ahogadas, meaning 'drowned sandwiches', hail from Guadalajara, Mexico, and they are a belter.

My great friend Julian Ornelas Jimenez owns one of Mexico's great wine bars and restaurants. It's in Guadalajara and called Rayuela Bodega de Vino and in early 2023 we did a pop-up version of my Sandwich Shop there! Obviously my sarnies were amazing but they weren't the real treat, the ones Julian took me out to eat were!

One of the standouts was a Torta de Labio, a sandwich made from Mexico's salsa verde (page 232) and braised cow's lips. My favourite ones of all though were both torta ahogadas, one hot and one cold, and here they are.

The idea of putting a sandwich in a bag, or on a tray, and literally drowning it in sauce is antithetical to everything I was ever told made a sandwich a sandwich. Before eating one of these, many of us would surely have argued that if you couldn't pick it up, it wasn't a sandwich?! What the hell did we know? As the phrase now goes: 'Even if you can't pick it up, if it's between two bits of bread, it must be a sandwich....'

In the second half of this book there are recipes for carnitas (page 166), both the fresh and the cooked salsas from these sarnies (pages 234–235) and the mashed black beans (page 208) so you can make these, but I'm loath to give you exact recipes because I think the things these sarnies teach us don't come from recreating them exactly, but from giving us a completely new way of thinking about sandwiches. When sauciness/wetness levels no longer determine whether something can, or cannot, go in a sandwich, it is the dawn of a new day. Take a risk, do something weird, enjoy yourself, you never know what might happen.

Turn to pages 92–93 for an attractive photo montage of how to eat a sandwich out of a bag.

TORTA AHOGADA 1

THE FRESH SALSA ONE, FROM DON JOSÉ, EL DE LA BICICLETA

Julian and I got to the front of the queue, and it was time to order our sandwiches. There were two men at the counter, or in this case, the bicycle. One seemed to be in charge of sauce and the other meat. The meat man asked whether we wanted fatty, or less fatty. Fatty (of course), Julian said, and the man began to fill a little torpedo bun with a just warm mix of slow-cooked fatty bits of pork – cheeks, belly, skin, various other bits of the head and all sorts. He licked the insides of the bun with a vibrant, poppy-red salsa he leant over and nicked from the sauce guy. Mr Sauce then asked how spicy I like things and I answered a tentative '7?' An appropriate amount of habanero was thrown into a clear plastic bag half filled with the same red salsa. Some finely chopped red onion went inside the little sandwich and it was plunged into the bag and completely submerged. More red onion followed it in, and I was presented with my bag of tricks.

I was about to have one of the great sandwich experiences of my life. It was refreshing and hydrating on a very hot day, spicy enough to keep me on my toes but not to make me uncomfortable and the meat was so sweet, fatty and rich, it balanced out the extraordinary freshness and acidity of everything else. To top it off, Julian ushered me into the elite club of people who know how to eat a sandwich out of a bag without ending up looking like a Jackson Pollock. Turn to the photo guide overleaf and I'll show you how to do it too.

TORTA AHOGADA 2

THE COOKED SALSA ONE, FROM EL PRINCIPE HEREDERO

Once I had sucked the last of the sauce from my bag (again, see overleaf), Julian whisked us off for the second torta ahogada of the day. This one was very different! Less drowned than the first and served on a tray with a knife and fork. The sandwich was filled with hotter, softer meat, a silky black bean pureé and melted Oaxaca cheese. The sauce was way (temperature) hotter, richer and smoother and enriched with dried chillies. I liked it very much!

We controlled the chilli heat and zing in this one ourselves, from a bowl of chopped white onion, habanero and lime juice sat on the table.

When buying beans in cartons/jars/tins make sure the ingredients don't contain 'firming agent' or anything other than beans, salt and water. In my experience, as soon as they're meddled with, the skins just don't break down properly, which is what we need them to do today.

If you can't buy Oaxaca cheese, a decent enough substitute would be good mozzarella, drained, ripped into shreds and dried out in the refrigerator for a few hours.

1. Roll down the top of your bag.

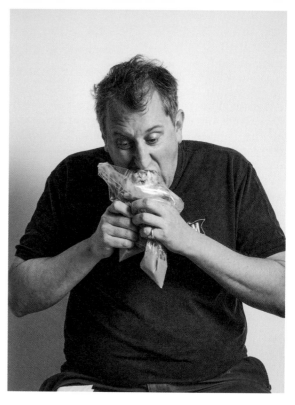

2. Eat most of the sarnie.

3. Shake everything to bottom.

4. Roll top of the bag back up.

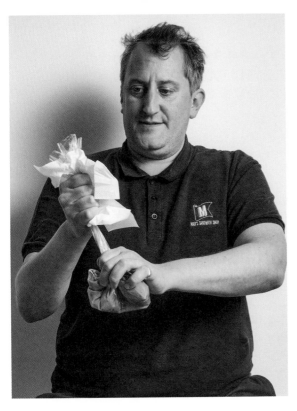

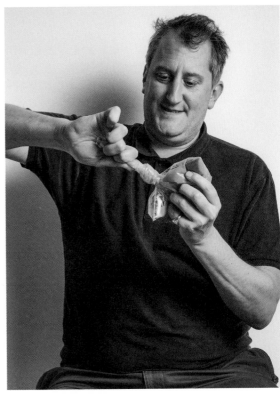

5. Grip bag tightly with napkin near base and slide to top to clean.

6. Tie tightly in a knot.

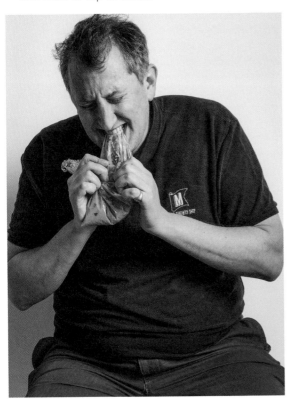

7. Turn bag on side and bite off one of the bottom corners.

8. Suck remaining sandwich and saucy goodness from bag. Discard. Order another.

A SALCHI-TACO HOTDOG WITH ONIONS, ONIONS, ONIONS AND ONIONS, AND AMERICAN MUSTARD

My wife Magali is Mexican (and amazing), and we go to Mexico every year to see her family. Even the smallest towns tend to have a tortilleria (a place that makes and sells tortillas), and in bigger towns there will be many, many more. It is almost impossible to under-egg the cultural and culinary importance of the tortilla (and corn) to Mexico and Mexicans.

I know in much of America there is easy access to decent tortillas (corn and flour), but that just isn't the case here in England and buying (good) corn (or flour) tortillas is very difficult if verging on impossible. Magali and I buy packs from the Cool Chile Company sometimes, as I would recommend you do, freeze them in stacks of ten in little bags and defrost them slowly in the refrigerator and then they don't tend to fall apart too much when you heat them up.

Mostly, Magali makes them though, as she has done since childhood, but I'm not gonna tell you to do that. If you're interested, *Tacopedia* by Deborah Holtz and Juan Carlos Mena will tell you A LOT about the variety of tacos that exist, and *The Essential Cuisines of Mexico* by Diana Kennedy is as good a place as any to start learning how to make tortillas. *My Mexico City Kitchen* by Gabriela Cámara (who owns Mexico City's amazing Contramar) is also full of gold!

I came across the Salchi-taco at a street food stall in Guadalajara. I'd ordered a sandwich and a portion of salchi-pulpo on the side for the lols. Salchi-pulpo are 5-cm (2-in) long pieces of frankfurter, with one half of them cut into from the end to make little 'legs', so when the sausages are deep-fried the 'legs' splay out and they look like little octopuses, or octopi or whatever. Luckily, the lady on the stall thought my excitement at the idea of salchi-pulpo warranted giving me some salchi-tacos to try and the idea for this hotdog was born.

She took the same (whole) cheap frankfurter-type sausage as for the octopuses/pi, wrapped it tightly in a corn tortilla, pinned this in place with cocktail sticks (toothpicks) and chucked it in the fryer. What came out was the Mexican version of a corndog. The Mexicans LOVE crisps and due to the deep-frying and its effect on the tortilla, this is essentially a sausage wrapped in a giant crisp, another of Mexico's legion culinary gifts to the world!

If you come across decent corn tortillas, the rest of this hotdog is pretty easy to do. Just take your time with those sloppy onions.

---

1 litre (34 fl oz/4¼ cups) vegetable oil

1 frankfurter (Unearthed? But you never get hurta with a Herta hahaha, sorry)

1 fresh corn tortilla and 3 or 4 cocktail sticks (toothpicks)

2 tablespoons Fried, Sloppy Onions (page 186)

1 hotdog bun (see Tinkerings on the opposite page for an apology)

1 teaspoon chopped pickled silverskin onions (the little, pale ones pickled in clear vinegar)

1 heaped tablespoon Pico de Gallo (page 230)

1 zigzag of American mustard (I like French's)

1 teaspoon store-bought crispy onions (you know the ones)

Right, you gotta deep-fry this, there's just no way round it. If you have a deep-fat fryer at home, set it to 180°C (350°F), otherwise you know the drill: get a saucepan on, put the veg oil in it and start heating it up. When it reaches 180°C (350°F), the point at which a piece of bread sizzles and goes golden in 20 seconds, roll your sausage of choice tightly in the tortilla, poke the cocktail sticks (toothpicks) right through the thing to keep the tortilla in place and slip it into the oil, roll it about occasionally with some tongs or a fork.

Warm your sloppy onions up in a little pan. Once the tortilla has turned completely golden (remember the sausage is already cooked), whip it out with some tongs, take the oil off the heat, and let the sausage sit on a wire rack or some paper towels to cool a little.

If you didn't steam the bun, cut it down its length, but not all the way through and pull out the cocktail sticks. If you did, do the same thing. Smear the sloppy onions in the crevice. Sprinkle the chopped silverskin onions on top. Put the sausage in and spoon the pico de gallo down the length of it. Zigzag back and forth across the whole thing with the mustard and sprinkle crispy onions on top of that. Have a massive bite and feel that amazing giant crisp crunch.

TINKERINGS

Steaming the bun is one of the secrets to a really good hotdog. I just feel bad asking you to do it because I know it's a faff and I already got you to deep-fry, track down corn tortillas AND take a day off to cook those onions. You can steam buns in one of those bamboo steamers or in any kind of vegetable steamer, they only need 30 seconds. They go so soft (always cut them before steaming), that the hotdog becomes completely about the sausage and the filling, which is the dream really.

Instead of a frankfurter, you could try this with a nice fat kielbasa from your local Polish shop/deli (and sometimes the supermarket). Instead of a corn tortilla you could try one of those big flour tortillas we get in the supermarkets in England and cut it down to size (the diameter should be just less than the length of the sausage) but I haven't done it and can't vouch for the crispness/burning potential. Tweet me, or X me, or whatever.

BIFF, BAFF, BOFF BIFANA

I love Portugal, and the Portuguese love crisps. We're a match made in heaven. There are loads of good sandwiches in Portugal: Porto's Francesinha, which makes the Croque Madame look like diet food, a cheese and steak sandwich called a Prego which is also excellent and legion others. My favourite, though, is Lisbon's Bifana. Very doable at home, the meat is happy cooked in a pan or licked by fire on the barbecue, my method of choice here.

The best bifana I've ever had – sorry Portugal – was at a restaurant in London. But it was cooked – thank you Portugal – by the legend Nuno Mendes. It was truly delicious, a kind of prego hyprid, unconventional, quite expensive and verging on impossible to replicate at home. It had grilled Ibérico presa (shoulder/collar, the same cut used by Meng in the Tātā Eatery classic discussed on page 116), yeast mayo (one of the cheesiest things ever not to be made of cheese), and from what I remember, some kind of fennel arrangement.

Launching the careers of many chefs, Nuno has done many great and many weird culinary things over the years. After writing *Lisboeta* it's a scandal if he hasn't been given the key to the city or whatever they do in Portugal. The book is chock full of gold, and while I lament the loss of his old, crazy bifana due to that restaurant not existing any more, he does give a still slightly tricksy, but at least doable, recipe for one in *Lisboeta*. This version of that sandwich removes the need to ferment anything and adds some crisps and mayonnaise OBVS.

If it isn't barbecue season, you can cook the meat in a frying pan (skillet) instead (don't forget to marinate it the night before), but I for one will wait for sunshine, up the recipe amounts, get some beers cold, make a margarita mix and invite some friends round for a sarnie barbie because this baby is hot to trot.

---

150 g (5½ oz) pork shoulder steak, bashed between 2 sheets of greaseproof paper with the bottom of a small saucepan to flatten and rough it up a bit
1 papo secos (a floury, crusty-ish white roll) or something similar
Extra virgin olive oil for drizzling
1 garlic clove, peeled
2 tablespoons chorizo mayo (page 223)
Handful of Dalimar Potato Sticks (Batata-Palha – you can buy these AMAZING crisps online) or your favourite brand of ready salted crisps, crushed
A nice wedge of lemon, for squeezing

Knob of butter

For the pork marinade:
1 roasted, skinned red (bell) pepper (page 203 for a method, but you can buy these in jars everywhere now, if you're lucky they'll be called piquillo peppers)
1 fat garlic clove, peeled
1 teaspoon each of white wine and sherry vinegar (or other good wine vinegars, not balsamic)
½ teaspoon salt
½ teaspoon sweet smoked paprika
2 tablespoons extra virgin olive oil

Put all the marinade ingredients in an appropriate receptacle and blend with a stick blender or in a Nutribullet or something. Pour the goo into a little Tupperware, put the meat in and squeeze it with your hands, squeeze, squeeze. Wash your hands, put the lid on and refrigerator the tub until the following day. If you remember, every few hours, give the whole lot a shake in the tub.

Now it is tomorrow, if you are barbecuing, light it and get the meat out of the refrigerator. If you're frying in a pan (skillet), get the pan on the heat in about 30 minutes, once the meat's not so cold.

When the barbecue's ready, grill your meat for a few minutes a side, getting a nice bit of colour and until it is just cooked through. Set it aside to rest.

Cut the bread in half, drizzle the insides with olive oil and grill them until they look toasty and nice. Let the bread cool a little and rub the grilled sides with the garlic clove, then slather the top in your chorizo mayo and cover it in the crisps. If you're really naughty you COULD butter the bottom, but I wouldn't bother. Slice the rested meat and heap it onto the bottom of the bun along with its juices and squeeze lemon juice all over. Add a bit of extra salt if the fancy takes you, lid on, bit of a squish, GO, GO, GO!

If you're frying in a pan rather than barbecuing, make sure you get the pan nice and hot, put a good slug of olive oil and a knob of butter in, get that nice and hot, and do everything as above. If the pan is too burned once the pork is cooked, you could toast the insides of the bun under the grill (broiler), but ideally you wanna cook them in this pan.

Thank you, Nuno.

TINKERINGS

Garlic mayo (page 220) would be lovely instead of the chorizo mayo, as would extra lemon juice and plain mayo, as long as it's Hellmann's.

Some insist that leaner loin meat should be used here, rather than the shoulder, but I think it dries out too much and doesn't get to know the marinade as well.

The Macau-style Fried Pork Chop, beloved of Anthony Bourdain and discussed on page 152, is allegedly derived from the Bifana, but probably not this Bifana. Biff, baff, boff.

My love of the Greeks, the Greek islands, my Greek godson Zephyr, Greek hospitality and nearly everything about Greece runs deep and strong and true. The Greeks love squid and octopus and often dress them, when grilled, with vinegar AND lemon juice, which is unheard of and a gift from the flavour Gods. I love Greek beer, Greek wine, Greek food generally, and the Greek attitude to life. They have given us so much, not least, this joyful sandwich with chips in. Yamas!

My friend Alex Gkikas owns a brilliant coffee roastery and lunch spot on Grays Inn Road in London called Catalyst. If you've been to my Sandwich Shop, you will almost definitely have dunked a mac 'n' cheese ball or chicken wing in his extraordinary coffee sriracha. Alex is from Thessaloniki (in northern, mainland Greece) and is one of the world's great lunchers. I've had many good gyros, but I turned to him for advice on this because it's so good it needs to be classic, not purposelessly innovative or trying to be clever. Having this sandwich at home, a few beers in, sitting in the sun, feet up, with nothing to do for the rest of the day, was as swift a route to happiness as I am yet to discover.

3–4 big fat slices of tomato (from a tomato they'd be proud of in Greece)

A sprinkling of salt and sugar

1 litre (34 fl oz/4¼ cups) vegetable oil (optional)

100–150 g (3½–5½ oz, marinated, cooked pork shoulder (page 154) depending on the size of your pitta

2 handfuls frozen (oven?) chips

A generous sprinkling of dried oregano (the good, good stuff you get in bags in delis)

1 good-quality pitta bread

3 tablespoons tzatziki (page 239)

A splash of red wine vinegar

1 heaped tablespoon finely sliced red onion

An hour in advance, cut the core out of the tomato, slice it nice and thick, put the slices on a plate and sprinkle them with the salt and sugar.

Get the fryer on for your chips (you could bake them in the oven too of course, but it's not the same). If you have a deep-fat fryer get it on to 180°C (350°F), if you don't, you know the drill: get a high-sided saucepan on the heat, whack the veg oil in it and get it up to 180°C (350°F), the temperature at which a piece of bread crisps and goes golden in about 20 seconds.

Re-fry the pork in a frying pan to get it nice and crisp. When that's a few minutes off ready (it'll probably take 5-ish minutes total), plunge the chips into the oil. When they're super crunchy, whip them out, if you're using a saucepan to fry in, use a small sieve (strainer) or a slotted spoon to get them out, into a bowl and give them a good hit of salt and a sprinkling of oregano. Remember, there is nothing sadder on earth than an underseasoned potato.

Pop your pitta in the toaster and get it nice and hot. If it's round crack it open and if it's oval chop it in half and build as two hot pockets. Smother the insides, all over, with half the tzatziki. Lay the tomato slices in, after giving them a little shake then cover them in the meat. Drizzle the remaining tzatziki in and sprinkle more oregano everywhere. Ram the chips in and drizzle in the red wine vinegar. Crack a Mythos and say it with me: *GEIA SOU NAFTI!*

TINKERINGS

Don't you dare! Alex tells me his parents' generation would never, ever, have had the chips in there... We won't tell anyone if you won't.

LABOUR

OF LOVE

MAX'S MEATLOAF SARNIE
AKA MARCELLA HAZAN'S
MEATLOAF IN A SARNIE

Years ago, some guys from Vice turned up in the Sandwich Shop and asked if I'd like to make some videos with them, which of course I did!! I banged on to them about how I use plates of food as inspiration, rather than just trying to 'come up with sandwiches'. Bearing that in mind, and before filming an episode proper, we had to shoot a test and they asked if I could make an 'unexpected sandwich'. This was it. Pommes purée instead of mayonnaise? That's what I call a surprise.

I had leftovers at home from the night before of Marcella Hazan's meatloaf, pommes purée (bougie mashed potato) and some julienne carrots I'd made as the veggie accompaniment. I thought these wouldn't be crunchy enough, so I made a quick batch of pickled carrots and popped home for the other leftovers. Remember, if you want to make this sandwich, you really need to do the pickles 24 hours in advance.

---

3 thick, leftover slices of Marcella Hazan's Meatloaf,
  plus a nice bit of the sauce (page 163)
A generous slathering (about 8 tablespoons)
  Pommes Purée (page 189)

Handful of pickled carrots (page 257)
1 mini supermarket ciabatta
1 tablespoon finely chopped flat leaf parsley

Preheat the oven to 110°C (225°F). Pop the meatloaf slices on a little metal baking tray, slather them with the sauce and pop in the oven to warm for about 10 minutes.

Get the mash in a pan, and blip, blip, blip, gently heat it up, stirring regularly.

Using tongs, take the pickled carrots out of the pickling liquor and pop them in a sieve (strainer) to dry a bit.

Ready your bread for sandwiching and slather the inside top and bottom with mashed potato. Lay the warmed slices of meatloaf on top of the mash on the bottom and cover in any extra sauce you have on the tray. Put a big handful of pickled carrots on top of the saucy meatloaf, sprinkle them all over with the parsley. Put the lid on and it's lights, camera, action.

TINKERINGS

This little beauty was made out of leftovers and GODDAMN was it good. Rather than suggesting tinkerings to this one, I'd like to encourage you to look at your leftovers a bit differently. Don't see them as things to reheat, to remake last night's meal, see them as an opportunity to get creative with what you can put between two bits of bread. The most unexpected things can be blitzed up and mixed into mayonnaise, and as long as you don't forget to have contrasts in there, hot and cold, sweet and sour, crunchy and soft, you can adapt nearly anything into a sandwich when you think about it a bit.

If you don't want to go through the hassle of making pommes purée, you can of course just use normal leftover mash.

RACHEL RODDY'S BOILED MEAT BANGER

Rachel Roddy can do no wrong. She is a fantastic cook, a hoot to talk to, writes like Elizabeth David in the form of her life and (generously) gives the best travel recommendations. When it comes to breakfast, lunch or dinner, she knows what delicious is, like the atomic clock knows what time it is.

If you turn to page 170 you will find her method for boiling beef, which will bring you joy and a sense of spiritual well-being similar to when your mum scratches your head and tells you everything's going to be alright and that you've been worrying about nothing.

Served in its broth, with a whole (peeled) carrot also cooked in the broth, a splash of olive oil, a sprinkle of salt and a good squeeze of lemon juice, a fat slice of this is one of those magical things.

I make Rachel's boiled meat at home often, especially in the spring, but I found out about it in Florence's central market (Mercato Centrale) at a place on the first floor called Nerbone, where it is at its finest between two bits of bread. At Nerbone many years ago, on the recommendation of my wise, head-scratching mother, I had two of the great sandwiches of my life: a Panino Bollito, a boiled meat one, and a Panino Lampredotto, a tripe sandwich. Tripe?! Not exactly, it's from the fourth part of a cow's stomach not the first or second like the stinky, chewy stuff. There isn't the faintest lingering smell of anything dodgy about it, however it is they do it (page 165).

You order the sandwich(es) and they ask you: 'Verde o rossa?' Verde being salsa verde (page 232) and rossa being red, spicy salsa (page 233). 'Entrambi' ('both' in Italian) is the only answer, of course, and adding a 'bagnato' (wet) and a 'per favore' will get your sandwich quickly dunked in broth, if that's what you fancy. If you have the sandwich dunked it will be served to you in a bag, and you will likely need a fork to eat it. Sadly, it won't quite be wet enough to refer to the photos on pages 90–91 for a handy guide to 'How to Eat a Sandwich Out of a Bag', but you can't have everything.

---

1 big, fat, warm, wet slice of Rachel Roddy's Boiled Beef that you have reheated, slowly, over about 15 minutes, in some broth (page 170)
At least a small ladleful of the broth you used to reheat the meat

1 crusty roll (a soft one won't take the dunking)
Salt, a big squeeze of lemon juice and a little good extra virgin olive oil
2 tablespoons Salsa Rossa (page 233 – optional)
2 tablespoons Salsa Verde (page 232 – optional)

Open the roll, put the meat in, put the sauce or sauces on and in and fill a little bowl with the reserved broth, squeeze a little lemon in it, sprinkle on some salt and a schploof of olive oil.

Sit yourself down and get a napkin ready. While you eat the sarnie, dunk it in the broth, which you should drink at the end.

I know at first boiled meat can seem weird, when (as I have) you've been brought up to think of grilled, roasted and fried meat as delicious, but the tender softness is warming, comforting and delicious.

TINKERINGS

Instead of dunking you could wet the bread inside with a tablespoon or two of the broth and have the best of both worlds. Loads of Dijon mustard, a splash of olive oil and a squeeze of lemon are also great in this sandwich instead of the red or green sauce. A load of butter and a big spoon of really punchy homemade horseradish (page 240) would also be wonderful.

THE KATI ROLL

As far as I can figure out, the story is that Nizam's Restaurant in Kolkata got so busy that they wanted to start serving takeaway (takeout) versions of their famous skewered meats. Eating a skewered meat on the hoof is not only difficult but dangerous, and it would be silly to give away iron skewers. As a solution they started using bamboo skewers (kati) instead of iron just generally, and for takeaway, flopping a paratha over the meat and whipping the skewers out. And so the Kati Roll was born.

As if you needed an excuse to get the barbecue out, invite your friends round, try and drink 650 beers and realise too late you never have enough skewers... If you don't want to/can't barbecue, you can grill (broil) these in the kitchen, no worries.

---

150 g (5½ oz) lamb leg, cut into
   2-cm (¾-in) chunks
2 tablespoons of butter
½ onion, coarsely grated into a bowl
1 heaped tablespoon full-fat yoghurt
1 frozen paratha (if you struggle to find these, there's a
   flatbread recipe on page 142, or at a push you could
   use one of those rough piadina flatbread/wrap things)
10 big mint leaves
6 sprigs of flat-leaf parsley, leaves picked
6 sprigs of coriander (cilantro), leaves picked
1 lime wedge, for squeezing
Salt

For the marinade:
1 tablespoon mashed papaya or mashed pineapple
   (you can use tinned, but fresh is best)
½ teaspoon garam masala
1 teaspoon grated ginger
1 teaspoon grated garlic
½ teaspoon ground coriander
1 teaspoon finely chopped red chilli
¼ teaspoon salt

You will also need:
1 skewer, if wooden, soaked in water for 30 minutes

Mix all the marinade ingredients together and chuck the lamb in. Mix the hell out of it. Give it at least 2 hours in there before commencing sandwiching.

Put a little saucepan on a low–medium heat and put a knob (pat) of butter in it. Once it's melted, chuck the grated onion in with a pinch of salt. Stir, then let it cook slowly for 10–15 minutes until it's browned, thickened and caramelised.

Take the pan off the heat, let it cool and mix the yoghurt into it. Set aside.

Once the 2 hours are up, put the lamb on a skewer. Keep the marinade if it hasn't all clung to the meat.

If you're cooking these on a barbecue, you should already have lit it, otherwise get your grill (broiler) 9 out of 10 hot. Grill (broil) your lamb skewer with half the extra marinade smeared on top of it. After about 3–4 minutes, turn the skewer over and smear the rest of the marinade on and put it back under the grill for another 3–4 minutes. You want it caramelised really nicely and at the beginning of burned on its edges.

Smear the other knob of butter on both sides of your paratha and pop it under the grill, or on the barbecue for 30 seconds, then grill the other side. These can also be done in a frying pan (skillet): put a dry frying pan on a medium-high heat and get it hot. Put the frozen paratha in (no butter). It will puff (some do so more than others) and colour nicely and go floppy in a good way. Flip it over, same again and you're done. Apart from buttering one side of it. Do that now.

Lay the paratha on a chopping board, buttered side up, and smear the onion/yoghurt mixture all over it. Mix up the herbs and put them in an even layer all about the place. Put the lamb skewer off centre and fold the bread over it and press your hand down firmly on the bread where the meat is. Whip the skewer out leaving the meat inside.

Open the thing up again and squeeze the lime on.

Roll it up, pat yourself on the back, YOU'RE AN ABSOLUTE BADASS!

TINKERINGS

The chilli paneer on page 196 is AMAZING in one of these! Kati Rolls come in many forms. There are ones with eggs and cheese, different meats, different marinades, the possibilities are endless. A big smear of the coconut chutney on page 228 would be wonderful in here as would Meera Sodha's Coriander Chutney (page 239).

When my dad and I get a takeaway from our local Indian restaurant, Chutneys in Shaftesbury, I mostly order a Peshwari naan, a large portion of chicken tikka (dry), an onion salad and extra of the green, minty, yoghurty sauce. At home I smear the sauce all over the naan, put the meat down the middle, put the onion salad all over that, roll it up and eat it as a kebab. Life is a joy.

A BREAKFAST BAO

Having lunch at Bao (the brilliant restaurant on Lexington Street) in Soho years ago I had my tiny mind blown about what could go in a bao. As a man who often wakes with a headache, there's something about the softness and snugness of a bao that makes me feel like everything's going to be alright.

Is a bao a sandwich? Well it's here, so you know how I feel... In the first sandwich book I put a whole fry up (beans and all) in between two pieces of bread for a breakfast sandwich, so I thought I'd go the opposite way this time and do something lighter, more delicate and veggie.

Years ago, my dear friend Ben Falk made a 'tiny food' film of my sarnie shop's Ham, Egg 'n' Chips sandwich which you can find on the @lunchluncheon YouTube channel. This isn't that small by any means, but it's what made me think of doing this – just the look of the fried quail's eggs and little rösti makes me want to well up with joy.

---

4 shop-bought, frozen bao (the Yutaka brand will do the job)
4 small tomatoes (a bit bigger than cherry)
1 medium potato, peeled
4 slices of smoked tofu (the Tofoo Co.'s is very good)
Plain (all-purpose) flour, for dusting

Vegetable oil, for frying
4 quail's eggs
Any sauce you like, on the side, for dunking (brown sauce, bulldog sauce, ketchup, hot sauce?)
Salt

Ideally an hour before you want to put your bao together, trim the top and bottom off the tomatoes leaving just the plump middle slices, sprinkle them with salt, turn them over, sprinkle the other side with salt, and leave them on a plate.

Reheat (re-steam?) the bao according to the packet instructions.

Coarsely grate 2 heaped tablespoons of peeled potato into a little bowl and season it generously with salt. This is all you need for your rösti.

Slice the smoked tofu about 5 mm (¼ in) thick and a bit wider than your bao buns. Then roll the slices in the flour.

Pour veg oil into a large frying pan (skillet) until the whole bottom is coated in oil. Get it on a medium heat. Once it's heated up, put 4 generous teaspoons of the shredded potato into the pan in neat, little heaps. Press them down with the back of the spoon into round-ish shapes. Put the slices of smoked tofu in. Let everything sizzle for a bit. Once golden, using a spoon, flip the rösti and the tofu, fry the tomato slices on both sides and finally, crack the quail's eggs in and sprinkle a tiny bit of salt on them.

The quail's eggs are surprisingly tricky to crack. I recommend using a butter-type knife to break into the egg and then use your fingers to pull the shell's halves apart.

Once golden on both sides, remove the rösti onto some paper towels for just a moment, and do the same with the tofu slices and the tomatoes. While the yolks are still runny, if that's how you like them, whip the eggs out.

Prise open your reheated bao and put in the tofu, followed by the tomato, the egg and lastly a rösti. Close the thing up, watch the yolk run, pick one up, dunk it in the sauce you chose and gobble it down. Isn't that tofu great! So redolent of bacon! Go again.

TINKERINGS

You could make bao if you want to, of course. If you'd like to, buy the book *Bao* by Erchen Chang, Shing Tat Chung and Wai Ting Chung. You could drop the smoked tofu and replace it with any number of meaty treats: pieces of black pudding, a sausage taken from its skin and split into patties, a rasher of good (Denhay, or premium supermarket own) smoked streaky bacon cut into 5-cm (2-in) lengths. OMG, you could poach the quail's eggs! The breakfast world is your oyster.

111

PORCHETTA SANDWICH

Gremolata might sound posh, but it really isn't, it's just a tiny salad and it's delicious and ridiculously useful. As good sprinkled on barbecued prawns, as on slices of rare steak, a fillet of fried fish or a plate of chickpeas (garbanzos). As culinary weapons go, this is another flavour scud missile.

Ben's porchetta recipe is fantastic: intimidatingly large, not cheap and taking a long time to cook, it is a labour of love and all the better for it. Having said that, if you want to feed 10-ish friends all at the same time, without having to do much in the moment, it's about as simple as it gets.

The secret to this sarnie is to have a load of thin slices of porchetta rather than one big thick one.

---

6 thin slices of Porchetta (page 161)
Olive oil, for drizzling
1 floury bap (bread roll)
1 heaped tablespoon mayo (Hellman's or page 220)
1 lemon wedge, for squeezing
Salt

1 heaped tablespoon gremolata:
    1½ tablespoons parsley, really finely chopped
    Zest of ½ lemon
    ½ decent garlic clove, cut into tiny, tiny pieces

Preheat the oven to 100°C (210°F).

As it says in the recipe at the back, remember that porchetta is best sliced cold, upside down, with a serrated knife, and eaten warm.

Pop the prochetta slices on a baking tray, drizzle some olive oil on and squeeze the lemon wedge over. Season with salt and pop the tray in the oven to warm for about 20 minutes and get everything else ready.

Mix all the gremolata ingredients together in a small bowl. Cut the bun in half, toast the insides if the fancy takes you, and spread the mayo over the top and bottom. Put the warmed porchetta slices in a heap on the bottom with a generous sprinkling of gremolata between each slice. Put the lid on and hit it.

TINKERINGS

Vegetables? You could put some rocket (arugula) in here, but there's a good chance that's an abomination. Fennel cut very thinly (on a mandoline, or with that julienne peeler you bought), soaked in cold water to crisp and curl, then dressed with lemon juice might be nice, but what a faff!

Maybe the best thing to do, if you want to do anything, is to make it even simpler: ditch the mayo and gremolata and try just meat and Salsa Verde (page 232), or if you want to go a bit rogue, just the meat and some Chimichurri (page 231). Or, why not have a go at just meat? Tweet me, or X me, etc.

THERE AIN'T NO TREAT

LIKE A BREADED MEAT

(OR FISH)

A TUNA KATSU SANDO
TOTALLY RIPPED OFF ANA AND MENG'S
TĀTĀ EATERY WORK OF GENIUS

Refer to previous page. Nuff said.

Tātā Eatery's Katsu Sandwich (Google it, or ask the chatbot about it or whatever) is THE BEST, MOST DELICIOUS version of the classic Katsu Sando EEEVVVEEERRRRR. Much as I would love to steal it wholesale, Ibérico pork collar (presa) is very difficult to buy and I can't tell anyone to sous vide anything, so I give you this instead, which is still a belter obviously. The raspberry jam mixed with brown sauce is, I believe, Meng's invention and SUCH a fun and delicious play on tonkatsu sauce!!!

---

1 breaded, fresh tuna steak (page 178), put in the freezer for 1 hour after breading
1 teaspoon raspberry jam
1 teaspoon brown sauce (HP is best, OBVS)
A little splash of Worcestershire Sauce
1 litre (34 fl oz/4¼ cups) vegetable oil
2 slices of brioche, from one of those loaves the supermarket sells (or 2 slices of Hovis-type, supermarket sliced white bread)

1 tablespoon room temperature butter
1 tablespoon store-bought XO Sauce (the Way-On (Scallop) one is great and Lee Kum Kee's one will do)
Handful of really finely shredded raw cabbage – hispi, sweetheart or classic white (not Savoy) (there should be way more cabbage than in the sandwich I made for the photograph)

Against conventional wisdom, Shaun Searley, one of my culinary heroes and the man in charge of the food at one of my favourite restaurants The Quality Chop House, cooks his steaks straight from the refrigerator. This allows him to get more crust and colour on the meat without overcooking the inside.

After breading the tuna steak, you have put it in the freezer so that when you deep fry it the fish won't overcook, or really, cook at all, and the breadcrumbs can get crisp and golden.

Toast the brioche slices. Once done, lean them together in an upside down 'V' to cool. (If using Hovis-type bread, toast just one side under your grill.)

Mix the raspberry jam, brown sauce and Worcestershire sauce together in a little bowl.

If you have a deep-fat fryer, get it on to 180°C (350°F). If you don't, you know the drill: get a high-sided saucepan and put the veg oil in it. Bring it up to 180°C (350°F), the temperature at which a piece of bread sizzles and goes gold in about 20 seconds.

Trim the crusts from the brioche (or the white bread) very gently with a serrated knife. Butter what will be the bottom slice and slather it in XO sauce. (The reason we toast both sides of the brioche but only one side of the Hovis-type bread is because the brioche just falls apart otherwise – the toasted sides of the Hovis-type bread will be the insides of the sandwich, so if you're using the sliced white, slather the toasted side of one of the pieces in butter and XO sauce.)

Take the tuna out of the freezer and fry it. It shouldn't take more than 2–3 minutes to go really golden. Once it has, let it rest for a few minutes on some paper towels, or ideally on a little wire rack, then pop it on top of the XO sauce and give it a sprinkle of salt.

Slather your other slice of brioche with the jam mixture. Scatter the cabbage evenly over the tuna and in larger quantity than in the picture. Put the lid on, cut the sandwich in half the way you like it (triangles, rectangles or squares, who cares?) with your sharpest, sharpest knife and do not press down on it at all, just saw the knife back and forth in long motions and let it cut through rather than pressing on it. Once you're through, look at the cut through and admire the beauty that sits before you. Congratulations, you've made a sandwich with a degree in architecture.

→

TINKERINGS

If you don't have an Asian supermarket within reach, or you don't buy stuff from souschef.co.uk, you could arguably make this without the XO sauce. Any breaded meat could go in here, or even some kind of breaded vegetable perhaps. All the recipes in this half of the book are to inspire you to think about what you might be able to sandwich, as much as telling you what to sandwich.

A BIG, BAD, BOURBON-Y
CARAMELISED BANANA HOTDOG

Come on, I had to! If there's a banana hotdog of a menu... Look at that picture overleaf! It looks SO much like a hotdog doesn't it?! Hahaha!

1 teaspoon Banana Nesquik (milkshake powder)

1 heaped tablespoon mascarpone

1 brioche hotdog bun, or another long, sweet bun or at a push, a regular hotdog bun

1 Bourbon Caramelised Banana (page 215)

½ slice of pineapple (fresh or tinned), core removed and chopped into tiny pieces

½ teaspoon sprinkles or hundreds and thousands or whatever

Beat the Nesquik into the mascarpone in a bowl. When these are combined, they are known as 'Jack Storer's Banana Cream'. Thank you, Jack.

Cut the hotdog bun if it isn't cut already and pop it in a steamer if you can be arsed (it's not essential here). It can be steamed in a vegetable steamer or one of those perforated metal things (or the bamboo ones) that sit on top of a saucepan of boiling water. It will only need about 30 seconds to become very soft and pliable.

Put Jack's Banana Cream all down the length of the bun inside the crevice. Pop the caramelised banana on top of that, with more of the boozy caramel from the pan on it. Sprinkle the little bits of pineapple on that and lastly, a good sprinkling of sprinkles.

Three bites? That's what I did mine in.

TINKERINGS

The best sprinkles in the world, which I sadly forgot to take to the photoshoot but did have, are definitely the Expen$ive Sprinkles made by Rich Myers, the man behind Get Baked! Check them out!!!

Different crunchy things, crushed up, would be really good: nuts, biscuits, caramelised nuts, Crunchy Nut Cornflakes, etc. To make it even more banana-y, you could blend up some of those dried banana chips and whack them on top to keep the sprinkles company. A little drizzle of pomegranate molasses or some desiccated coconut would be great! Different flavour Nesquik? You could try it with jams, all manner of chocolate and hazelnut or speculoos type spreads (Nutella, Biscoff, etc etc). If you think it too sweet, you could use cream cheese, thick (strained?) yoghurt or posh crème fraîche instead of the mascarpone. You could cover the entire thing in a mountain of squirty cream, get in there face first with your hands behind your back and play find the caramelised banana?!

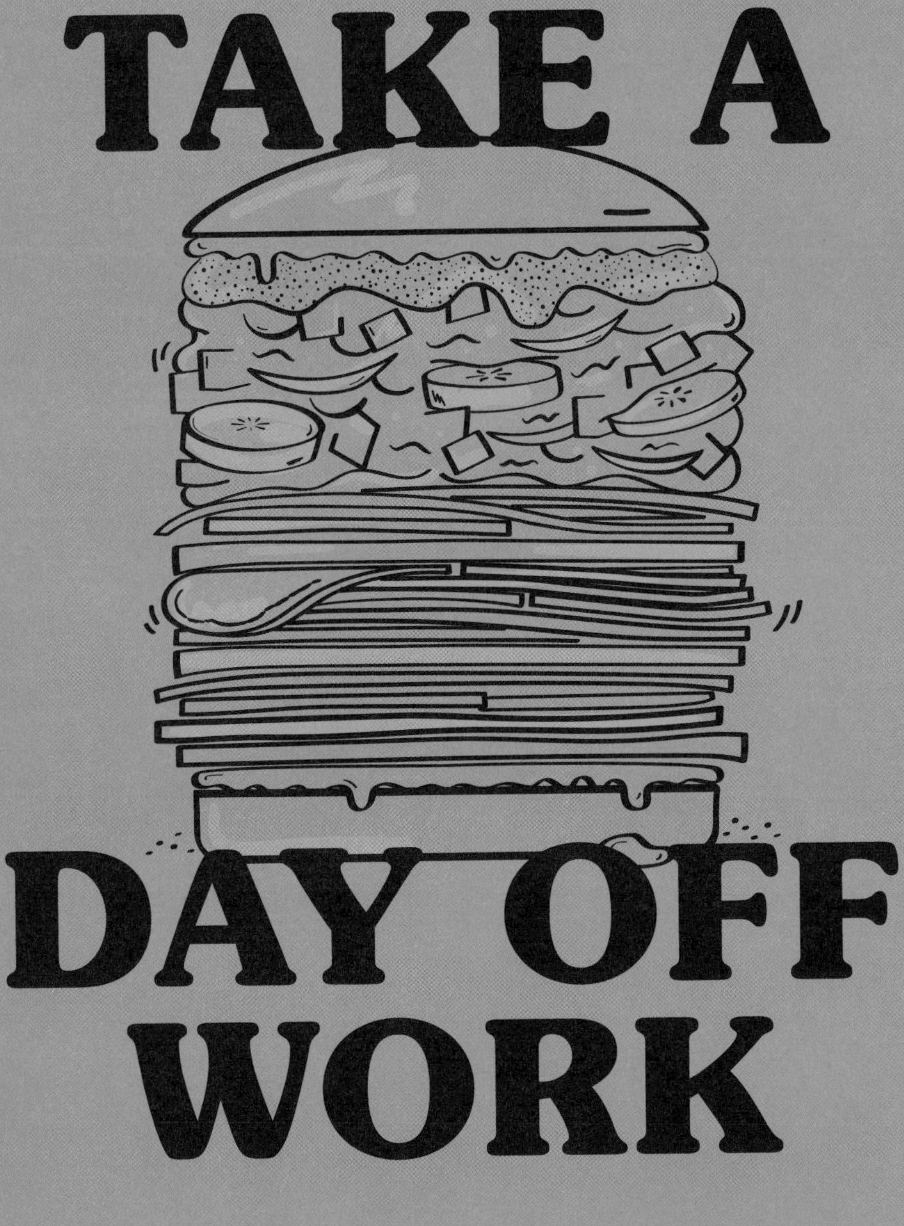
TAKE A
DAY OFF
WORK

TIKKANOTHER LITTLE PIECE OF MY HEART

This is a Sandwich Shop favourite, but the shop's focaccia recipe isn't in this book, because it's in first one and I was worried people would think I was lazy, so you're gonna have to buy some focaccia to replicate this totally (which is arguably easier I guess). You could also buy the first sandwich book, but that's gonna make this sandwich EXPENSIVE. I tell you what, I'll whack a video of how to make it on the @lunchluncheon YouTube channel too, to save you the cash! If I were you, I'd just forget about the focaccia element, buy a mini supermarket ciabatta and have done with it.

When we went to Lyndy's Fish and Chip Shop as kids, my darling sister Lydia always had a chicken burger, and I always had a chicken tikka pizza. A lifelong tikka love affair began.

110 g (3¾ oz) Goat Tikka Masala Braise (page 160)
1 massive slab of focaccia
2 heaped tablespoons Lime-pickle (and Gravy?) Mayo (page 224)
Handful of Bombay Mix (if you can find it, London Mix is better because it's finer – I like CoFresh)

1 teaspoon pomegranate molasses
50 g (1¾ oz) Lime-pickled Onions (mixed with 1 teaspoon nigella seeds – page 261)
4 sprigs of coriander (cilantro), leaves picked
4 sprigs of mint, leaves picked
4 sprigs of flat leaf parsley, leaves picked

Put the meat in a pan with a splash of water and get it nice and hot. Split the focaccia in half and cover the inside of the top in the mayonnaise and cover that in the Bombay/London Mix.

Put the hot meat onto the bottom of the bread in an even layer and drizzle it with the pomegranate molasses.

Spread the lime-pickled onions and nigella seeds over the meat in an even layer.

Mix the herbs together and pile them on.

Put the lid on and imagine you're in Finsbury Park and some handsome bloke in a black polo shirt is shouting and waving and probably drinking a shot and the lights are a little too low and the music is a little too loud and someone's getting upset after they've put their suggestion for a fish finger sandwich into the shredder suggestions box, and you're basically at the Sandwich Shop.

DRE'S SILKY BÉCHAMEL
LASAGNA SANDWICH

SILKY BÉCHAMEL, the best rapper ever. Before telling you how to do this Sandwich Shop classic I gotta tell you how it came about!

One of my guiltiest pleasures is putting a slice of leftover lasagna in a croissant and toasting it in my toastie machine (page 32). I wanted to recreate the deliciousness of that croissant, but it felt antithetical to the Sandwich Shop's way of doing things to just bang some lasagna in a sandwich, so I came up with this.

It tastes just like all the things we like about lasagna but doesn't have lasagna in it and has become a huge customer favourite. Sometimes, when it's on the menu, it even outsells the Ham, Egg 'n' Chips!

If I was making this at home, I would definitely make too much bolognese when I make spaghetti bolognese and use that for this, rather than getting the goat in and stuff.

---

120 g (4½ oz) Goat Bolognese (page 172), or leftover Bolognese

50 g (1½ oz) 'Nduja Mayonnaise (page 223)

75 g (2½ oz) Taleggio Béchamel (page 245)

A handful of boiled, Deep Fried and Crushed Macaroni, AKA The Blender Destroyer (page 207)

2 heaped tablespoons Pickled Mirepoix (page 255)

1 huge slab of focaccia (the Sarnie Shop's focaccia recipe isn't in here as I explained on page 125, so feel free to use a supermarket mini ciabatta)

Baby Gem and Rocket Salad (50/50), dressed with vinaigrette, the moment before using it (page 241) – this is the salad I always have with lasagna

---

Get the grill (broiler) on hot and get the meat and some of its sauce nice and hot in a pan. Ready the mayonnaise, béchamel and crushed pasta.

Cut your bread in half and cover the bottom in the hot meat and the top in mayo. Smear cooled béchamel all over the meat (you might be able to slice it!) and pop the bottom of the sarnie under the grill to melt the béchamel.

When it's melted and bubbled, whip it out, let it cool for a moment and sprinkle pickled mirepoix all over it. Dress the salad and put on top of the pickled mirepoix, sprinkle the crushed up pasta all over the mayo, put the lid on and HUSTLE. Does it remind you of lasagna? Please say it does!

I love how the pasta gives the sandwich a back teeth crunch rather than a whole mouth crunch like a crisp gives you! Know what I mean?

LEFTOVER ROAST LAMB, RATATOUILLE, ONION SOUBISE, SAFFRON MAYO, TAPENADE

Now I look at it, this sounds like something out of *Lulu's Provençal Table* but never mind that. As a plate of food it is magnificent, but it will take you all of the day, and possibly half of the night. On the plate you want a heap of lamb shoulder or leg, doused in some of its gravy, sitting on top of a little lake of the soubise. A big spoon of ratatouille on the side, a scoop of tapenade, a scoop of saffron mayo and some crusty bread. Heaven. Then tomorrow, you can make this sandwich. As I wrote in the first sandwich book: 'Together, Ben and I would like to encourage just generally, the idea of making a delicious dinner for tonight, with a sandwich in mind for tomorrow.'

Harry Mackintosh, the man who taught me to cook, showed me how to make this ratatouille and while labour intensive, it is the bee's bloody knees and a welcome relief from the usual mooshy chunks of courgette.

1 really sturdy crusty bun or bap (this is juicy!)

1 tablespoon tapenade (page 238), mixed with
  1 scant tablespoon mayonnaise

1 heap of leftover roast lamb leg or shoulder (whichever one you have) reheated in some gravy if you have any (pages 148–149) or a splash of water

2 tablespoons Onion Soubise, warm (page 186)

4 heaped tablespoons ratatouille (page 213), warmed up a bit – it is also good cold though

2 tablespoons saffron mayo (page 226)

Cut your bun in half and spread the bottom with tapenade. Pile the hot meat on top of that, then slather the meat with onion soubise. Ratatouille next – did you heat it up?

Lastly, smother the top bit of bread, from edge to edge, in the saffron mayo. Bang the lid on, give it a squish and get going sharpish before the structural integrity of the thing begins to slip.

TINKERINGS

Of course, some kind of crushed-up crisp arrangement might be nice, sprinkled all over the mayo before you put the lid on.

PART TWO
COMPONENTS

Dearest lovely everyone,

That may be the end of the sarnies, but it is only the beginning of everything you need to make them yourself, and to come up with amazing things all of your own.

Many of the recipes that follow are Ben's and they are brilliant. He's an extraordinary cook, obsessed with deliciousness and more fun than Hunter S. Thompson's birthday party. Oh, and one last thing: PLEASE remember that you do NOT need to make your own bread or mayonnaise to make amazing sandwiches. But if you want to, there's recipes for everything here.

Big Love,

Max

BREADS

How-to
videos

We are not saying, in any way, that you need
to make your own bread to make great sandwiches,
but you can if you want.

In the first sandwich book we gave you the
Max's Sandwich Shop Focaccia recipe, and we want
to give you a few similarly useful ones in this book,
without repeating ourselves and looking lazy.

There are how-to videos for both the breads that
follow (and that foccacia recipe) in the 'Max's World
of Sandwiches – Bread Recipes' section of the
@lunchluncheon YouTube channel – check 'em out!
With much of this stuff, pictures are easier than
words. Speaking of which, here come those words…

A NICE EVERYDAY SANDWICH BREAD

Most of the sandwiches in this book are best made in sauce-soaking, loose-crumbed rolls, baps, buns or small breads of some kind. This isn't a bread book though, it's a sandwich book, so we've come up with this hopefully one-stop shop for you. Versatile, easy to make into different shapes (a whole big loaf, baguette-ish stick, nice round bun-ish, etc) and hopefully pretty simple as long as you have some time on your hands.

Makes 4–6 rolls

40 ml (2½ tablespoons)
  extra virgin olive oil (plus extra
  for greasing)
8 g (¼ oz) fine sea salt
500 g (1 lb 2 oz/3½ cups) strong
  white bread flour, plus extra
  for dusting
300 ml (10 fl oz/1¼ cups)
  warm water
1 sachet or 7 g (⅛ oz)
  dry active yeast

MOST OF THE WORK FOR THESE NEEDS TO BE DONE THE DAY BEFORE.

This is an overnight dough, which admittedly requires some planning, but the benefit is that it doesn't really require any kneading. So, and sorry, but the night before you need these for sandwiching:

Mix the oil and salt together in a little ramekin or cup or something.

Combine the flour, water and dry yeast in a mixing bowl and bring together into a very loose dough with your hands. This'll happen quickly (1 minute) and loads will stick to your fingers. Add the oil and salt and mix and squeeze and knead about again, so that everything is incorporated (2 minutes) and you have a nice ball of dough and a cleaner bowl. Everything should have mostly come off your fingers now and things should be looking better. Cover the bowl with a clean tea towel (dish towel) and leave it somewhere warm (airing cupboard, top shelf in a cosy kitchen) for 30 minutes to start the proving process.

After 30 minutes, and before you pop it in the refrigerator for its long, gentle overnight proving, you need to quickly wet your hands under the cold tap (faucet) and perform a few folds of the dough.

Put the bowl in front of you and imagine the dough is a square with four sides, top, bottom, left and right. Reach out using both (wet) hands, pinch a few centimetres (about an inch) of the dough starting at the top, between your thumb and four fingers (not forefingers), lift it up in the air, stretching it up a bit (about 15 cm/6 in) and press it down into the centre of the bowl. Turn the bowl 90 degrees and do the same again. And again. And again. Now all four 'sides' of the dough have been lifted, stretched and pressed into the middle of the bowl. Your work is done.

Replace the tea towel and pop the bowl in the refrigerator while you idle the night away (10–12 hours).

The following morning, take the dough from the refrigerator, wet your hands again and perform a second series of folds exactly the same as last night. Leave the bowl somewhere warm again with the tea towel still over it and let the dough double in size, which should take an hour, at worst, two, depending on warmth, humidity, luck and all sorts of annoying things that affect the life of the baker. Perform one last folding session and let the dough prove again for another hour. By now the dough should be pretty smooth and full of air, with amazing nice bubbles just below the surface.

Once it has proved, dust your work surface and the surface of the dough with a little of the flour you used to make it and carefully flop the dough out onto your counter, top side down, using the tips of four fingers as a make-shift scraper to get everything out of the bowl. Dust the exposed side of the dough with flour and prepare to shape your rolls.

Flour your hands and gently shape the dough into a roughly rectangular shape before cutting it in half lengthways with a knife or dough scraper and cutting each length into 2 or 3 equal-size chunks, depending on how big you want your rolls/breads to be.

Line a baking tray (pan) with baking parchment cut to the size of the bottom of the tray. If you put a touch of oil (veg/olive/whatever) on the bottom of the tray and smear it around everywhere, this will help the parchment stick to the bottom. Once the parchment is stuck down, add a further dusting of flour and carefully place on the rolls you have, one by one, with as much space as you can between each other and the edges of the tray – remember they will rise. They'll be a bit wonky; they could even stick together like hot cross buns if your tray isn't really big enough, but this is nice and rustic, innit. Cover the tray with your tea towel again and leave to one side while you heat your oven to its top heat, which should be about 250°C (480°F) or perhaps even higher.

Once the oven has reached temperature, place the baking tray (pan) with the dough in it, on a shelf in the centre of a hot oven and splash/throw a spoon (1 tablespoon) of water straight onto the floor of the oven. Shut the door immediately, turn the oven down to 200°C (400°F) and bake the rolls for 20–25 minutes, or until golden brown on top and hollow sounding when tapped on their underside.

Once cooked, leave to cool on a wire rack and resist sandwiching until completely cooled.

These guys freeze very well. Once they've cooled, feel free to bag 'em up, suck the air from the bag, twist it, tie it up and chuck 'em in. To reheat, pop them in a 180°C (350°F) oven for 6–8 minutes, straight from frozen on a baking tray (pan) lined with baking parchment..

BEN'S LOVELY FLATBREADS

A flatbread is a useful weapon in any culinary arsenal. They can easily turn any barbecue, or any meal, into a sandwich/wrapwich affair and they are puffy, fluffy and delicious rubbed with butter and dunked in just about anything.

Makes 6–8

200 ml (7 fl oz/scant 1 cup) warm water

1 teaspoon caster (superfine) sugar

1 pack dried instant yeast (they tend to be 7 g (⅛ oz), which is what you need here, weigh it if you're unsure)

500 g (1 lb 2 oz/3½ cups) strong white bread flour, plus extra for dusting

1 teaspoon fine sea salt

120 g (4¼ oz) good Greek yoghurt

2 tablespoons extra virgin olive oil

THESE CAN BE MADE, BAKED AND EATEN/SANDWICHED ALL IN ONE DAY.

You can knead these by hand, but let's not beat around the bush – an electric mixer with a dough hook is gonna make your life a million times easier and help this whole affair not be a complete disaster.

Use a measuring jug (pitcher) for the water and throw the sugar and yeast into it. Whisk it vigorously and put to one side for 15 minutes to get bubbly and frothy. If it doesn't get lively in this time, it's likely been in your cupboard for ten years and needs sacking off. Buy some new yeast and start again.

While your yeast and water mix sits, put the flour, salt, yoghurt and oil in the bowl of your electric mixer (or a big bowl) and give it a cursory mix on a low speed to combine everything.

Once the yeast mixture is good and frothy, and 15 minutes is up, toss it into the flour/yoghurt mixture and set the mixer off again for 3 minutes on the lowest speed (or knead in the bowl for a few minutes, then turn it out onto a floured surface and knead properly by hand for 5 minutes).

Pull the dough from the mixing bowl and form it into a rough ball in your hands. Hold it from underneath with both hands like someone is passing you a watermelon or a bowling ball and using your fingers tuck both the sides under and in on themselves so it starts to look like a Super Mario turtle shell. After every tuck, turn the dough in your hands 90 degrees until you've gone all the way round twice.

It should now have a smooth(ish) top and a less smooth bottom. Sometimes it's really smooth, sometimes it isn't, it'll be alright. Plonk your ball (turtle shell) into a big bowl, cover with cling film (plastic wrap) and leave it somewhere warm to prove for 1 hour or at least until doubled in size.

All that remains after that, is to take the risen dough from the bowl and gently knock it back (give it another gentle knead with your hands for 10 seconds or so), then shape it into a round-ish loaf shape. Cut it into 6 or 8 equal-size pieces (like a cake) with a knife, depending how big you want your flatbreads, then roll each piece into a ball, either between both hands, or deftly, with one hand, on the work surface like a pro.

Leave these to one side while you warm a nice wide frying pan (skillet) on a medium heat.

Finally, working on a floured surface, use a rolling pin or wine bottle to roll each ball into a 5 mm (¼ in) thick, roughly round shape. One at a time, put a rolled-out piece of dough into your hot, dry pan, and don't move it until you start to see big bubbles/air pockets forming. Flip the bread and watch it puff up and cook on the other side. Once both sides are flecked with little golden brown patches/attractive burny bits and the bread feels light and puffy, remove from the pan, and put inside a folded-in-half tea towel (dish towel) (in a 50°C/120°F oven) and repeat for all the remaining breads.

If you only need a couple of breads at a time, you can freeze the balls of dough, bring them out of the freezer to defrost a few hours before you need them and then roll out on a floury surface and cook as above.

MEAT

& FISH

BEN'S FANTASTIC CEVICHE

This isn't for a sandwich, it's just delicious. Ben pinched this recipe from a New Zealander who pinched it from a Fijian. An untraditional route to ceviche maybe, but the end result is banging and provides plenty of leche de tigre (the milky liquid often drunk as a hangover cure) to lap down like a dog with heat stroke.

Serves 4

400 g (14 oz) nice, skinned white
  fish fillets, such as bass, bream,
  hake, haddock (prawns/shrimp
  and slices of the white bit of
  scallops are also good)
Juice of 6 limes
Big pinch of salt
2 long, not crazy hot, red chillies,
  deseeded and finely chopped
½ red onion, very finely chopped
Big handful of coriander
  (cilantro), leaves set aside,
  stalks finely chopped
2 ripe passion fruits

If you haven't got your fishmonger to skin the fillets for you, watch a YouTube tutorial, it's easier than you might think, but there is a knack.

Once skinned, cut the fillet (not lengthways) into slices about 1 cm (⅓ in) thick, then cut those slices into smaller chunks also about 1 cm (⅓ in) wide. Toss these into a glass or plastic bowl with the lime juice, salt, chillies, onion and coriander stalks.

Cut the top off the passion fruit and empty their insides into a sieve (fine mesh strainer) over the fish bowl, and scrape everything about with a spoon so you only get the juice, not the seeds (if you don't mind the crunchy seeds – as many don't – just empty the passion fruit straight into the fish bowl without the sieve).

Give everything a really good but gentle stir and leave it in the refrigerator for 2–3 hours to do its thing. Eat it straight from the refrigerator with gusto and sprinkled with the coriander leaves. Using baby gem lettuce leaves as little edible cups is a lovely way to go.

Stored in an airtight container in the refrigerator this will last for 48 hours or so before the fish becomes a bit pappy, which is never nice.

PICKLED PRAWNS
KIND OF À LA GABRIELLE HAMILTON

Gabrielle Hamilton owned New York restaurant Prune, which has now closed down but apparently might re-open. Jeopardy huh?! There were pickled shrimps on the menu there, for which there is a recipe in her cookbook, also called *Prune*. They're a lovely idea, but a massive hassle so this is a simplified (if still relatively laborious) version along very similar lines. Buy wild, not farmed shrimp if you can/care. Do this in a plastic or glass Tupperware with a lid – nothing metal. This isn't cheap. Sorry!

Makes enough for 4 sandwiches

500 g (1 lb 2 oz) nice, big, raw prawns (jumbo shrimp), heads removed if present and peeled (and deveined if you care/can be bothered)

For the pickle liquor:

2 lemons, 1 halved and sliced, 1 juiced (just keep the juice, not the lemon)

1 small onion, peeled and thinly sliced

4 garlic cloves, thinly sliced

1 celery stalk, quite thinly sliced

4 bay leaves (either fresh or dried, I don't mind)

500 ml (17 fl oz/2 cups) extra virgin olive oil

500 ml (17 fl oz/2 cups) vinegar (Hamilton uses rice vinegar but white wine vinegar is fine if you haven't got that)

¼ teaspoon salt

8 grinds of black pepper

You will need: a sheet of baking parchment cut to the same size as the container you'll be pickling your prawns in.

First, you boil, then you pickle.

Before you start on the boil, combine all the pickle liquor ingredients in the airtight container large enough to hold them (and later the prawns) and leave to one side.

Bring a pot of water large enough for all the prawns to the boil. Throw all the prawns in the boiling water and count to 60. That's it.

Drain the prawns into a colander.

Put them into the pickling liquor (make sure they are all submerged) and allow to cool completely. Press the baking parchment sheet onto the top of the liquid, which will keep everything below sea level, put the lid on and leave them to pickle for 24 hours in the refrigerator before tucking into them or making a Bánh Mì (page 85) or a crispy bacon and shrimp salad or something.

If kept under the liquid in the refrigerator, these will probably keep for a week at least, but they're seafood and the publisher's lawyers are busy enough, so give them 2 days and nothing more.

ROAST LAMB SHOULDER

Like your grandma used to make, if she ever cooked lamb shoulder, and it was a bit like this.

Makes enough to serve 4 and then have some leftover for a sandwich or two the next day, or makes a lot of sandwiches straight up

1 whole head of garlic, halved horizontally
3 big onions, halved
5–6 sprigs each of rosemary, thyme and sage
1 lamb shoulder (bone in), roughly 2 kg (4 lb 8 oz), removed from the refrigerator at least 1 hour before cooking
1 tablespoon extra virgin olive oil
1 tablespoon fine sea salt
200 ml (7 fl oz/¾ cup) white wine
50 ml (3 tablespoons) red wine vinegar
125 ml (6 fl oz/½ cup) water

Preheat the oven as hot as it will go.

In the middle of a large roasting tray, place the halved garlic, onions and the herbs. These are going to act as a very tasty trivet/plinth.

Rub the lamb shoulder all over with the oil and salt and place it on the tasty plinth. Add the liquids to the tray, then cover with a layer of baking parchment followed by two layers of kitchen foil and seal the tray nice and tightly.

Place in the hot oven and immediately reduce the heat to 150°C (300°F). Cook for 3½ hours.

The meat will easily pull away from the bone(s). Any sauce left in the tray can be reduced to a lovely gravy, while the meat sits and rests somewhere covered in tin foil (for 20 minutes).

I like a lamb leg to still be a little pink once cooked (but never rare – whatever they say in posh restaurants in France), and so that's what we're aiming for below. And please buy a temperature probe.

Makes enough to serve 4 and then have some leftover for a sandwich or two the next day, or makes a lot of sandwiches straight up

3 onions, halved

1 whole head of garlic, halved horizontally

1 lamb leg (bone in), roughly 2 kg (4 lb 8 oz), removed from the refrigerator at least 1 hour before cooking

4 garlic cloves, thinly sliced

Handful of rosemary, thyme and sage, leaves picked, finely chopped and mixed together

1 tablespoon extra virgin olive oil

1 tablespoon fine sea salt

200 ml (7 fl oz/¾ cup) white wine

Preheat the oven as hot as it will go. Take a big roasting tray and pop the halved onions and head of garlic in its centre as a tasty trivet/plinth for the leg to sit on.

Pop your lamb leg on a board and, using a sharp little knife, make a load of holes (10?) into the lamb all the way down to the bone. Using your finger, stuff a slice or two of garlic and a good pinch of the herb mix into the incisions. This is all quite Jamie Oliver, who I'd imagine got it off Simon Hopkinson, but it is nice and gives a very old-fashioned feeling to the thing, which I like, even if it doesn't really do THAT much. Once done, smother the meat all over with the oil, then the salt and transfer to the roasting tray, sat on the onion, garlic and any of the herbs you have left and pour the white wine around it.

Bang this in the hot oven and roast for 20 minutes at full blast. Reduce the temperature to 180°C (350°F) and cook for another 40–50 minutes, depending on how pink you like your lamb. You could easily check the internal temperature of the meat with a probe, if you want to nail that blushing pink – it needs to come out at 55°C (131°F) for medium (pink) and 65°C (149°F) for cooked through/well done as it will go up at least 5°C (41°F) more while it rests. So pull the thing out when it's somewhere between those windows.

Once cooked, cover the lamb with kitchen foil and rest for 20 minutes to give things a chance to settle before you carve it up.

As always, the tray juices and oniony gubbins make a banging little sauce, even if it's only a few spoonfuls underneath all the liquid fat (which you can spoon off and discard, or retain in a little cup in the refrigerator, thinking you will use it for frying something, then throw it away in 3 weeks when you find it again and wonder what the hell it is).

SPICY CUMIN LAMB

This is roughly what you'll find in a Rou Jia Mo (or *meat in a bun*, to give the direct translation). There are pork and beef versions of Rou Jia Mo available in London, but this smoky, lamby little number is inspired by (and a slightly livelier version of) slightly livelier version of the one I've had at Xi'an Impression, near the Arsenal football stadium.

From what I understand, made classically with thin strips of lamb shoulder, but we're making it with minced (ground) lamb as he says it is quicker, cheaper, and arguably more delicious. Banged in a sandwich it is an absolute joy but eaten as it comes over rice with some vinegary (or even better, smacked) cucumbers (page 259) it is also a great treat, so make plenty and try that too.

When crushing things in a pestle and mortar, I find if you put some salt in too, it really helps get things (such as Sichuan peppercorns) broken down into a good, fine powder.

Makes 4 sarnies

2 tablespoons vegetable oil
1 tablespoon cumin seeds
500 g (1 lb 2 oz) good, fatty minced (ground) lamb
1 tablespoon ground cumin
½ teaspoon chilli (hot pepper) flakes
¼ teaspoon Sichuan peppercorns (red and green, or just one, red is easier to find), crushed to powder (a pestle and mortar is just the job here)
½ teaspoon salt
2 garlic cloves, grated
1 tablespoon light soy sauce
2 tablespoons Shaoxing rice wine
6 spring onions (scallions), top 5 mm (¼ in) and rooty bottoms discarded, finely sliced (green and white bits)
Small handful of coriander (cilantro), chopped

In a large frying pan (skillet) on a medium heat, heat the oil, toss in the cumin seeds and, after a few seconds of sizzling, add the lamb, and then use a wooden spoon to work it into a single layer. Leave it to cook for a good 2 minutes before breaking it up and turning it, then repeat your actions. Keep going like this until you have nicely browned lamb.

Add the ground cumin, chilli flakes and Sichuan peppercorns that you have, crushed into a powder in a pestle and mortar with the salt. Add the garlic, soy sauce and Shaoxing wine and bring to a simmer. Cover the pan with a lid, reduce the heat to a whisper, and leave to blip away for 15–20 minutes, by which time you should have thick, rich, almost dry lamb mixture that is spiced and seasoned to its highest capacity. Add the spring onions and coriander, plus a little splash of water if you think it needs it, and use as and when you fancy, preferably sandwiched in a pitta.

You'll need a couple of good long skewers for this, little, short ones will be no use at all. Metal is best, ideally those slightly flat ones with the jazzy, brass ends, but wooden will do, soaked in water for 30 minutes prior to using.

Serves 4

Zest and juice of 1 unwaxed lemon

1 tablespoon red wine vinegar

50 ml (3½ tablespoons) extra virgin olive oil

1 whole garlic bulb, cloves peeled and grated

2 teaspoons ground cumin

1 teaspoon ground coriander

1 teaspoon fennel seeds, ground

2 teaspoons fine sea salt

12 grinds of black pepper

1 tablespoon dried mint

700 g (1 lb 9 oz) boned lamb shoulder, cut into very thin strips

You want to give your lamb plenty of time in the marinade, so get this done and it can sit in the refrigerator overnight.

Combine the lemon zest and juice, vinegar, oil and garlic in a large bowl and whisk to combine. To this add the cumin, coriander, ground fennel, salt, pepper and dried mint and mix again.

You want your lamb shoulder cut into nice, even, thin strips, about 7–8 cm (2¾–3¼ in) wide, 3–4 cm (1¼–1½ in) high and less than 1 cm (⅓ in) thick. Then they'll go nicely on your skewers. The shape of your meat will dictate exactly how the strips come out of course. If you're handy with the steel if you know what I mean, do this yourself, if not, sweet talk your butcher.

Add your lamb to the marinade and mix well before covering with cling film (plastic wrap) and leaving in the refrigerator overnight.

When ready to cook, heat your grill (broiler) to full blast. Take your two skewers and line them up parallel on the bench in front of you 2.5 cm (1 in) apart. You're going to make a horizontal style spit for this shawarma. All you need to do is to slide the strips onto the skewers like sleepers on train tracks. Poke skewers through the left- and right-hand side of each slice. When you finish you should have a reconstituted piece of lamb made up of loads of thin slivers. Press these nice and close together, imagining that you're creating a doner kebab (kabob)-style spit. All that remains is to place this in a tray and pop it under the grill. Give it 3 minutes before turning it, then repeat this again and again. You want a nice mix of charred edges, on the brink of burning, and a nicely cooked inside. You'll likely need to give your shawarma 3–4 turns at 3 minutes a side before the meat is suitably burnished on the outside and cooked enough inside.

Once ready, hold the skewers vertical on a chopping board using a tea towel (dish towel) or oven glove or something and slice slithers of lamb from your shawarma just like they do in kebab shops on the high street. Rolled up in a flatbread with a load of goodies, this would be amazing.

P.S. These would be great treated exactly the same on the barbecue in the summer.

MACAU-STYLE FRIED PORK CHOP

Popularised in the West, I guess, by Anthony Bourdain, this culinary mash-up (allegedly), originally based on the Bifana (pages 98–99), delivers an insanely good bit of tasty, breaded meat, which just begs to be sandwiched or quite frankly, sliced and eaten with honey mustard or anything you might fancy.

Makes enough for 2 sandwiches

2 x 200 g (7 oz) pork chops, deboned (about 150 g/5½ oz without the bone)
2 garlic cloves, grated
2 star anise
½ teaspoon fine sea salt
Pinch of caster (superfine) sugar
2 teaspoons light soy sauce
8–10 grinds of black pepper
1 tablespoon white wine vinegar
100 g (3½ oz/1¾ cup) plain (all-purpose) flour
2 large free-range eggs
150 g (5½ oz/1½ cups) panko breadcrumbs
Vegetable oil, for frying

First, we need to make the marinade and prep the chops. If your chops have only a very thin layer of fat on them, just nick with a knife a few times into the fat along the length of the chop. You only need to cut about 2 mm (1/16 in). If they have a thicker layer of fat along one side (which I hope they do), cut down through the fat at 1-cm (½-in) intervals all the way from the base of the chop to the top (not all the way to the flesh but 90% of the way through the fat) – this is so the chop doesn't curl up too much while cooking. If you're really lucky and your chops have skin on, remove the skin, slice it into pieces, and chuck it in a 180°C (350°F) oven until it turns into amazing scratchings.

Add the pork chops, grated garlic, star anise, salt, sugar, soy sauce, pepper and vinegar to a glass/plastic bowl or a Tupperware and mix well with your hands, being a little rough on the pork to ensure the marinade gets well distributed and has every chance to penetrate evenly. Cover with cling film (plastic wrap) or put the lid on. Refrigerate overnight, or for at least 6 hours.

When you're ready to cook, put the flour on one plate in front of you, beat the eggs on another and sprinkle breadcrumbs on another. Pick the star anise out of the marinade and take out a chop. Press both sides of the chop and the fatty edge into the flour and shake off any excess. Dunk the chop into the beaten eggs, all over. Lastly, put it into the breadcrumbs, pressing them all over, including on the fat and in the little crevices, if they are there. Do the same with the other chop – they should be completely covered in breadcrumbs. If you have enough egg and breadcrumbs left, you could repeat the egging and breadcrumbing stages for a real thick coating, but I'll leave that to you.

Put enough oil in a frying pan (skillet) to come 3 mm (1/8 in) up the sides and put it on a medium heat. Once the oil is nice and hot, put the chops in and fry for about 4 minutes on each side. When deep golden brown and stupidly crisp, transfer the chops to a plate lined with paper towel (or ideally a little rack so they don't go soft) and sprinkle with salt. In his book *Appetites*, Bourdain toasts the white bread when making a sandwich with one of these, which I don't agree with, the meat is crunchy enough. He did also put an indeterminate chilli paste in there though, which I do agree with.

Crackling's difficult in a pot with a lid on, so this puppy is skinless. What a piece of pork though! Much like the Italian porchetta, slicing this thick gives you naughty, juicy, soft slabs of pork to eat with your choice of sides, or slicing it thin can give you a fantastic pork sandwich.

Makes enough to serve 4 and then have some leftover for a sandwich or two the next day, or makes a lot of sandwiches straight up

1.5–2 kg (3 lb 5 oz–4 lb 8 oz) piece of skinless rolled pork loin
2 tablespoons extra virgin olive oil
2 teaspoons fine sea salt
1 tablespoon English mustard
1 tablespoon good, dried oregano
1 teaspoon sweet, smoked paprika
2 onions, peeled and cut into wedges
1 tablespoon red wine vinegar

Place your rolled pork on a board and rub it with a little oil. Season all over with salt. Get an oven-proof (ideally Le Creuset-type) pan with a lid, big enough to hold your pork, on a medium heat. Slather the meat with the mustard, then the oregano and paprika. Add the onion wedges to the middle of the pan, then the vinegar, before placing the pork on top, add 500 ml (17 fl oz/2 cups) of water to the pan and bringing to the boil. Place the lid on the pan and reduce the heat to a whisper, leaving the pork blip, blip, blipping away for about 1½ hours until completely cooked through. You might want to check it after 45 minutes or 1 hour and top up the water a bit if needs be and things are looking dry.

If sandwiching with this, allow the meat to cool completely before slicing it. If using it for something else, slice as and when you wish. The sauce that results from cooking is very delicious indeed and can be used as a gravy, mixed into mayo for sandwiching, or simply drunk by the glass as an elixir for everlasting youth.

PORK GYROS

As in the shawarma recipe on page 151, you'll need a couple of good long skewers for this, little ones just won't do. Ideally, they should be metal and flat, as opposed to wooden and round. I like the ones with ornate brass ends. If you're using wooden ones, soak them in water for 30 minutes first.

Serves 4

2 tablespoons red wine vinegar
50 ml (3½ tablespoons) extra virgin olive oil
1 whole head of garlic, cloves peeled and finely grated
1 tablespoon sweet smoked paprika
2 teaspoons fine sea salt
1 teaspoon freshly ground black pepper
1 tablespoon dried oregano
700 g (1 lb 9 oz) pork shoulder, cut into loads and loads of very thin strips

You want to give your pork plenty of time in the marinade here, it could handle up to a day, so get this done ahead of time and relax.

Bang the vinegar, oil and garlic in a large (non-metal) bowl or Tupperware and whisk to combine. Add the paprika, salt, pepper and oregano and mix again.

You want your pork shoulder cut into nice, even, thin strips, about 7–8 cm (2¾–3¼ in) wide, 3–4 cm (1¼–1½ in) high and less than 1 cm (⅓ in) thick. Then they'll go nicely on your skewers. Your piece of pork shoulder will dictate exactly how the strips come out though. If you're good with a sword, do this yourself; if not, try and sweet talk your butcher. Good luck!

Add your pork to the marinade and mix well before covering it with cling film (plastic wrap) and leaving it in the refrigerator overnight.

When ready to cook, heat your grill (broiler) to the max. Take your two skewers and line them up, 4 cm (1½ in) apart, parallel on the bench. You're going to make horizontal-style spits for these gyros. All you need to do is to slide the strips of meat onto the skewers a bit like sleepers on train tracks. Poke the skewers through the left- and right-hand side of each slice. When you finish you should have a reconstituted block of pork made up of loads of thin slivers. Press these nice and close together, imagining that you're creating a doner kebab (kabob)-style spit. All that remains is to place this in a tray and pop it under a full heat grill (broiler). Give it 3 minutes before turning it, then repeat this again and again. You want that nice combination of charred edges, right on the verge of burning, and a nicely cooked inside. You'll likely need to give your gyros 3–4 turns at 3 minutes a side before the pork is suitably burnished on the outside and cooked inside.

Once ready, hold the skewers vertically on a chopping board with a tea towel (dish towel) and slice slithers of pork from your gyros just like they do in the gyros shops on holiday. Of course this is intended for the sandwich on page 101 but equally, you could serve it with nice bread and chopped salads and some tzatziki or tarama and imagine you're sat with your hot little feet in the Aegean and an ice-cold Mythos dripping condensation on the table.

N.B. If it's summer and you're considering lighting the barbecue, this would work just as well being turned in the same fashion over hot coals and sandwiched immediately rather than being refried as in the sandwich on page 101.

A cornerstone of the Cubano (one of the world's most loved sandwiches and essentially a jazzed-up ham and cheese toastie), this is normally made with a shoulder of pork marinated and then cooked in salsa of (at least) sour orange, cumin and oregano. It can be tough to find sour oranges though, so for pragmatism's sake any orange will do, but taste it, if the juice squeezes sweet, sour the marinade a little further with lemon juice.

Makes enough for sandwiches for DAYS for many people or feeds a ton of people as part of a meal, throw a party!

2.5–3 kg (5 lb 8 oz–6 lb 8 oz) skinless, boneless pork shoulder

Zest and juice of 2 medium unwaxed oranges

Zest and juice of 1 large unwaxed lemon

3 teaspoons fine sea salt

2 teaspoons ground cumin

10–12 grinds of black pepper

4 tablespoons good dried oregano

1 whole head of garlic, cloves separated, peeled, then grated

1 tablespoon extra virgin olive oil

1 onion, unpeeled and cut horizontally into 1-cm (½-in) slices

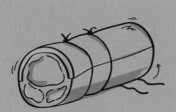

We've treated this a bit more like a porchetta than a traditional Cuban mojo pork in terms of how it's cooked. In a home kitchen it is easier to get consistent results this way. It does however, mean you'll need some butcher's twine, or some string soaked in water in order to roll this little porker up before cooking.

Preheat the oven to 230°C (450°F). Your deboned pork shoulder, which your butcher should have happily done for you, will be able to open out almost flat. If you need to, use a sharp knife to help it on its way, or to slice into it and even out any sections. Do so until you have a relatively uniform flat piece of pork laid out on a board in front of you, cut side facing up.

Drizzle half the orange and lemon juice on the pork and rub it all over, massaging it into the flesh. Then season the pork all over with 2 teaspoons of salt, then with the cumin, black pepper, dried oregano, orange and lemon zest and lastly the grated garlic.

Next, with the short edge of the pork shoulder facing you, measure out lengths of twine that are at least twice the height/length of the piece of pork in front of you. You'll likely need 5 or 6 lengths. Shuffle these evenly spaced under the pork from left to right. Roll the pork up like a jam roly-poly and tie it tightly with the first piece of string. Repeat this with each string, tightening it all each time, so that by then end you have a nice, tight, rolled and tied piece of pork. Rub the outside of the pork with the oil, then season with the final teaspoon of salt.

Place the onion slices, the squeezed lemon and oranges, any remaining juice and perhaps a few unpeeled garlic cloves in the middle of the base of a roasting tray. Place the pork on top of the goodies, add 200 ml (7 fl oz/scant 1 cup) of water to the roasting tray and cover with baking parchment and two layers of foil. Place in the hot oven and roast for 20 minutes, then reduce the temperature to 160°C (325°F) and cook for 2½–3 hours, or until the pork comes away like pulled pork when picked at with a fork or tongs.

Leave to rest for 30 minutes, before slicing, eating or sandwiching. You should be left with a delicious sauce in the roasting tray, this can be spooned over the cooked pork or chilled and beaten into mayo if you're naughty.

If you wanna make a Cuban Sandwich, get some of this meat, 2 slices of a good melting cheese (one put above and one below the meat inside the bread), some pickles, American mustard, cooked ham and some slices of salami (optional), put everything in a supermarket ciabatta/panini, mayo the outsides of the bread and fry and squish it in a pan (on both sides) until the cheese has melted and everything is hot inside.

ROAST HAM

Who doesn't love a roast ham? I mean it's Christmas, innit?! This is useful for knocking up a Jambon Beurre (page 30) or the Ham and Celeriac Rémoulade Sandwich on page 63 or for about 100,000,000 other things.

Please remember this is how you make a ham from scratch. You can of course buy a ham/gammon from the butcher already brined and/or already cooked and jump straight to the boiling or glaze bit of this recipe.

Makes enough to serve 4 and then have some leftover for a sandwich or two the next day, or makes a lot of sandwiches straight up

500 g (1 lb 2 oz) fine sea salt
250 g (9 oz/1¼ cups) caster (superfine) sugar
2 kg (4 lb 8 oz) boneless ham joint (unbrined)
5 bay leaves
1 tablespoon black peppercorns
2 big onions, unpeeled, chopped into about 8 wedges
4 celery sticks, chopped into big pieces
4 carrots, unpeeled, chopped into big pieces

For the glaze:
2 tablespoons runny honey
1 tablespoon English mustard
½ tablespoon poaching liquor

You'll need to get your ham into brine 3 days before you plan on cooking it. To make the brine, combine the salt and sugar and 5 litres (170 fl oz/5 quarts) of water in a big pot, mix well and bring up to the boil. Stir it to make sure all the salt and sugar have dissolved and allow it to cool completely (which will take HOURS) before submerging the meat in a non-metal container and weighing it down with a plate. Leave in the brine for 72 hours.

Remove the meat from the brine and rinse well under cold running water, leaving it submerged for an hour or so in clean water if you have the time.

To cook the ham, place it in a big pan with the bay leaves, peppercorns, onions, celery and carrots and cover with cold water. Bring to the boil, reduce to a gentle simmer, and cook, covered loosely with a lid, for 1 hour. Leave the ham in its cooking liquor with the lid on tightly to cool completely, which itself will take a few hours. At this point, you have a very passable ham, and a delicious ham stock that can be used for soups and stews and millions of other things.

To finally roast the ham, preheat the oven to 200°C (400°F).

Mix the honey, mustard and cooking liquor to give you a nice runny paste. Use more cooking liquour if needs be. Sit your ham, fat side up and cut the fat all over in a checkerboard pattern. Then cover it in the delicious paste, ensuring that you get it onto and into every conceivable surface. Place the ham in a roasting tray, ideally on a wire rack to keep it off the base, or on a few sticks of celery if you don't have a rack. Pop it in the hot oven for 15 minutes (or less if you're worried about the glaze going too dark), checking a few times and baste gently with any sticky juice accumulating in the base of the pan. Once mahogany brown and glazed, remove from the oven, allow to cool, and slice as thinly as humanly possible for all your sandwiching needs.

SLOW-COOKED HAM HOCKS

This is the recipe that started it all; the star of the very first sandwich at my Sandwich Shop, the Ham, Egg 'n' Chips. As I said in the first book, you could use these ham hocks to fill a pie, or serve the meat with mashed potato, or polenta, or roasted vegetables. You could set the picked meat in a terrine with pistachios and pickled vegetables. Like me you could win five Michelin stars by putting it in a sandwich. The cooking method here is just the same as in the first book because it's still how we cook the ham hocks at the restaurant, and it is how we think you should make them at home too.

Makes enough to serve 2 as a meal and then have plenty left over for a sandwich or two the next day, or makes enough for 4–6 sandwiches straight up

2 ham hocks (probably weighing about 2.5 kg (5 lb 8 oz) all together) (we use unsmoked at the shop)

3 celery stalks, cut into 7.5-cm (3-in) pieces

2 carrots, unpeeled, split in half

1 large white onion, unpeeled, cut into quarters

6 bay leaves (dried or nicked from the neighbour's garden)

75 ml (5 tablespoons) apple cider vinegar (or white wine vinegar)

1 teaspoon coriander seeds

2 teaspoons black peppercorns

Bunch of parsley (stalks and all)

In a large, heavy-based saucepan, place the ham hocks, celery, carrots, onion, bay leaves and apple cider vinegar and enough water to just submerge the meat. Add the coriander seeds and peppercorns, as well as the bunch of parsley, and bring to the boil. Skim any scum that's easy to spoon off the top. Reduce the heat to the gentlest of simmers and cook for 2½ hours, or until the ham falls easily off the bone. Sometimes this takes 3 hours, sometimes it takes 1½ hours.

Drain (by putting a colander in a big bowl or another big saucepan), reserving the liquid (which is delicious when used as a base for soup, stews and other sauces – you can make velouté with it by using it instead of milk to make a bechamel). At the shop we keep litres of it for reheating the ham in when we make the sandwiches, so I'd recommend keeping aside at least 250 ml (8 fl oz/1 cup) to heat your ham up in if you're making a sandwich with it as well as enough to cover your cooked meat in once you've picked it.

When the ham is cool enough to handle, pick the meat from the bones and separate out the skins, discarding the bones and any funny bits you don't like the look of. The skins can be blended up with herbs and some cooking liquor to make an amazing setting agent for terrines, deep-fried in strips as makeshift scratchings, or thrown away.

Put the picked meat in a Tupperware or non-metal bowl and tip some reserved cooking liquor onto the meat until it's completely covered. It will set and look weird after it's been in the refrigerator but it'll all melt and be delicious when you heat it up again to make your future sandwich.

To reheat, simply spoon out as much as you need and pop it in a pan on a low heat, making sure you get a good amount of the set liquor too. As this heats, everything will melt and after 4–5 minutes you'll have nice chunks of ham hock warmed in a tasty sauce. You can always add more of the extra reserved sauce too if the pan doesn't look juicy enough.

Please note that if you're cooking this to use the hocks for a regular meal, you can skip picking the meat from the bones and simply serve the bone-in hock (skin removed) alongside your polenta, mash, etc, like some sort of marauding Viking rewarding yourself after a full day of pillaging.

A SORT OF RED BRAISED PORK

A Hunanese dish from central China, sometimes known as Chairman Mao Red Braised Pork Belly due to his alleged love of it, this is a sweet and spicy firecracker of a braised pork dish.

Normally, the whole thing would happen in a nice hot wok, but I don't have a wok at home, and was taught to make this by braising it in the oven, which still works really well, so I am going to use that method here.

Makes enough to serve 2 as a meal and then have some leftover for a sandwich or two the next day, or makes about 8 sandwiches straight up

750–800 g (1 lb 10 oz–1 lb 12 oz) pork belly (skin on but deboned), cut into 3-cm (1¼-in) chunks

2 tablespoons good veg oil, such as organic rapeseed (canola) oil

1 fat thumb-size piece of fresh ginger, sliced into rounds

3 garlic cloves, peeled and sliced

6 spring onions (scallions), sliced (white and green parts kept separate)

2 tablespoons caster (superfine) sugar

3 tablespoons Shaoxing rice wine

2 tablespoons light soy sauce

1 tablespoon dark soy sauce

1 cinnamon stick

2 star anise

1 teaspoon chilli (hot pepper) flakes

400 ml (14 fl oz/generous 1½ cups) water

Traditionally you'd poach the pork belly before caramelising it in a wok with sugar and all the tasty aromatics, but I'm going to save you that trouble. Do try the OG version if you want a side-by-side, there are loads of good recipes for it on the internet or in books such as Fuchsia Dunlop's *Revolutionary Chinese Cookbook*.

For this version, preheat the oven to 180°C (350°F).

Get either a heavy roasting tray or Le Creuset-type casserole dish hot on your hob and bang all the ingredients (apart from the water) in it. Give everything a good mix so that all the tasty stuff gets good contact with the pork belly, and everything is combined. Add the water and bring to the boil. Cover the tray/pot with kitchen foil, or put the lid on, and place in the oven.

After 1½ hours, increase the heat to top whack, mine goes to 250°C (480°F), remove the foil or lid, and place the tray back in the oven for 15 minutes. After 15 minutes, check the pork, it should be super soft and starting to go nice and dark. Flip the pieces of pork belly to allow the undersides to get a bit of love, add a little more water if it's looking dry, and give it another 5–10 minutes until all the pork belly pieces are uniformly dark and delicious looking.

This is wonderful served alongside smacked cucumbers (page 259) and plain rice, or, of course, in a sandwich with both those things. At the Sandwich Shop we use all kinds of meat braises in sandwiches and they often need balancing with crunchy, acidic things – hello smacked cucumbers. I love rice in a sandwich too. Its stickiness keeps everything together and it adds a wonderful chewiness to proceedings.

A GOAT TIKKA MASALA BRAISE

To cook legit chicken tikka masala, you marinade chicken, then grill the marinated meat and then add that to a separately made sauce. At the Sarnie Shop we don't have the time (or equipment) to do that, so this is really a stew that has taken chicken tikka masala as its inspiration and combined the marinade and sauce ingredients into a nice stew. If you'd like to make legit chicken tikka masala instead of this abomination, please buy Pushpesh Pant's magnificent *India Cookbook* and get stuck in.

You could deffo switch the meat for beef, lamb or indeed chicken (thighs), if you wouldrather/can't get goat. This will make enough for at least 8 massive sandwiches and the leftovers would be GREAT in a toastie with some cheese, and dunked in some lime-pickle mayo (page 224).

This will make enough for at least 8 massive sandwiches and the leftovers would be GREAT in a toastie with some cheese, and dunked in some lime-pickle mayo (page 224)

1 x 440 g (15½ oz) tin of tomatoes, chopped up if whole
2 medium onions, peeled and chopped
6 garlic cloves, peeled and chopped
1 big fat thumb-sized piece of ginger, peeled and chopped
100 ml (4 fl oz/scant ½ cup) double (heavy) cream
100 g (3½ oz) good thick, full fat yoghurt
1 tablespoon tomato purée (paste)
1 tablespoon sugar
½ teaspoon ground turmeric
2 teaspoon ground cumin
2 teaspoon ground coriander
½ teaspoon ground cardamon
½ teaspoon cayenne pepper
½ teaspoon freshly ground black pepper
1 teaspoon paprika
1 teaspoon of salt
100 ml (4 fl oz/scant ½ cup) water
1 kg (2 lb 4 oz) boneless goat meat good for braising (neck and/or shoulder are perfect), cut
into 2 cm (¾ in) cubes
Vegetable oil and butter, for frying
Salt, for sprinkling
1 lime, for squeezing

Preheat the oven to 180°C (350°F). Put all the ingredients apart from the meat, lime, salt for sprinkling, vegetable oil and butter in your food processor and wazz the hell out of it until it's nice and smooth. You could also do this with a stick blender.

Get your biggest, oven-safe, lidded, thick-bottomed pan out and put it on a medium heat. Put a big schploof of veg oil and a teaspoon of butter in it. Once it's hot, brown the meat all over in four or five batches (of about 5 minutes each), without letting the pan get TOO hot. Sprinkle salt on the meat when you put it in the pan. Put the meat in a bowl once browned. Add some fresh oil and butter to the pan before frying each batch. When finished, if the bottom of the pan is black and burned, wash it out. If everything on the bottom of the pan is looking more brown and golden than it is black, it's good to keep.

Bang the pan back on the heat and when hot, add 25 g (1 oz) butter and let it melt, foam and subside. Put the meat and all its juices back in pan and roll everything about it to get it hot and get the party started. Empty all the sauce into the pan. Bring the whole thing up to the boil stirring regularly. Put the lid on and stick it in the oven for 1½ hours. If you used lamb or beef, it might need at least 2 hours for the meat to soften. If you used chicken, it might only need an hour.

To establish if it is cooked, bring the pan out, dig a bit of meat out and squish it on a plate with a spoon. If it squishes and breaks into nice soft looking fibres, you're done and you can just leave it out with the lid on to cool down before sandwiching merrily. If the cube of meat bounces back at you and stays as is or only breaks down a bit, back in the oven it goes for another half an hour, at which point you can check again.

Now, you need to sort the sauce out. If it's too runny, you could boil it on the hob for a while to reduce it, stirring it regularly to avoid it burning on the bottom. But, you want it nice and saucy for your sandwich so I wouldn't worry too much. If it's too sweet/ rich, add some of the lime juice and try it again. Try it, if it lacks oomph, add some salt, stir it up and try again. You could consider putting some more cream in if you're a bit naughty. I'll leave it up to you. Nice one.

Traditionally this would be made using a young piglet, stuffed and trussed and cooked over an open fire. It would likely be sliced roughly and layered in crusty country rolls, likely at a village gathering, likely by a sabre-wielding farmer whose wife had prepared a coarse but delicious salsa verde to cut through the fatty pork. This is not our reality though, obviously, so here's one made with a pork shoulder and cooked in an oven cut up by yourself.

This is going to cook for a good long time and go all soft and yielding and delicious. Old school bods would prescribe loin with the belly attached for this dish, and if your butcher is compliant, go for that and treat it in exactly the same way as below. I find it harder to find, so tend to request a good piece of boned and rolled shoulder with the skin left very much in place.

Makes enough to serve 4 and then have some leftover for a sandwich or 6 the next day

2.5–3 kg (5 lb 8 oz–6 lb 8 oz) boned and rolled pork shoulder (skin on)

2 teaspoons fine sea salt

1 teaspoon fennel seeds

1 teaspoon chilli (hot pepper) flakes

Zest and juice of 1 unwaxed lemon

4–6 garlic cloves, peeled and grated, peels kept for the roasting tray

4 sprigs of rosemary, leaves picked and finely chopped, stalks kept for the roasting tray

4 sprigs of sage, leaves picked and finely chopped, stalks kept for the roasting tray

2 big red onions, cut into 1-cm (½-in) thick rounds unpeeled (skin and all)

200 ml (7 fl oz/scant 1 cup) white wine (or water if you wish)

Buy the meat the day before you're cooking, remove all packaging and paper from the joint and place it (skin side up) in a tray on a load of paper towels in the refrigerator. This will help dry the skin and thus leave you with a savage brittle crackling, which is just what you want. If you don't have the time, pat dry with paper towels and keep it dry between now and the oven.

Preheat the oven to 160°C (325°F).

Next, remove the joint from the refrigerator and ease off any strings or butcher's elastics used to keep the joint rolled up. Keep these to one side as you'll use them again later. If you had to cut the string, cut new lengths much wider than the pork, and you can re-tie it later.

Open up the shoulder joint and let it roll open on your chopping board, skin down, flesh up. Take a sharp knife and cut and prod at the meat in order to ease it into as flat a piece of meat as possible. As long as you don't cut all the way through the meat to the skin, be as rough as you like. Any deep lesions will better allow the gubbins you're about to add to penetrate the meat.

Once you have the shoulder open and flat, the seasoning can begin. Sprinkle each seasoning on in an even layer starting with the salt. Next the fennel seeds, chilli flakes and lemon zest. Then the grated garlic, rosemary and finally the sage.

Now, roll the shoulder back up the way it unrolled and do it up nice and tight. If you've kept the butcher's strings/elastics, ease these back over the rolled pork, spacing them evenly so that the thing is held in a neat roll. If you are using your own string, soak it in water and tie the rolled shoulder tightly, at 4-cm (1½-in) intervals.

Pleasingly rolled, find a suitable-size baking tray (pan) and add the onion rounds, herb stalks and garlic skins to the base of the tray to act as both seasoning for the cooking juice and a trivet for the pork to sit on. Settle the pork skin-side up on top and add the wine or water and lemon juice around the base of the tray. For good measure, pat the skin dry one last time and place the whole thing on the shelf in the centre of the oven, and leave it there for up to 3 hours.

After 2 hours, check your porchetta. Add more water if the tray is looking worryingly dry and cook for up to another hour, or until the exposed ends of the porchetta are darkening nicely and might pull away easily if your greedy fingers were to try and sneak a premature treat. Once happy, turn the oven up to full whack (mine goes to 250°C/480°F), and give the porchetta a final 30 (ish) minutes to crisp the crackling. Keep an eye out for burning. If it looks like it's gonna burn, or begins to burn at any stage, whip it out – it is what it is.

Coppery crackling and soft, soft meat doubtless achieved, remove the porchetta from the oven and leave it to rest for 30–40 minutes. This is crucial for slicing, which you should always do with a good, serrated knife, like a bread knife. If you have really crisp crackling, which happens sometimes, and not others, and your joint has cooled nicely, turn the thing upside down, crackling at the bottom, and cut your slices that way.

MARCELLA HAZAN'S TUSCAN MEATLOAF

My dear dad, the legend Ned Halley, has made this since I was a tiny kid and it's been a favourite of mine as far back as I can remember. Rich and soft, it's just lovely and really comforting. This recipe is originally from Marcella Hazan's seminal *The Classic Italian Cookbook*, now published as *The Essentials of Classic Italian Cookery*, which is one of the best cookbooks ever, without a doubt. The squid and peas recipe and the squid and potatoes recipe are second to none, as is the ragù method.

Makes enough for about 4 big sandwiches, or 4 people as a meal

3 tablespoons milk
1 slices of good-quality white bread, crusts removed
500 g (1 lb 2 oz) good-quality minced (ground) beef
1 tablespoon very, very finely chopped onion
1 teaspoon salt
10–12 grinds of black pepper
50 g (1¾ oz) chopped mortadella, prosciutto or pancetta (I always use mortadella but Marcella never specifies)
100 g (3½ oz/1⅓ cups) freshly grated Parmesan
1 garlic clove, finely chopped (or grated)
1 large egg yolk
Plenty (150 g/5½ oz) of fine, dry, plain breadcrumbs spread on a baking tray (pan) or something large and flat
15 g (½ oz/1 tablespoon) unsalted butter
2 tablespoons extra virgin olive oil
100 ml (4 fl oz/scant ½ cup) white wine (whatever's in the refrigerator)
25 g (1 oz) dried porcini, soaked in 100 ml (4 fl oz/scant ½ cup) water straight from the kettle for at least 20 minutes, then drained into a bowl, through a sieve (fine mesh strainer) lined with paper towels (soaking water reserved) and mushrooms chopped into little pieces
400-g (14-oz) tin plum tomatoes, emptied into a bowl (juice and all) and chopped into little pieces

If you're having this for dinner, do all this first bit just after lunch because the meatloaf wants to sit in the refrigerator firming up for at least 4 hours before you cook it, otherwise it always falls apart.

Put the milk in a small saucepan and get it warm. Put the bread in, which will immediately soak up the milk. Mash it to a sticky pulp with a fork. Remove from the heat and allow to cool completely – this (and the egg yolk) are your tasty food glue.

Put the minced beef along with the bread and milk moosh, the onion, salt, pepper, chopped mortadella (or whatever you went for), the grated Parmesan, garlic and egg yolk in a large bowl.

Knead the mixture thoroughly with your hands to get everything completely mixed together. When everything's come together, shape the meat into a big fat, stubby sausage shape (you could say a meatloaf-shape), and make sure it'll fit in whatever you're gonna cook it in with plenty of room for sauce. Slap the loaf all over to drive out air which will help keep your meatloaf from breaking apart. Roll the whole thing in the breadcrumbs until coated completely and keep squeezing it together from the ends. Put it in the refrigerator on something flat, and with some baking parchment underneath it, to set and chill for at least 4 hours.

Bearing in mind you're cooking this on the hob, not in the oven. Ideally you want to cook it in something with not too high sides (and a lid) so you will be able to turn the meatloaf over, in the initial browning process and once during the cooking. That is perhaps a tough piece of equipment to come up with. Sometimes I have used a Pyrex baking dish that can go on a gas flame and then covered it with kitchen foil during cooking rather than with a lid. Often the meatloaf breaks in half when I roll it over, and if yours does too, never mind. It is what it is.

Once you've chosen your cooking vessel, put it on a medium heat and put the butter and oil in. When the butter foam subsides, take the loaf out the refrigerator and pick it up using the baking parchment and put it in the pan (without the parchment). Brown it all over as best you can, turning carefully with two spatulas or whatever seems best, to try and keep it from breaking up (which it might well do anyway – but hopefully only in half).

When you have browned the meat, add the wine and let it bubble until it has reduced to half its original volume, shaking the whole pan gently to nudge the loaf this way and that and baste it with a spoon rather than trying to turn it again.

Reduce the heat to medium–low and add the chopped, reconstituted porcini mushrooms. Add the tomatoes and all their juice to the pot together with the filtered mushroom liquid and bring it to the boil. Give everything a really good stir and baste the loaf a little. Cover and adjust the heat to cook at a gentle but steady simmer. Every 10 minutes or so, use a spatula to just move the loaf about rather than turning it, so it doesn't stick too much, unless you feel bold about the potential break up and fancy giving it a turn. After 30 minutes move the lid so it's slightly askew and cook for another 30 minutes, turning the meat once, but only if you dare, and basting regularly if you don't dare.

Once that hour is up, your loaf is cooked. Doesn't it smell AMAZING?! Let the whole caboodle sit for 5–10 minutes, then transfer the loaf to a chopping board and cut it into slices about 2 cm (¾ in) thick. If the juices left in the pot are a little too runny, boil them down on a high heat, using a wooden spoon to scrape loose any cooking residues stuck to the bottom and sides.

If eating as a plate of food, Marcella recommends coating the bottom of a warmed serving platter with a spoonful or so of the sauce, placing the meat slices over it and slathering them in more sauce. This would be unbelievable with wet polenta, or little Tuscan roast potatoes and greens (or the great Greek potatoes I had in Tinos on page 191), or indeed with pommes purée (page 189) and julienne carrots (page 187).

If sandwiching, sandwich away boss.

OK, s**t just got serious.

What we're dealing with here is the preparation of the lining of the fourth stomach of a cow. Someone told me that stomach thing is a myth, and cows only have one after all, but it's split into compartments or something. What do I know, I'm not a zoologist.

The tripes from this bit of the cow (abomasum) are lighter and less, um, pungent, than from the previous stomachs or compartments or whatever they are. In Florence there are lovely places (like Nerbone in the Mercato Centrale) where you can get rolls filled with chopped, braised lampredotto and a choice of salsas. In your home kitchen however, there's a chance the smell of boiling tripe might just put you off ever eating again, so do be warned.

Right, if you're still here, warning issued, strap in and let's boil.

Makes enough for 4–6 sandwiches

4 celery stalks:
  2 broken in half, 2 finely diced
2 carrots: 1 cut into big chunks,
  1 peeled and finely diced
3 onions, peeled: 1 halved,
  2 finely diced
1 tomato, halved
1 kg (2 lb 4 oz) lampredotto
  (see intro)
2 tablespoons extra virgin olive oil
4 garlic cloves, finely grated
2 tablespoons tomato purée (paste)
500 ml (17 fl oz/generous 2 cups)
  red wine
75 ml (5 tablespoons) red wine
  vinegar
Salt and pepper

Making the lampredotto happens in two parts. You boil the tripe first, then braise it in a tasty sofrito with wine and tomato purée.

To start, bring a pot of water to the boil with the broken celery, the chunks of carrot and the halved onion and tomato in it. Add the tripe, reduce to a simmer and cook at a gentle simmer for 1½ hours, topping up the water if necessary keeping the goods below sea level.

Meanwhile, warm the olive oil in a heavy-based saucepan on a low heat. Add the diced celery, carrot and onion as well as the garlic, season with ½ teaspoon of salt and 10 good grinds of pepper and cook slowly for 20 minutes or so, stirring occasionally, until you have something nice and soft and sweet. Increase the heat to medium, add the tomato purée and cook, stirring regularly, for 2 minutes. Add the red wine and the vinegar, bring to a boil, then reduce the heat to a simmer, add your cooked tripe (get it out of the other pot with tongs or a fork) and simmer it down for 35–40 minutes until the tripe has released its juice, the wine has reduced to a lovely sauce and it's all nice and thick and tasty. Taste the sauce and adjust the salt and pepper to your preference.

To make a panino con lampredotto, make a sandwich in exactly the same way as the boiled meat sandwich on page 106. These tripes would also be lovely with someone who already fancies you, served on a plate, sprinkled with grated Parmesan and chopped mint, alongside, soft polenta, good bread and a bottle or two of Chianti Classico.

NOT TECHNICALLY CARNITAS

Soft, fatty, largely unadorned carnitas are integral to both the Tortas Ahogadas on pages 90–91. They make a great base for many delicious Mexican things and when coupled (quadrupled?) with Mexico's Salsa Verde (page 243), raw onion, and fresh coriander (cilantro) they are the bedrock of many a wonderful taco.

Carnitas are normally pieces of pork cooked (you could say aggressively confited) in massive copper pans full of boiling, rendered pork fat, but it's extremely unlikely you're going to do that at home.

If you wanna try a more home-appropriate, plainer carnitas method, you can slice the pork shoulder into thin strips, including ALL the fat, but with no skin. Put the meat in a big pan, JUST cover it with water, chuck the salt in, bring it to the boil, lower the heat and simmer it until all the water has evaporated. Then, keep turning the meat regularly to brown it in the fat that has rendered out of it and you're done, OR you can try this lovely, but slightly different thing instead, just for the lols! These are also AMAZING in a torta ahogada.

Makes loads, enough for sandwiches and tacos for a week, or would feed 4 with leftovers as part of a Mexican spread with rice, tortillas, salsas, etc

About 2 kg (4 lb 8 oz) fatty pork shoulder, skin removed, all the fat left very much intact, cut into 5-cm (2-in) chunks
2 teaspoons fine sea salt
1 tablespoon dried oregano
1 cinnamon stick
1 onion, quartered, unpeeled
1 large orange, halved and juiced
1 whole head of garlic bulb, halved (horizontally)
100 ml (3½ fl oz/scant ½ cup) good vegetable oil, such as organic rapeseed (canola), or extra virgin olive oil at a push
100 g (3½ oz) lard (shortening)
100 ml (3½ fl oz/scant ½ cup) water
2 tablespoons apple cider vinegar

Preheat the oven to 200°C (400°F).

We do this in a baking tray (pan) by combining all of the ingredients, tossing in the squeezed orange halves and juice, and adding the onion and garlic, skin and all. Once combined, mix so that everything is coated and cover tightly with a double layer of kitchen foil.

Place in the oven and immediately reduce the oven temperature to 150°C (300°F). Cook for 3 hours. Check your chunks of pork, they should be holding their shape but be squishable with very little effort.

Once cooked, you can eat as is, nice and soft and saucy. Equally, you can do as they do in Mexico and squish and crisp up the nice little bits of soft pork. You can do this in a hot pan, frying the squished bits for a minute or so per side until golden and crispy, or you can pop the squished chunks on a tray and pop them under the grill (broiler) for a few minutes per side.

These are good wrapped in tortillas with the things discussed above (and many other things of course), in tortas ahogadas and just about anything else you can think of.

This is here so you can make a steak tartare burger for yourself and people you love (page 82), but it is also great as an actual steak tartare. It isn't innovative, it's not trying to be clever, it's uber traditional and all the better for it. Really, what is with the constant need for innovation?

Ideally use fillet, talk to the butcher – sirloin is also very nice, just don't use the hard white fat across the top of the steak. See the pictures on pages 168–169 for how to best cut the steak.

Makes enough for 4 burgers/ servings, or could feed 8–10 as a little nibble, in Baby Gem lettuce cups if you're feeling bougie

500 g (1 lb 2 oz) very good, lean beef, ideally fillet

2 squash-ball-sized shallots, very finely diced

1 tablespoon capers, drained and chopped (if salted, soaked in cold water for 10 minutes, then drained and chopped) (if you can buy those tiny capers, some times called Lilliput Capers (Oi Oi Gulliver), just leave them whole)

½ teaspoon freshly ground black pepper

½ teaspoon salt

1 teaspoon lemon juice

1 tablespoon Dijon mustard

A good few dashes of Tabasco sauce

2 large free-range egg yolks

1 tablespoon ketchup

Small handful of finely chopped parsley

A good few dashes of Worcestershire sauce

When it's going to be eaten as steak tartare, not as a burger, I like to make this at the last minute so that the acids (etc) in the lemon juice, capers and mustard don't get time to work on the steak and start to 'cook' it before you're ready to devour it. I also cut it chunkier. If you're gonna make the burger, leave out the lemon juice, cut the meat finer and do it long enough in advance for the patty to sit in the refrigerator for an hour or two, to firm up and bind itself together. Never be tempted to mince the meat; if you do, Ben and I will never talk to you again, and I'm sure that would be the last thing you'd want.

To cut the steak, follow the instructions on pages 168–169. This will be even easier if you use your sharpest knife and your meat is refrigerator cold.

Once all the beef is cut into nice small bits, add it to a bowl and add everything else. Mix to combine and serve in whatever fashion you intend, which could well be with a few mates and some chips, roast potatoes or crisps. If this is for the burger on page 82, then mix everything, form into tight patties and refrigerate on a plate for at least 2 hours.

1. Cut the steak into strips.

2. Cut strips into half lengthways, or even into three if the steak is very thick.

3. Cut those strips into little chunks.

RACHEL RODDY'S BOILED BEEF

There is a wonderful passage on page 179 of Rachel Roddy's cookbook *Five Quarters*, where she talks of her love of a sandwich shop in her local market (Mordi e Vai, Testacchio Market). It serves classic Roman dishes, 'boiled beef, chicken with tomato sauce, boiled tongue with sauce or oxtail stew', and stuffs them in sandwiches. She goes on to give a recipe for how to boil beef (find something EXTREMELY close to it below) and it's just wonderful. The meat is plain, soft and comforting, juicy and delicious. A slice of it served in a bowl of the broth with some great olive oil and lemon juice is one of the great lunches and it also makes a fantastic sandwich. The meat looks a bit odd and anaemic when you put it in the bun but once you've slammed some salsa verde (page 232) or fiery salsa rossa (page 233) in there it really comes alive; I mean just look at the photo on page 107.

Serves at least 4 of the world's greediest people for lunch or makes a load of sandwiches

1.5 kg (3 lb 5 oz) piece of rolled, tied, fatty beef good for boiling (ask the butcher, this is what brisket is made for)

2 onions, cut into 6, unpeeled (I find the skin adds a lovely colour to the final broth)

Small bunch of flat leaf parsley, tied together tightly with string

2 celery stalks, cut into large chunks

1 carrot, unpeeled, cut into chunks

2 garlic cloves (still in their skins), half crushed with a knife

A few bay leaves

1 teaspoon salt

Put the meat in a pan large enough to accommodate it submerged with all the vegetables and salt. Cover the whole lot with cold water and bring it all to the boil. When it boils, immediately reduce the heat to a blip, blip, blip simmer, skim any scum off the top and let it do its slow, blippy thing for 4 hours. It might only take 3 hours, depending on how big your beef is, or what your definition of 'blipping' is. You can tell how cooked the meat is by how easily a sharp little knife goes right through into the middle and out the other side. Very easily? Ready. Met with even the slightest resistance? Not ready.

Once the path of least resistance has been met, you're done. Turn the heat off, put a lid on and let the meat and liquid cool completely, which will take a few hours. Strain the broth and discard the bits. You can keep the meat in the broth in the refrigerator for a few days. When you want some, slice a slab off and heat it up gently for 10–15 minutes in a small pan of broth, with a lid on, and go again and again, and always serve it in the broth. I also like to gently cook whole peeled carrots and tiny potatoes in the skins in some more of the broth, in a separate pan. Then I combine the meat-heating and carrot cooking broths and serve everything together in one big bowl with lashings of olive oil and lemon juice (as I mention above).

Or, of course, you can use it to make a sandwich like the one on page 106.

Thank you, Rachel.

Oh come on, it's a simple pleasure but one of the greats. In a sandwich with coleslaw and some punchy horseradish, it's one of the best things ever. Topside is lean, but good value, and works perfectly as a thinly sliced hot roast and also as a wafer-thin deli-style, cold roast beef, which is what we want here. Read all this before cooking, there's some gravy chat at the bottom.

Makes enough to serve 4 and then have some leftover for a sandwich or two the next day, or makes a lot of sandwiches straight up

1.5 kg (3 lb 5 oz) topside beef
2 tablespoons extra virgin olive oil
2–3 teaspoons fine sea salt
3 onions, quartered but not peeled
4 celery stalks, cut into big chunks
1 whole head of garlic, halved, horizontally not vertically
Small bunch of thyme
3 large carrots, unpeeled and cut into chunks

Remove your beef from the refrigerator at least 1 hour before you plan to cook it.

Preheat the oven to 250°C (480°F). Take an ovenproof frying pan (skillet) or a good roasting tray and place it on a medium heat.

Rub the topside with 1 tablespoon of oil before seasoning really generously with salt. Don't skimp. Remember this is a thick piece of meat and this is your only seasoning.

Once the pan or tray is hot, brown the topside for a good 2 minutes per side or until a nice bark is created all over. Once suitably browned, turn off the heat and bang the beef on a plate or something. Add the onions, celery, garlic and thyme to the pan and settle into a single layer, this is just for the beef to sit on while cooking, although it will also flavour a very good gravy, if needs be, at the end.

Sit the beef on top of the veg and place in the oven, immediately reducing the heat to 180°C (350°F) before cooking for 50–55 minutes for a blushing pink roast. Go a little more if your preference is for medium cooked beef. A lot of how cooked it will be depends on your oven. Please buy a temperature probe, they don't cost much and make things like this mad easy. Stick the temperature probe into the centre of the meat after 40 minutes of cooking and see where it's at. You want to take it out at about 50°C (122°F) as it will come up at least 5°C (41°F) more while it rests.

Once cooked, whack the beef on a plate or carving board, cover loosely in kitchen foil and leave to rest for 30 minutes. Meanwhile, a 500 ml (17 fl oz/generous 2 cups) jug/pitcher of chicken stock added to your roasting tray, boiled and reduced for 5–10 minutes and passed through a sieve (fine mesh strainer) will make a very good gravy indeed.

If you're eating this straight away, slice nice and thin and serve with your usual accompaniments. If sandwiching, allow to cool a little more and slice as thinly as possible with a very sharp knife.

GOAT BOLOGNESE

This recipe is here because it is what we use for the lasagna sandwich (page 127) at the sarnie shop. If I was making that sandwich at home, I'd make my usual spaghetti bolognese-type recipe, have spaghetti bolognese for dinner and use the leftover sauce in the sandwich tomorrow.

However, if you are this way inclined, here you go. Goat meat should be eaten way more; it's delicious and we use it at the Sarnie Shop because it braises beautifully and (wrongly or not) after watching *Cowspiracy*, I was worried about how much beef the shop used. Chat to your butcher, you never know, they might be able to get you some.

Minced (ground) beef, 50/50 beef and pork, veal or even lamb could all be used here instead. Once you've cooked this, you can of course have it with spaghetti or whatever, in a lasagna (with the Taleggio Béchamel on page 245), or even on toast with a fried egg. The real deal though, of course, is in that sandwich.

Makes enough for 1 lasagna, for 6–8 sandwiches, or for a meal for 4 with leftovers

4 tablespoons extra virgin olive oil
4 slices of smoked streaky bacon, chopped into little bits
1 large carrot, peeled and finely diced
1 large onion, peeled and finely diced
2 celery stalks, finely diced
1 teaspoon fine sea salt
1 teaspoon fennel seeds
20 grinds of black pepper
700 g (1 lb 9 oz) boned goat shoulder, minced (ground), or cut into small (2-cm/¾-in) cubes and mashed at the end of cooking if easier
210 g (7½ oz) tomato purée (paste)
150 ml (5 fl oz/scant ⅔ cup) good white wine
750 ml (25 fl oz/3 cups) chicken stock (made with one of those Knorr jelly pots)
2 strips of lemon zest from an unwaxed lemon, removed with a veg peeler
2 fresh or dried bay leaves
¼ nutmeg, grated

Place a large pan (with a lid, but not with it on) on a medium heat and warm the oil. Once shimmering, add the bacon, and cook until it's started to brown, and the fat has begun to render (about 4 minutes). Add the carrot, onion and celery, a big pinch of salt and cook until it has softened and lost some of its structural integrity (about 10 minutes). Add the fennel seeds and black pepper, mix them in and cook for another 5 minutes.

Add the goat meat, be it minced or little cubes, and turn the heat up a bit. Cook for 5–10 minutes, stirring regularly, until it has all changed colour and bits of it have browned a little. Add the tomato purée and stir until all combined with the meat. Add the white wine and cook until reduced to almost nothing. Add the stock and scrape at the bottom of the pan, getting any stuck on bits off. These are all flavour gold. Add the lemon zest, bay leaves and the grated nutmeg, mix everything in and reduce the heat to a mere blip, blip simmer.

Now is the time for that lid. Give everything a final stir and pop the lid on. It needs to stay on for 30 minutes. Have a check every 10 minutes to see that nothing is sticking to the bottom of the pan, scrape it off if it is and mix everything in and reduce the heat.

Once the 30 minutes is up, keep doing everything the same but take out the lemon zest and bay leaves and cook with the lid off for another 45 minutes, keeping a beady eye to ensure the heat is not too high and nothing is sticking to the bottom of the pan, and until the oil has split out beautifully and is floating about on top.

A LOAD OF BREADED MEATS

(AND SOME BREADED FISH)

CARL CLARKE'S FRIED CHICKEN

There are (many) times when you must accept, and celebrate, that people are better at things than you are, and this is one of them. I would love to pretend that I had figured this out, and was the badass behind the method, but I've copied Carl Clarke's way of doing things, from his mad and brilliant book *The Whole Chicken*, because he is just so damn good at it.

Makes enough for 4 sandwiches

4 big boneless chicken thighs,
   skin on if possible
2 litres (68 fl oz/2 quarts)
   flavourless oil (rapeseed/canola
   or sunflower), for deep-frying

For brining the chicken:
284 ml (9½ fl oz/generous
   1 cup) buttermilk (that seems
   to be the size of the containers
   supermarkets sell)
½ teaspoon fine sea salt
¼ teaspoon MSG powder
   (optional)

For the wet bit of fried chicken:
1 free-range egg
120 ml (4 fl oz/½ cup) whole milk

For the dry bit of fried chicken:
50 g (1¾ oz/6 tablespoons) plain
   (all-purpose) flour
65 g (2¼ oz/scant ½ cup) rice
   flour
20 g (¾ oz/3 tablespoons)
   cornflour (cornstarch)
½ teaspoon fine sea salt
¼ teaspoon freshly ground
   black pepper

To brine the chicken, whisk the buttermilk and salt and MSG (if you're using it) together in a glass or plastic bowl or a Tupperware or something. Submerge the thighs in it and stick it in the refrigerator for at least 12 hours. Turn the thighs over every now and again if you remember.

When you want to cook the chicken, make the wet bit by whisking the egg and milk in a bowl until completely combined and set aside. For the dry bit, combine all the ingredients in another bowl, whisk them all together well, using a dry whisk, and set that aside too.

Take the chicken thighs out of the buttermilk, give them a shake and dip them, one by one, into the flour mix and then into the wet batter, then back into the flour mix. Carl says to work/squeeze the coating around the thighs with your hands so it has a texture 'almost like cornflakes'.

Carl double-fries these babies, so I'm gonna tell you how to do that, but quite frankly, at home, once is probably enough, so skip past this bit to the last paragraph, unless you wanna really go for it.

Set your deep-fat fryer to 140°C (275°F), or if you're frying in a saucepan, you know the drill: take a large, high-sided pan and heat the oil to 140°C (275°F) which is the temperature a piece of bread sizzles and goes golden in about 40 seconds (as opposed to the usual 20). Fry the thighs two at a time, depending on the size of your pan/fryer, for 7 minutes, then take them out, put them on a rack and ramp up the heat in the oil (like you're making French fries). This time heat the oil up to 180°C (350°F) – when a piece of bread dropped into the oil sizzles and goes golden in 20 seconds.

Fry the chicken again, this time for 3–4 minutes and rest back on that rack to cool a little while you ready all the other bits for Coronation Chicken Fried Chicken BANGER!

If you're only frying once, heat your oil to 180°C (350°F) from the off and fry the chicken for about 7 minutes until it is cooked through and over 70°C (158°F) inside. If your fried thighs are long and flat, you might wanna cut them in half once they've been fried and stack 'em on top of each other in your sarnie.

Thank you, Carl.

In 1979 the Chicken Kyiv hit the shelves of Marks and Spencer and became Britain's first ready meal! Try to buy nice plump chicken breasts from your butcher for this and remember it is a bit of a palaver (or as my wife Magali says: pavlova), but it's really fun and always a treat.

Makes 2

125 g (4½ oz) salted butter, at room temperature

6 garlic cloves, finely grated

Handful of parsley, very finely chopped

2 skinless chicken breasts

200 g (7 oz) dried breadcrumbs

3 eggs, beaten

50 ml (3½ tablespoons) milk

150 g (5¼ oz/1 cup plus 2 tablespoons) plain (all-purpose) flour

1 teaspoon fine sea salt

Plenty of freshly ground black pepper

Extra virgin olive oil, for the baking tray and for drizzling

Combine the softened butter, garlic and chopped parsley in a bowl (or even better, a food processor) and beat so that everything is perfectly mixed. Lay out a 30-cm (12-in) (ish) square of baking parchment on your work surface and dollop the garlic butter in the middle of the edge nearest you. Roll the paper over and over into a sausage shape by squeezing the butter sausage forming in front of you as you roll it. When you reach the end, twist the ends of the parchment like an old-fashioned sweetie (candy). Pop this in the refrigerator for an hour or so and chill until solid.

Next, take each chicken breast, lay on your chopping board cut side up and remove the 'mini fillet' (the bit that flaps about), keeping it for something else tomorrow. Put the breast between two sheets of baking parchment and bash them out, bang, bang, bang, with the bottom of a small saucepan, a rolling pin or a meat hammer, until they are about 5 mm–1 cm (¼–⅓ in) thick all over.

Remove your butter from the refrigerator and cut it into two even sticks just over half as long as your bashed out chicken breats that'll fit inside once you roll it up. Put the butter sausage on one side of your chicken breast and roll it up, round the sausage, tucking the ends up and in, folding them over the butter so you create a sealed chicken wrapping around the butter. Roll this tightly up in cling film (plastic wrap) and bang it back in the refrigerator for 1 hour.

In three trays, or on three plates, make three breading stations. One for the breadcrumbs, one for the eggs and milk whisked together, and one for the flour seasoned with salt and pepper.

You're gonna get messy here but you can clean up afterwards. Take each breast and, being careful to keep it completely sealed, remove the cling film, roll it about in the flour, then the egg, then into the breadcrumbs, patting them about everywhere, then back into the egg and finally a second coat of breadcrumbs, patting them on where necessary and making sure there are no gaps anywhere at all.

Put these on a plate and back into the refrigerator for 30 minutes while you preheat the oven to 200°C (400°F).

To cook, line a baking tray (pan) with kitchen foil and give it a good oiling with some of the olive oil. Put it in the oven for 5 minutes so it's hot as hell. Take it out and put the Kyivs in with the end of the roll (if you can tell where that is) facing up. This helps make sure the butter doesn't leak out. Drizzle the Kyivs with more olive oil and cook for 15 (ish) minutes, or until golden brown and cooked through.

CHICKEN SCHNITZEL
COOKED IN THE METHOD FROM *ALPINE COOKING*

Yup, another breaded meat recipe. This time borrowed almost wholesale from Meredith Erickson's brilliant book *Alpine Cooking*. Meredith formed a schnitzel team (definition of Dream Team?) to perfect the recipe and ended up eating over 200 schnitzels in her search for perfection, so as an opportunistic recipe snaffler at the best of times, this one's a no brainer. Having said that, and ignoring Meredith completely, I've switched veal for chicken here because chicken's better. Tweet me, Meredith. Please feel free to take the bull by the horns, ignore me and switch chicken for pork, veal or even turkey, if you so wish. Do everything exactly the same.

Makes 4 schnitzels

4 skinless chicken breasts, about 150 g (5½ oz) each, mini fillet (the bit that flaps about) removed
200 g (7 oz/1½ cups) plain (all-purpose) flour
4 free-range eggs, beaten
300 g (10½ oz/3¾ cups) fine dried breadcrumbs (panko works well but who knows how Meredith would feel. If you fancy making your own, see page 206)
About 1 litre (34 fl oz/4¼ cups) vegetable oil (or any flavourless oil – Meredith uses groundnut/peanut, so maybe that if you can get it)
Fine sea salt and freshly ground black pepper

Ask your butcher to pound out the meat for you to about 5 mm (¼ in) thick. If you don't have a butcher and bought the chicken from the supermarket like most peeps, cover a chopping board with baking parchment and lay a chicken breast down (one at a time) and cover with another sheet of parchment. Use a meat mallet and pound the meat to the desired thickness. I know, I don't have a meat mallet either, I just like saying it. Use the flat bottom of a small saucepan or a rolling pin or something. Once appropriately pulverised, season both sides of the meat with salt and pepper and set aside. Repeat until you've done all the ones you're doing. If you're lucky the parchment will last two schnitzels, if it starts ripping at all, start afresh.

Put three plates and a shallow bowl in front of you. From left to right, go plate, bowl, plate, plate. Starting on the left, put the flour on plate, crack the eggs into the bowl and whisk them up with a fork if you hadn't already done so, then put dried breadcrumbs on the next plate, and leave the last plate empty for putting the breaded meats on.

One at a time, put the seasoned meat in the flour, move it all about, flip it over, shake off the excess and put it into the egg. Turn it over, making sure everything has been egged. Then go into the breadcrumbs, making sure every little bit is covered, pressing breadcrumbs on where needs be and bang it on the empty plate. Repeat, and put parchment between each one.

Pour the oil into a large pot – if you think this should (officially) be clarified butter not oil, you haven't read Meredith's book, have you? The oil should be about 2 cm (¾ in) deep, which should be enough to completely submerge the schnitzel (if you're using a very large or slightly smaller pan, increase/decrease the amount of oil accordingly). Slowly warm the oil on a low heat to 130°C (265°F), using a temperature probe to track its progress (sorry, but how else are you gonna do it?). Also, cover a baking tray (pan) or big plate or something with loads of paper towels for the finished schnitzels to sit on. A wire rack would be even better, with paper towels underneath it.

Once the oil has hit 130°C (265°F), slip a schnitzel in. Erickson advises using tongs, which I would too, as this is boiling oil, after all. I would also recommend putting the bottom of the schnitzel into the oil on the side closest to you and lowering the rest in slowly going AWAY from you so that if you drop it, the boiling oil splashes the wall behind the cooker or

whatever, NOT YOUR GOOD SELF. Do you see what I mean? This is important, you don't wanna get burned.

Erickson reckons the perfect cook will be achieved once the meat treat has been in the oil for 3–3½ minutes – of course, to some extent, this is reliant on the meat being close to 5 mm (¼ in) thick and you maintaining the temperature of the oil at 130°C (265°F) by turning the heat under the pan up or down. Sorry.

Make sure that none of the schnitzel rears its head above sea level while it fries. If it does, poke it back under with your tongs and swill the pan gently. The idea is to allow the breadcrumb layer to set and rise, away from the meat, allowing the meat to steam in its bready jacket, rather than fry per se. This will result in a better breadcrumb crust and more tender meat. The. Dream.

When the time is up and the goose is cooked, with tongs, transfer the golden, beautiful schnitzel to the wire rack or lined baking sheet and recalibrate your oil temperature before frying the next one. Repeat with all four schnitzels, or however many you are making, keeping the cooked ones warm in a warm oven.

These little beauties are wonderful eaten classically, with some boiled potatoes, a wedge of lemon and a nice over-cooked vegetable of some kind. I like them best in a sandwich though, and I always go Holstein (page 88).

I know this isn't easy, and the oil temperatures and stuff are tricky, but that's how it is if you wanna cook a schnitzel as one is meant to cook a schnitzel. What kind of pound-shop cookbook would this be if I told you to sack off all that malarkey and just fry it in a pan in a big splash of oil like you might fry anything else?!

TONKATSU

If you're making the sando on page 116, switch the pork for tuna steaks.

Makes 4/Serves 4

4 butcher's best pork chops,
  skin removed (or fishmonger's
  finest tuna steaks) (2 cm/¾ in
  thick is ideal)
1 teaspoon fine sea salt
½ teaspoon ground white pepper
  (black pepper will do if you haven't
  got any white)
4 large free-range eggs
200 g (7 oz/1½ cups) plain
  (all-purpose) flour
200 g (7 oz/4½ cups) panko
  breadcrumbs (or other good,
  dried breadcrumbs – page 206)
400 ml (14 fl oz/generous 1½ cups)
  sunflower or rapeseed (canola) oil

While it might seem fun and aesthetically pleasing to bread the pork chops while still on the bone, it's a bit of a nuisance in the long run, so ask your butcher to remove the bone or use a sharp knife and carefully work the meat from the bone yourself. If your chops have a thick layer of fat along one side, lucky you, but do cut some incisions down through the fat, not so deep as to go into the flesh, at 1 cm (⅓ in) intervals. This will make sure that the chop doesn't curl up too much as it cooks. Season the chops with salt and white pepper and press them into the flesh.

To breadcrumb, set three stations in front of you. Two plates and a shallow bowl in the middle. Crack the eggs into the bowl and whisk them with a fork. On the left plate, put the flour and into the right, the panko breadcrumbs.

Take your seasoned chops (or tuna steaks) and completely coat them in the flour, then into the egg mix and, finally, press them into the panko and make sure you get a very good coating on all sides, you really need to have no gaps at this stage. You're creating a breaded cage for the cutlets within which they will steam and cook.

If you are doing the tuna not the meat here, put the breaded fish bits into the freezer for 1 hour. They won't freeze solid but they'll be so cold you can fry them and keep them really, really rare.

Finally, heat the oil in a wide shallow pan on a medium heat. Once hot (you can test this by dropping some breadcrumbs into the oil and watching them sizzle and brown – this should take 10 seconds or so, slower, keep heating your oil; faster, turn down the heat), lay your chops into the pan in a single layer, work in batches if they don't all fit. Cook for 3–4 minutes on the first side, carefully turn (two spoons work well), then 3–4 minutes more on the second side. You should now have golden breaded chops that will be cooked to perfection inside (a little pink is no worries these days but buy them from a butcher not a supermarket if possible). All that remains is to rest on a tray lined with paper towels, or even better on a wire rack, for 6 minutes before slicing and eating however you see fit. If you are doing the Katsu Sando on page 116, cook your tuna exactly like this but straight out of the freezer and only until the breadcrumbs are a deep golden brown (you don't need to cook the fish). You could also use these breaded pork chops to make the same sarnie as the tuna one, but with meat in it. This book's good, innit?!

The recipe for Tonkatsu on the opposite page gives us breaded pork (and tuna), the schnitzel on page 176 gives us breaded chicken, hell, there's even (sort of) breaded prawns (shrimp) on page 83. To bring two pairs up to a full house, here's a Milanesa, an Argentinian breaded steak. Once you've read this one, or even better cooked it, you're tooled-up-to-the-nines and could pretty much bread anything. Welcome to Dicky's meadow, where the sun is always shining, the birds swoop and sing and the smell of fresh cut grass hangs verdantly in the air.

Argentina is rich in many things, two of which stand out here: cows and people of Italian heritage. As cows don't do much cooking, it's the people of Italian heritage who have turned to their motherland's culinary wardrobe for inspiration. Where the Italians might have breaded veal, pork or even chicken, these guys have ended up breading steak and serving it with tomato sauce and cheese. The similarity this has to Middlesborough's Parmo, also of Italian descent, hasn't passed me by.

Argentinian cooks tend to do three things with their Milanesa that I find exciting. One, there's not much flouring of the meat prior to meeting the egg. Two, they season their egg mixture, and three they often add grated cheese to their breadcrumbs. So we will do all of those things here.

Makes 4 Milanesa

4 rump steaks, bashed out to about 1 cm (½ in) thick with something blunt and heavy, like the base of a small saucepan, between two pieces of baking parchment/greaseproof

½ teaspoon fine sea salt

¼ teaspoon freshly ground black pepper

4 large free-range eggs, beaten

250 g (9 oz) dried breadcrumbs (panko work well, but if you fancy making your own, see page 206)

50 g (1¾ oz/⅔ cup) grated Parmesan

About 1 litre (34 fl oz/4¼ cups) rapeseed (canola) or sunflower oil, for frying

Optional:

300 ml (10 fl oz/1¼ cups) tomato passata (sieved tomatoes)

200 g (7 oz) grated or finely sliced, hard, cow's milk cheese that melts well, such as Cheddar (or anything you have knocking about really)

To breadcrumb, set two stations in front of you. One plate and a shallow bowl. Season the steaks with some of the salt and pepper. Crack the eggs into the bowl, with the leftover salt and pepper and whisk them with a fork. On the plate, put the breadcrumbs and Parmesan, and mix them together.

Take your steaks and one by one dump them into the egg mix, turn them over to cover every bit, and finally, press them into the cheesy panko and make sure you get a very good coating on all sides. You really need to have no gaps at this stage. You're creating a breaded cage for the steaks within which they will steam and cook.

To cook, fill a wide shallow pan with about 1 cm (⅓ in) depth of oil. Heat this on a medium heat and, once hot (you can test this by dropping some breadcrumbs into the oil and watching them sizzle and brown – this should take 10 seconds or so, slower, keep heating your oil, faster, turn down the heat), lay your breaded steaks into the pan in a single layer, working in batches if they don't all fit. Cook for 2–3 minutes on the first side, then turn and give them the same on the other side. Once golden and delicious, remove to a paper towel-lined tray and leave to rest for a few minutes.

If you're going all out, preheat the grill (broiler) on your oven to full whack. Place the breaded steaks in a baking tray (pan) and top each one with passata and cheese. Place under the grill, and grill (broil) as briefly as possible until the cheese is melted and just starting to brown.

**Makes enough for 4 sandwiches,
or for 2 as part of a meal**

600 g (1 lb 5 oz) mini or larger
 squid (fresh or frozen and
 defrosted), cleaned
200 ml (7 fl oz/scant 1 cup)
 whole milk
1 litre (34 fl oz/4¼ cups) vegetable
 or rapeseed (canola) oil (optional)
250 g (9 oz/2 cups) cornflour
 (cornstarch)
½ teaspoon fine sea salt, plus extra
 to serve

I was taught by a Spaniard to tenderise squid in milk, which
is what we're doing here, because it works.

Ideally the squid wants to go in the milk at bedtime and be
cooked for lunch tomorrow, but even 30 minutes is better than
nothing. Whether using fresh or defrosted, frozen squid, cut it
into rings about 1 cm (⅓ in) thick, stick in a bowl and pour milk
on until it covers the squid. (If your squid has tentacles, lucky
you, cut the bunch in half and chuck them in too.) Leave this
for at least 30 minutes as discussed.

Turn the deep-fat fryer on to 180°C (350°F). If you're frying
in a saucepan, you know the drill: put the oil in a medium,
high-sided pan and place on a medium heat and bring up
to 180°C (350°F), the temperature at which a piece of bread
sizzles and goes golden in 20 seconds – ideally use a
temperature probe to track progress.

Meanwhile, add the cornflour and salt to a shallow bowl
or tray and mix well. Working a handful at a time, remove the
squid rings from the milk, toss in the cornflour, ensuring a good
coating, then fry in batches for 2–3 minutes, or until nice and
golden. Remove to a paper towel-lined plate and sprinkle with
a little extra salt.

Sandwich these guys while hot, or simply cover in lemon juice
and dunk into a punchy garlic mayo (page 220).

BATTERING FISH
(LITTLE OR LARGE, FOR A VARIETY OF THINGS, INCLUDING WHITE BREAD, MAYO AND LEMON JUICE SANDWICHES)

This is all about the batter. Once you have an indomitable batter, all bets are off and you can fry anything and make it tasty as hell.

Get the fishmonger to fillet and skin you something nice that will like being battered and fried. Haddock, pollock, etc, all fry excellently as fillets or cut into chunks, but there's also things like monkfish cheeks, sprats, prawns (shrimp), scallops and who knows what else?!

It's worth mentioning that you don't just have to use fish, and that you could cook off a nice large sausage, let it cool and batter and deep-fry that. And yes, you could also get a load of Celebrations (or other small chocolates), freeze them, take them from their wrappers, and then batter and deep-fry them, like my friend Neil Gill used to do. You could even do vegetables like Tenderstem broccoli and stuff.

Below is a messy hodgepodge of the recipe and the method I use for battering and frying just about anything.

Because the liquid in the batter (and batter just generally) wants to be mad cold when hitting hot oil, we don't want it sitting around, these aren't Yorkshire puddings. Consequently, my order of service tends to go like this:

1. *Start heating 2 litres (68 fl oz/2 quarts) of vegetable or rapeseed (canola) oil in a big pan or in a deep-fat fryer to 180°C (350°F).*
2. *Make my batter (see below).*
3. *Dust the piece of fish (taken from the refrigerator) with flour, shake off any excess (put some flour on a plate, don't worry about the temperature).*
4. *Dunk the fish in the batter.*
5. *Plunge it into the oil, holding it carefully just in the oil for a second or two at the side nearest you, then carefully lowering it in away from you and letting it fry for 3–5 minutes, or until golden brown and delicious. If you're frying in a deep-fat fryer rather than a saucepan, wiggle the basket about immediately on putting the fish in so it doesn't stick.*

MY GO-TO BATTER

120 g (4¼ oz/1 cup, minus 1 tablespoon) plain (all-purpose) flour (put in the freezer for 30 minutes before you make the batter)

100 g (3½ oz/1 cup) cornflour (cornstarch) (also put in the freezer for 30 minutes before using)

1 tablespoon baking powder

1 teaspoon salt

300 ml (10 fl oz/1¼ cups) ice-cold beer straight from the refrigerator (a good flavoursome lager is perfect)

Combine all the dry ingredients and whisk them thoroughly with an actual whisk. Steadily add the beer, whisking as you go. Once you've hit a single (light) cream consistency, you're done. If you dip a finger in and the batter coats it, but you can still see the detail of your knuckle, you're in the right territory. Needs to be thicker? Bit more flour. Needs to be thinner? Bit more beer. Easy.

Melissa M. Martin's brilliant book *Mosquito Supper Club* is full of Cajun gold, including a lovely recipe for fried shrimp which this one is based on. These shrimps are here because they are so damn good, and because they're a classic component of one iteration of Louisiana's, and more specifically, New Orleans' Po' Boy sandwich. In Nawlins, you might find Po' Boys (from the 'poor boys' (workers) for whom they were originally made) filled with any number of fried fishy treats (oysters, crayfish, catfish etc) and even braised beef and gravy. If you wanna make a Po' Boy at home, hollow out a little baguette and fill it with the fried, breaded fishy goodness or braised beef and gravy filling of your choosing, along with shredded iceberg lettuce, American mustard, hot sauce (Tabasco for me) and either the Po' Boy Mayo on page 225 or just some mayo with lashings of grated dill pickle in it.

Makes enough for 2 sandwiches

1 litre (34 fl oz/4¼ cups)
  vegetable oil (optional)
250 g (9 oz/1⅔ cups) fine
  polenta (cornmeal)
150 g (5½ oz/1¼ cups) cornflour
  (cornstarch)
1 tablespoon onion granules
1 tablespoon garlic granules
10–12 grinds of black pepper
2 teaspoons cayenne pepper
1 teaspoon celery salt (you could
  use regular salt, but just use
  half a teaspoon)
2 large, free-range eggs
1 teaspoon Tabasco
1 tablespoon American mustard
  (I like French's)
350–400 g (12–14 oz/about 20)
  large, raw, peeled king prawns
  (jumbo shrimp) (deveined if you
  care/can be bothered)

If you've got a deep-fat fryer, turn it on and set it to 200°C (400°F). If you haven't got one, you know the drill: put the oil in a high-sided saucepan and heat it to 200°C (400°F), the temperature at which a piece of bread sizzles and goes golden in about 15–20 seconds.

Meanwhile, set two large bowls in front of you, left and right. In the right one, whack all the dry ingredients and stir them all about (whisk?) until completely combined.

In the left-hand bowl whisk the eggs, mustard and Tabasco together until they are foamy and combined.

Throw all the prawns into the whisked egg mix and stir them all about with a spoon. Melissa wisely advises that using one hand (and continuing to use this hand for this task), one by one pull out a prawn, give it a little shake, and drop it into the dry ingredients bowl. Using your other hand, flick, flick, flick the breadcrumby mix all over the prawn and roll it around making sure every bit of wet is now dry. Take the prawn out, bang it on a plate or something and repeat until all the prawns are done. Wash your hands.

Finally, fry the prawns in two batches for 2–3-ish minutes until they are super crunchy and a sexy golden brown. Using a slotted spoon or a spider (ask the chatbot, not that kind of spider), transfer them to a wire rack or tray lined with paper towels and season with a little extra salt before sandwiching and shouting 'WHO DAT!' as you inhale the goodies.

VEGETABLES

You will never regret buying an OXO Good Grips Julienne Peeler (and unfortunately for me, they have not paid me to say that).

ONION SOUBISE

This stuff is naughty, and it isn't just good with roast lamb! The creaminess and softness of it are a great foil to roasted caramelised things generally. It's great with roast pork of course, and I made it once to go under roasted onions which worked super well.

Makes enough for 4 sandwiches (or maybe 40)

250 g (9 oz/2¼ sticks) butter
4 big onions, finely sliced
3 good pinches of salt

Put a saucepan on a low heat and melt the butter in it. Add the onions and season with the salt. Cook on a low heat for about 30 minutes, stirring regularly. The onions should not colour at all, and they should be extremely soft. Once they are super soft, blend the whole shebang with a stick blender until a beautiful smooth purée, and sieve it if you want it really smooth.

This will be good for a few days in an airtight container in the refrigerator and heated up again as necessary.

FRIED, SLOPPY ONIONS

These are sweet, sloppy, savoury and extremely handy for adding to sausage sandwiches of all kinds, including hotdogs of course.

Makes enough for 10(ish) hotdogs

6 tablespoons extra virgin olive oil
50 g (1 oz/3½ tablespoons) butter
4 onions, thinly sliced
½ teaspoon salt

Get the oil and butter in a saucepan, and heat until the butter has completely melted. Add the sliced onions and salt. Stir and cook on a low heat for about 1½ hours, stirring regularly until the onions have become a sweet, sloppy, gooey mess. If you leave them a little while without stirring, bits of them will catch on the bottom of the pan and when you then stir them back in you will get more caramelised flavours and a darker colour to the onions. If you're looking for just sloppy, never let that happen, but if you're looking for caramelised AND sloppy, go for your life.

When the onions have cooked, you can use them just as they are or experiment a little by adding goodies to them:

1 tablespoon ketchup
1 tablespoon French's mustard
(or whatever mustard you have in the refrigerator)
1 tablespoon red wine vinegar
1 tablespoon Worcestershire sauce
1 tablespoon just about anything

Try any or all of these things thrown in at the very end to really 'hotdog van' them up and see what you think.

These will be good for a few days in an airtight container in the refrigerator.

ISTANBUL ONIONS

Guess where I had these? The recipe here makes enough for four people/sandwiches, but scale it up or down as needed.

Serves 4/Makes 4 sandwiches

2 large red onions, very finely sliced

Huge handful of flat leaf parsley, finely chopped

1 teaspoon sumac

2 tablespoons pomegranate molasses

2 tablespoons extra virgin olive oil

½ teaspoon fine sea salt

Toss everything in a bowl and mix well with your hands to combine. Feel free to give the onions a good scrunch or two while you're in there.

You can eat these nice and crunchy straight away or give them a little while (an hour or two) to soften and become sloppier and juicier. Both ways are magic.

These'll keep for a day, then they go a bit funny and want chucking out.

JULIENNE CARROTS

Julienne, there's that word again! Tell me you've bought that peeler by now. The Oxo Good Grips Julienne Peeler y'all, buy it once, save ever going to hospital with a mandoline accident.

Makes enough for 4 people as an accompaniment to a Sunday roast, a Tuscan Meatloaf or to put in a sandwich with leftovers from said meatloaf and lashings of pommes purée if you can't be bothered to make pickled carrots because you've cooked enough today DAMMIT.

3 medium carrots

1 garlic clove, peeled and chopped into a few big bits

1 teaspoon caster (superfine) sugar

Good pinch of salt

50 g (1¾ oz/3½ tablespoons) butter

50 ml (3½ tablespoons) water

1 tablespoon finely chopped parsley

Top and tail the carrots, peel them with a normal peeler and then have at 'em with your julienne peeler until they're all little sticks. If you don't have a julienne peeler (which you should), top and tail them, peel them, then cut them into thin strips lengthways. Cut those in half, across not lengthways, then cut those lengthways into little strips a bit like matchsticks. Confused? Well, if you had a julienne peeler this wouldn't have happened!

Put your mound of carrot sticks into a small saucepan along with the garlic bits, sugar, salt, butter and water. Stir everything about. Bring the water to the boil, then put a lid on and put the pan on a 1 or 2 out of 10 heat for 20–30 minutes. Keep checking on the carrots and stirring everything about until they are cooked, and you think they are nice. You don't want them too soft, or too crunchy, just delicious and a pleasure to eat. Classic culinary instructions, sorry.

When you want to eat them, take them out with some tongs or a fork, put them in a warmed bowl and quickly razz the liquid left in the pan on a high heat to reduce it by half, tip it over the carrots and sprinkle with the parsley.

Enjoy yourself, these are lovely, and that sauce, OMG!

These keep for a day, in the refrigerator.

MASHED POTATO

Chef bros are always talking up Joël Robuchon's Pommes Purée and saying it's the best mashed potato in the world and stuff. It is really nice, but it's not really mashed potato, it's a potato sauce. 'He makes it 50/50 potato and butter, bruv', they say, which he doesn't. Of course, that mad buttery goo has many places where it is utterly delicious, like in the meatloaf sandwich on page 104, and I'm not saying it isn't just dinky doo, BUT sometimes you just want mash to be mash; a fluffy and soft affair, living in a world where a few little lumps are OK, and where potato tastes of potato, not butter. I wouldn't use one of those mashers that has a wibble of metal rather than holes, but I wouldn't obsess about smoothness either.

Makes loads innit

1 kg (2 lb 4 oz) good potatoes, peeled and quartered (I like red-skinned ones for mash, so Albert Bartlett is a friend indeed, Rooster, Désirée or Apache are all good)
100 g (3½ oz/7 tablespoons) butter
100 ml (3½ fl oz/scant ½ cup) whole milk
Salt and pepper

Bring a pan of salted water to the boil (1 teaspoon of salt per 1 litre/34 fl oz/4¼ cups of water, as a guide) and simmer the potatoes for about 15 minutes. Start checking after 10 minutes, and if a butter knife passes through a spud without any real resistance, they're done. Overcooking can leave them waterlogged, and we don't want that. Once cooked, drain into a colander and leave to steam dry in the sink for 10 minutes while you heat your butter and milk together in the potato pan on a medium–low heat.

Once the butter has melted and the milk is on the cusp of boiling and 10 minutes is up, add the spuds back to the pan. Using a masher, or the end of a sturdy whisk, mash, mash, mash the spuds into, well, mash. Once completely broken down, remove the pan from the heat and switch to a wooden spoon or spatula and start to beat the mash with some gusto. Taste as you go here, adding a little extra salt and a good few grinds of black pepper, before finishing with a beating flurry that could see a bead or two of sweat trouble your top lip. If you feel a little extra milk or butter would help grease the wheels, splash some in, be guided by your instincts. Once you've a smooth (ish) potato-y piece of heaven, serve.

As I said on the opposite page, chefs with loads of tattoos LOVE this stuff. It makes them feel cool because it's got so much butter in it. Which arguably, and sadly perhaps, is quite cool hahaha. Sometimes a classic mash isn't what you want, and you're after something runnier and sloppier. For those moments, one need look no further than Monsieur Joël Robuchon. He won Michelin stars with mashed potato. Maestro, take it away.

The recipe for this is in the brilliant book *The Complete Robuchon*, which I have tried to faithfully reproduce here, without getting the book pulped.

Joël Robuchon (RIP) wisely advises that you use a 'food mill or potato ricer' for this. Whatever Marco Pierre White says, a blender will turn your potatoes into PVA, leave that alone. You can force the cooked potatoes through a sieve (fine mesh strainer) with a spoon, but really, I'd say if you don't have a potato ricer, a food mill or a really good, really fine sieve and a desire to work extremely hard, sack this off entirely and just make some normal mash.

Serves 6

1 kg (2 lb 4 oz) potatoes, scrubbed but unpeeled (Joël specifies Ratte potatoes or something romantically called BF-15, and who are we to argue?)
Fine sea salt
250 g (9 oz/2¼ sticks) butter, cubed and kept in the refrigerator
250 ml (8 fl oz/1 cup) whole milk
Salt and pepper

Put 2 litres (68 fl oz/8½ cups) of water, the potatoes and 1 tablespoon of fine sea salt in a saucepan and bring it up to a simmer. When simmering, cover it with a lid and cook until the potatoes are soft enough for a knife to slip through them easily. Joël says this will take 25 minutes, so I guess we're on a slow simmer, but I'll resist commenting because this bloke had more Michelin Stars than I've had hot sandwiches.

When just so, drain the potatoes and peel them. (Joël was clearly extremely hard – my worry here is the temperature of the potatoes, so definitely wear rubber gloves for this.) The skin should come away easily but might need helping off with a little knife.

Put the potatoes through the ricer/vegetable mill (mouli légumes) with the finest disc in it or force them through a fine sieve (strainer) with a spoon (good luck).

Once you've done this, the 'mashing' is over and Joël says you should put the potato, dry, into a saucepan on a medium heat and stir it about with a spatula to dry it out a bit. You don't want it to stick to the bottom of the pan or to colour at all, so I'd only do this briefly, for a minute or so, two at the most, and stir it all the time.

Reduce the heat to low and beat the butter in bit by bit with a wooden spoon or spatula until all is incorporated and everything seems smooth. Most of the way through incorporating the butter Joël says to 'rinse a small saucepan and pour out the excess water but do not wipe dry. Add milk and bring to the boil.' So do that.

Once all the butter is in and the milk is super-hot, beat that in a bit at a time, incorporating each addition. Once the milk is in, taste the mash and season with salt and pepper. Joël casually says that for an even smoother mash you can then pass all this lot through a fine sieve AGAIN.

All that. For mash. It is good though...

POTATO SALAD

It's the vinegar on the hot spuds that's the key here. The rest is just seasoning and personal preference. There are many ways to skin a cat, and indeed to make potato salad. I'm imagining I'm in the Austrian mountains for this version, the schnapps has kicked in and everything's really rather nice.

If you'd like to close your eyes and imagine you're somewhere else and doing this differently, please go ahead. Use all the mayo, crème fraîche, sour cream, cubes of ham, boiled egg, peas or celery you like, it's only a potato salad innit.

Serves 4

500 g (1 lb 2 oz) new or little salad
   potatoes, skin on
1¼ teaspoons fine sea salt
1 tablespoon red wine vinegar
1 tablespoon extra virgin olive oil
1 tablespoon Dijon mustard
2 big shallots, very finely chopped
6 cornichons, finely chopped
6 sprigs of tarragon (or parsley, dill,
   etc, depending on your taste),
   leaves picked, finely chopped
10 grinds of black pepper

Put your potatoes whole into cold water, with 1 teaspoon of salt, and bring up to the boil slowly. Simmer for 10–12 minutes after the water has started bubbling. Make sure a sharp, little knife slides through the potato with NO resistance at all and then they're done. Drain, put them in a bowl and once they have cooled a bit, cut them into equal-size pieces, halves or quarters should do it, and cover in the vinegar and oil, sloshing everything about and leave them to almost completely cool, but not quite, while you get everything else ready.

In the bowl you'd like to serve the salad in, combine the mustard, shallots, cornichons, tarragon, the remaining ¼ teaspoon of salt and the black pepper. Add the mostly cooled spuds and any liquid and turn it all about in the bowl with a big spoon and it's ready to go.

Some naughty chefs might add some double (heavy) cream, crème fraîche or even mayo at this point, and it's hard not to endorse doing the same. So, if you have some to hand and feel the urge, add a heaped tablespoon or two of something naughty now and mix it all about.

MY FAVOURITE POTATOES
I EVER HAD IN GREECE

The Greeks certainly seem to love fried potatoes. Sometimes they're just potatoes cut into rounds, chunks, chips or whatever and fried in one go from raw, or sometimes they're more like these, which are kind of semi-fried/roasted. I had these at a restaurant by the harbour on the island of Tinos, cooked by a handsome man with a large ponytail called Marcos.

I like these in a fried egg sandwich, or they'd be great in the crisp omelette sandwich on page 37, and they'd also be lovely as an alternative to a more conventional chip in the Gyros on page 101. Quite frankly they're good with just about anything. And they LOVE garlic mayo.

Makes enough for 4 sandwiches

Juice of 1 lemon
100 ml (3½ fl oz/scant ½ cup)
  chicken stock (½ cube would do
  – if you're lucky though you'll have
  some of the good homemade stuff
  and this dish will really shine)
2 bay leaves (dried or fresh)
3 tablespoons extra virgin olive oil
4 big garlic cloves, peeled
  and cut in half
2 big fist-size potatoes
  (I understand all fists are different,
  so why don't we say 2 lemon-size
  potatoes? Wait, lemons are
  different too! Let's just say,
  2 nice, big potatoes)
1 teaspoon dried oregano
Loads of fine sea salt

Preheat the oven to 200°C (400°F) and put a rack on the top shelf so the potatoes can go at the top.

Put the lemon juice, chicken stock, bay leaves and olive oil into a roasting tray and stick it in the preheated oven to get hot.

Peel the potatoes and cut them lengthways into slices 1 cm (⅓ in) thick. Cut those slices into strips, also lengthways, and also 1 cm (⅓ in) thick. Then cut THOSE sticks/chips (fries) into cubes 1 cm (⅓ in) thick. Nifty. Some won't be cubes, obvs, but it doesn't matter.

Take the hot baking tray out of the oven and put all the potatoes and garlic in, give them a liberal sprinkling of salt and stir everything about, making sure all the potatoes are completely coated. Bang the tray back in the oven.

They are going to cook for 45 minutes–1 hour, so start a timer. On 15 minutes, 30 minutes (and 45 minutes if it goes on that long), take the potatoes out and stir them all about, turning them all over and gently rolling them about. When the time is up, everything should have gone a bit brown and sticky and chewy and extremely bloody nice. Sprinkle with oregano and a bit more salt. Yamas!

What's brown and sticky? THESE POTATOES, HAHAHA!

POTATO DAUPHINOISE

You probs already know how to make dauphinoise, but if you don't, here you go.

Serves 4, with plenty of leftovers for your naughty toasted croissant (see page 32)

200 ml (10 fl oz/1¼ cups) double (heavy) cream

200 ml (3½ fl oz/scant 1 cup) whole milk

1 teaspoon salt

800 g (1 lb 12 oz) potatoes, peeled and sliced whole as thinly as possible, on a mandoline if you have one (Maris Pipers or Roosters work well)

1 garlic clove, cut in half

50 g (1¾ oz/3½ tablespoons) butter

Preheat the oven to 200°C (400°F).

Pop the cream and milk into a large pan and bring just to the edge of a simmer, you know, when the little bubbles start to gather at the edge of the pot and the thing is steaming. Season with salt and add the sliced potatoes sloshing everything about. Remove from the heat and leave to stand for 10–15 minutes so that everything gets to know one another.

Rub a roasting tray (the sort you'd use for lasagna or brownies) all over with the cut garlic halves, then rub all over the inside with some of the butter using a small piece of baking parchment or butter paper. If you're finicky you can carefully lift the potato slices out of the cream and milk and arrange them in neat layers in the dish before pouring over the liquid. If you're more rough and ready, simply pour the potatoes and all the liquid into the dish, spread them out with your hands into an even-ish layer, give 'em a good pressing down and you're ready for action. The liquid element of this needs to come just over halfway up the inside of the baking dish. If the liquid comes all the way to the top, tip some off.

Put the remaining butter in little lumps all over the top of the potatoes, put the dish on a baking tray (pan) in case there's leakage and bake not quite at the top of the oven for at least 45 minutes, and up to 1 hour. Once cooked the dauphinoise should look nice and golden brown on top, if it doesn't give it longer. Use a sharp knife to check for doneness, it should pass through all the way to the bottom without resistance. If it doesn't, bang it back in.

Allow to sit for about 15 minutes before serving and pop any leftovers in the refrigerator for tomorrow's toasted croissant.

In mine and Ben's previous book about picnics, there was an arguably inappropriate, slightly unpicnicky recipe for McDonald's-style French fries. They were extraordinarily good, but fiddly. These are also fiddly, but less so. Think of them as two-thirds of Heston's Triple Cooked Chips – Double Cooked Chips, is that trademarkable? They are a bit thicker than a McDonald's French fry and, if we were in South Africa, they would be called slap chips. Sadly, not because they slap, but they do. I think slap means soft, but don't quote me on it.

Makes enough for 4 chip butties, with leftovers for snaffling

600 g (1 lb 5 oz) russet (or any floury) potatoes
Vegetable, rapeseed (canola) or sunflower oil, for deep-frying
Salt and pepper

Peel the potatoes and place them in a bowl of cold water. Remove the potatoes, one by one, and cut them lengthways into 1 cm (⅓ in)) thick slices, then stack the slices and cut those into 1 cm (⅓ in) thick slices, also lengthways. Now you've got fries. Drop the fries into some fresh cold water and leave for an hour or so in order that some of the starch is removed.

When you're ready to cook, drain the fries and rinse well in a couple of changes of cold water. Spread them out on paper towels and pat dry.

Pour enough oil for deep-frying into a deep-fryer or a large, heavy-based saucepan and heat to 140°C (280°F). This is roughly the heat at which a cube of white bread will float about frying but not colouring for a minute or so. If you had a temperature probe, this would be easy. Working in batches, and using a slotted spoon, carefully lower your fries into the hot oil, without overcrowding them. Leave to blanch for 5 minutes before removing and draining on a baking tray lined with paper towels. The fries will be very soft at this stage, and hopefully (unless your oil was too hot) won't have coloured much at all.

Once all the fries are blanched, heat the oil to 200°C (400°F) and, again in batches, fry the fries for a couple of minutes until golden brown. Drain on yet more paper towels and immediately hit the fries with a generous dusting of salt, remembering the maxim that there is nothing on earth as miserable as an under-seasoned, fried potato (unless it's a shoestring fry destined for a Ham, Egg 'n' Chips Sandwich).

Voilà! Perfect double cooked fries in the comfort of your own home. Have that Heston!

ALOO VADA

Battered, fried mashed potato? YES, PLEASE. This popular Mumbai street food, frequently found in a nice bun and called a Vada Pav, is often enjoyed alongside a curry, and as a snack on their own.

Makes about 12–15, depending on who's balling, and what a baller they are

500 g (1 lb 2 oz) potatoes (about 3 big ones), peeled
2 tablespoons vegetable oil, like rapeseed (canola) oil
2 teaspoons black mustard seeds (yellow will do)
1 teaspoon cumin seeds
About 20 curry leaves (fresh is best, dried will do, go with none but only if you can't get any)
1 teaspoon chilli (hot pepper) flakes
½ teaspoon ground turmeric
2 garlic cloves, grated
2-cm (¾-in) piece of fresh ginger, peeled and grated
Handful of coriander leaves, chopped
2 litres (68 fl oz/9 cups) vegetable oil, for frying
Salt

For the batter:
150 g (5½ oz/1⅔ cups) chickpea (gram) flour
¼ teaspoon chilli powder
¼ teaspoon ground turmeric
½ teaspoon salt
100 ml (3½ fl oz/scant ½ cup) water (be ready to use more if necessary)

Cut your potatoes up as you would for roast potatoes, boil them in salted water until just falling apart, as in a little bit longer than you'd cook them for boiled potatoes, then drain and leave them to steam in the colander for 15 minutes.

Next, in a frying pan (skillet), heat the 2 tablespoons of oil on a medium-low heat and once warmed, add the mustard seeds and when they begin to crackle, add the cumin seeds, curry leaves, chilli flakes and turmeric, letting each spice sizzle and toast for a few seconds. Add the garlic and ginger and fry for a minute before adding the potatoes and mashing them into the spice mix, with a sturdy spatula. You want quite a smooth and pliable mix. Add the coriander leaves, mix once more, then transfer to a bowl to cool. Once cool, shape into squash-ball-size balls and pick out the curry leaves as you come across them, without worrying too much.

If you've got a fryer at home, get it on to 180°C (350°F), otherwise you know the drill: heat oil in your biggest high-sided pot, and get it to 180°C (350°F), which is the temperature at which a piece of bread goes golden and crisp in about 20 seconds.

While the oil heats, make your batter by combining the flour, chilli powder, turmeric and salt, whisking together, then adding the water and whisking until smooth.

To cook the bonda, dip each potato ball into the batter then, using a slotted spoon or wire spider (good bit of kit), carefully drop into the hot oil. Work in batches of 4–6 so as not to overcrowd the pan.

Fry each batch for about 4 minutes until golden, before transferring to a plate lined with paper towels, sprinkling with a little more salt and keeping them in a warm oven.

You could dress a whole plate of these like Mumbai nachos, drizzling yoghurt, possibly some of the coconut chutney on page 228 dotted about, or the coriander chutney on page 229, or both. You could fry some curry leaves and mustard seeds gently in browning butter and tip them on. You could also use these to make a veggie meatball sandwich of sorts, now I think about it…! Wahey!

ALOO MASALA

Order a masala dosa in a South Indian restaurant and you'll often get an enormous disc of crisp-edged dosa pancake and a steaming pile of aloo dosa to scoop and swipe it through and all that business. Couple or triple this potato curry in a rolled paratha or flat bread (or on a plate) with the coconut chutney on page 228 and some London Mix (finer Bombay Mix – check out the Cofresh brand) to be transported somewhere really, really nice. You could use this in place of the meat to make a banging veggie version of the Kati Roll on page 108.

Serves 4

3–4 potatoes (about 500 g/
  1 lb 2 oz), peeled and cut into
  2-cm (¾-in) cubes
1 tablespoon cider vinegar
2–3 tablespoons vegetable oil,
  like rapeseed (canola) oil
1 teaspoon cumin seeds
½ teaspoon mustard seeds (ideally
  black, but yellow will do)
20 curry leaves, fresh is best
  (if you can find them), dried is
  fine (none is also fine if you can't
  find either)
2 green finger chillies or
  2–3 supermarket green chillies,
  finely chopped
Thumb-sized piece of fresh ginger,
  peeled and finely chopped
1 large onion, chunkily chopped
½ teaspoon fine sea salt
½ teaspoon ground turmeric
Small bunch of coriander (cilantro),
  leaves picked and roughly
  chopped
Salt

Boil the potatoes in plenty of salted boiling water for about 10–15 minutes until completely cooked through and collapsing at the edges, then drain in a colander, sprinkle all over with the cider vinegar and leave to one side to steam dry for about 30 minutes.

In a saucepan on a medium heat, warm the oil and add the cumin and mustard seeds and curry leaves, letting them sizzle in the oil for 30 seconds before adding the chopped chillies and ginger, cooking this all for a further minute and stirring regularly. Add the onion, salt and turmeric, reduce the heat to low and cook for 6–8 minutes, stirring occasionally, until the onion is sweated and soft but not browned too much.

Tip the cooked potatoes into the pan, add 100 ml (3½ fl oz/ scant ½ cup) or so of water and stir to combine. As you stir, allow yourself to be quite rough, it's nice when some potato gets mashed to a paste, but make sure the majority is left as nice chunks. Cook on a low heat, stirring every now and again, for a further 3–4 minutes, adding a little extra water if the mixture seems dry. All that remains is to add the chopped coriander and to check the final seasoning.

CHILLI PANEER

Oh my gosh, I love chilli paneer! A joyful meeting of Chinese and Indian cuisines and a textural delight. This is another little beauty that could easily be used instead of the meat for a veggie Kati Roll (page 108) that will knock the flavour socks off just about anyone. One thing to remember is that it holds the heat rather well, so proceed cautiously with that first bite.

Makes enough for 2 Kati Rolls (page 108)

4 tablespoons cornflour (cornstarch)
2 tablespoons plain (all-purpose) flour
½ teaspoon fine sea salt
6–8 grinds of black pepper (or ¼ teaspoon)
250 g (9 oz) paneer, cut into 2-cm (¾-in) cubes
5 tablespoons vegetable oil, like rapeseed (canola) oil
1 onion, chunkily chopped
2 green chillies, chopped (deseeded if you wish)
1 green (bell) pepper, deseeded and chunkily chopped
1 tablespoon light soy sauce
2 tablespoons tomato ketchup
1 tablespoon rice wine vinegar

In a bowl, combine the cornflour, flour, salt and black pepper and whisk a little. Add 50 ml (2 fl oz) of cold water and whisk to a smooth batter. Add a touch more water if it's too thick. Drop the cubed paneer into the batter and muddle to coat.

Heat the oil in a large frying pan (skillet) on a medium–high heat and, using two forks, carefully place the battered paneer cubes, one by one, into the hot oil. Brown for 30 seconds on each side, turning carefully with tongs or the forks to keep the nice crisp batter that's forming.

Once browned, remove the paneer to a plate lined with paper towels. Add the onion, chopped chillies and green pepper to the pan and fry nice and hard so that the edges start to colour. After 3–4 minutes, add the soy sauce, tomato ketchup and vinegar and allow it to sizzle and steam for a minute before tossing in the paneer and stirring so that everything gets to know one another. Cook for a minute or two so that the paneer is hot through, and the sauce reduces around it.

Serve hot, ideally in a Kati Roll (page 108) sandwich-wise, but I reckon it's equally good in a white bread sandwich with a load of coconut chutney (page 228) and very little else.

This zingy little spice mix is ideal for taking a tomato, cucumber, bits of celery or cubes of mango and turning them into a spiced and lively chopped salad to enliven any sandwich, wrap or curry spread. There are many varieties of chaat all over Southeast Asia. Something hot and fried (often potatoes or chickpeas/garbanzos), will be paired with something fresh, some curry leaves and some sauces, tamarind, coriander (cilantro) chutney or thinned yoghurt, and sprinkled with a masala like this. This mix would also work well on a roast potato or on top of a fried egg between two pieces of bread or rolled up in a paratha. Experiment; it's a real treat.

Amchoor is dried, unripe mango powder, which can be found in most South Asian groceries or on the venerable souschef.co.uk. It also crops up in the Amba on page 237.

Makes 1 small jar

3 teaspoons amchoor powder
1 teaspoon ground coriander
½ teaspoon ground cumin
½ teaspoon chilli powder
½ teaspoon ground cardamom
½ teaspoon ground cinnamon
1 teaspoon ground ginger
1 teaspoon fine sea salt

Sling all these things in a jar, shake it to mix everything, then keep it in that jar and sprinkle it on the things mentioned above and loads of other stuff too. To check your levels, dip a wetted finger into the jar (or sprinkle some on a slice of cucumber or piece of tomato) and give it a taste. You want zing (which comes from the mango powder) and pleasing fragrance (from everything else). Tweak as you like with amchoor, chilli and cardamom being the levers most usefully pulled.

Once jarred up, this will last for months, although, as with any ground spices, the vitality will start to ebb the longer you keep it.

VEGETABLE SAMOSAS

The recipe below includes a hopefully, relatively simple explanation of how you fold and cook these little golden triangles of joy, that we have lifted straight from Meera Sodha. The filling includes a demand for 750 g (1 lb 10 oz) of vegetables. These can be any vegetables but leaning towards hearty and rooty is always good as these tend to absorb and carry the spicing nicely in the finished samosa. Combinations of carrot, celeriac (celery root), parsnip, sweet potato, turnip, potato, cauliflower, peas, etc, all work nicely. You do you.

The final twist in this samosa recipe is that we suggest you bake rather than fry them. Madness, but baking at home is largely easier and less messy than deep-frying, so we thought we'd give you a break and let you just slam these in the jammer. Once you have made them, there is also no reason you couldn't deep-fry them, if you so wish.

Makes about 20

400 g (14 oz) filo pastry

For the filling:
100 g (3½ oz/7 tablespoons) butter
  (plus a knob more, melted,
  in a separate pan for samosa
  construction)
1 large white onion, diced
750 g (1 lb 10 oz) vegetables
  (see intro), peeled and cut into
  small dice a bit like the onion
2 teaspoons garam masala
1 teaspoon ground cumin
1 teaspoon chilli powder
½ teaspoon ground turmeric
2 teaspoons salt
Juice of 1 lemon
Handful of coriander (cilantro)
  leaves, torn

Start by heating the butter in a large frying pan (skillet). Add the onion and fry, stirring occasionally, for 10 minutes or until soft and golden. Add the potato (or whatever you went for) and cook for a further 10 minutes, stirring regularly and tossing the pan. Add the garam masala, cumin, chilli powder, turmeric, salt and lemon juice. Stir to coat and cook for a couple more minutes, then take off the heat and allow to cool. When cooled, add the coriander leaves and stir well.

To make the samosas, unroll a sheet of filo and place it on a work surface or large chopping board. Brush it lightly with melted butter and layer with another sheet of pastry and smooth them together. Cut the sheets into three horizontal strips. (Pic. 1, opposite)

Here is how Meera Sodha describes the process of filling and folding [with me making unhelpful shouts in these square brackets haha]:

'You make a cone shape at one end of the strip [by making a triangle then folding that over itself leaving one open side (Pic. 2, opposite)], place 1 heaped tablespoon of the filling inside the cone, then fold the open side of the cone into the rest of the filo strip to close the thing up. Keep folding over [and over (Pic. 3, opposite)] the rest of the pastry around the shape of the cone [samosa] until you come to the end of the strip... stick the strip down with a brush of melted butter (Pic. 4, opposite). Pop the samosa on a tray and repeat.'

All you need to do now is preheat the oven to 180°C (350°F). Brush the samosas with a little extra melted butter and bake for 30 minutes, or until golden brown. Allow to cool slightly before eating with a punchy chutney or indeed sandwiching in a similar manner. At the Sandwich Shop we have used samosas, spring rolls and all kinds of fried, filled crispy things in sandwiches with great success. Matched up with mayo or yoghurt, loads of herbs and something pickle-y, their crunch and soft interior richness are magic in between two bits of bread or wrapped in a flatbread of some kind.

A GUIDE TO FOLDING A SAMOSA

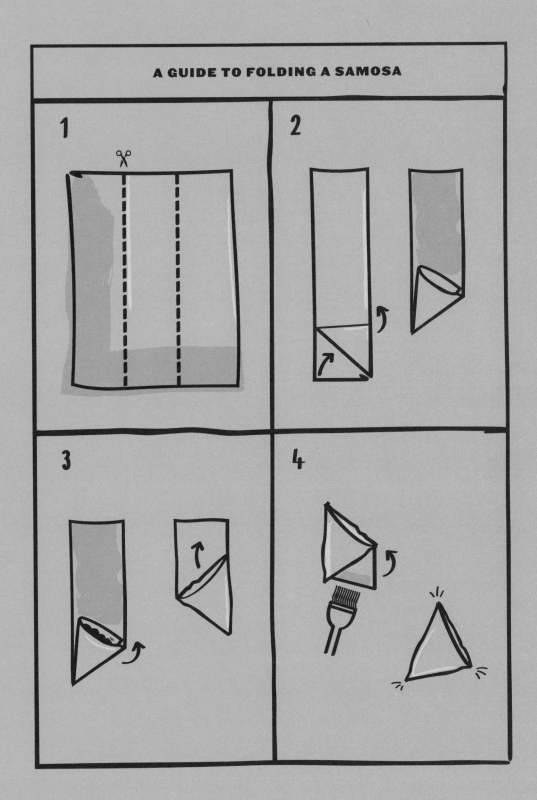

CELERIAC RÉMOULADE

You need to julienne the celeriac for this which is gonna take ages with a knife. Maybe save this recipe for after you've bought the Oxo Good Grips Julienne Peeler I keep banging on about. If you insist on doing it without one, you will need to peel and cut your whole celeriac into thin (2 mm/⅛ in) slices, then cut those slices into matchstick like slivers. Good luck and see you next year. Sadly, you cannot grate it because then it'd be weird coleslaw, not swanky rémoulade.

Makes enough for 4–6 people to eat however they may wish

Juice of ½ lemon
1 tablespoon wholegrain mustard
1 tablespoon Dijon mustard
100 g (3½ oz/scant ½ cup) mayonnaise (I like Hellmann's) or homemade (page 220)
1 tablespoon extra virgin olive oil
1 tablespoon red wine vinegar
½ teaspoon salt
10–12 grinds of black pepper
1 small celeriac (celery root), top and messy bottom cut off, peeled (but don't do any of this until you've made the sauce)

Put all the ingredients apart from the celeriac into a bowl and whisk them together. Taste it. Nice, huh?!

Now julienne the celeriac with that special peeler you've bought and mix the slithers into the sauce as you go, being careful not to julienne yourself. At the end, mix well – I like to use my hands for this one so that I can gently squish everything together.

Once mixed, leave for at least 1 hour, or ideally a few hours, for the flavour to develop and the celeriac to soften. My fried Owen, I believe, salts his celeriac slivers before putting everything together. I never bother!

This'll keep for 3 days in the refrigerator.

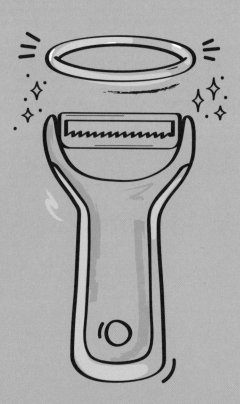

Not having the ability to see into the future or much inclination to cook dried beans, when I want hummus, I reach for a jar of cooked chickpeas (garbanzos). The best chickpeas, in my opinion, come from Brindisa, followed by Belazu and Bold Bean Co, and they come in big 660 ml (22 fl oz/2¾ cup) jars. That's too big for a regular batch of hummus, which is a good thing as it means you can use the rest of the jar for a lovely little stew or salad, or something.

When you buy tins, cartons or jars of chickpeas (or any beans/pulses), try and stick to organic options and always check the ingredients. If there is anything other than chickpeas (or whatever), water and salt, don't buy them! Those skins will never be soft, and your hummus will be ruined.

Someone once told me that the secret to amazing hummus is to put a few ice cubes in, but I always forget! Give it a try and let me know @lunchluncheon!

**Makes about 250 g (9 oz)
or enough for 4 sandwiches,
wraps, pittas, etc**

200 g (7 oz) chickpeas (garbanzos),
plus a little tin/jar liquor (buy the
nice big posh ones if you can)
Juice of 1 lemon
2 garlic cloves, grated
50 g (3½ oz/scant ¼ cup) tahini
(stir the jar first)
½ teaspoon ground cumin
1 teaspoon salt

To get the best blend on hummus, I find it helps to warm the chickpeas in their juice first. Weigh out the chickpeas into a small pan, then splash a good bit of jar juice over them if there is any (or 2 tablespoons of water if there isn't). Place this on a low heat and warm through for a few minutes.

Meanwhile, put the lemon juice, garlic, tahini, cumin and salt in a food processor and blitz together. This will give you a thick paste but do not be alarmed. Add the warm chickpeas and a splash or two of extra juice or water (or 5 ice cubes if using), and start to blitz. If it looks too stiff, add a touch more chickpea juice or water. Blitz until nice and smooth. Give it a taste. Depending on the chickpeas and tahini used, I find it can often take more lemon juice, and extra salt and cumin can also help bring out that pleasing background musk that the best hummus has. Once you think it tastes lovely, you're good to go.

ISRAELI SALAD

Quick to knock up, not too much chopping and absolutely delicious if your veggies are good. This one's a knockout if you do it properly and more than the sum of its parts.

**Makes enough for 2 people
(or enough for 8 Sabich)**
1 cucumber (or a few of those
dinky little, delicious ones if you
can get them)
2 good, big, fat, deep red tomatoes
1 red onion, peeled
Bunch of flat-leaf parsley, leaves
picked and very finely chopped
75 ml (2½ fl oz/5 tablespoons) mix
of 50 ml (1¾ fl oz/3½ tablespoons)
extra virgin olive oil and 25 ml
(2 tablespoons) lemon juice
Big pinch of salt

Chop the cucumber(s), tomatoes and onion into really small chunks, all of a similar size and put them in a bowl. Add the chopped parsley.

Put the olive oil, lemon juice and salt in a bowl and whisk them together. Stick your finger in. Try it. More acidic? Add some lemon. Needs to be saltier, add some salt. Too lemony, add more olive oil. You get the idea.

Put the vinaigrette onto the salad, toss it all about and stuff it in a sarnie or just eat it for your lunch.

COLESLAW WITH CREAM

There ain't nothing quite as dreamy, as when the coleslaw's nice and creamy.

100 ml (3½ fl oz/scant ½ cup) double (heavy) cream

4 tablespoons mayonnaise (Hellmann's or page 220)

4 tablespoons red wine vinegar

½ teaspoon fine sea salt

400 g (14 oz) finely shredded white cabbage (this is best done with a very sharp knife, you could grate it on a coarse grater, but it tends to go a bit mooshy and you could also use hispi/sweetheart type cabbage but never Savoy, NEVER, you'll be chewing it for weeks)

2 crisp eating (dessert) apples, such as Granny Smith

8–10 sprigs each of parsley, tarragon and lovage or celery leaves, roughly chopped (celery leaves, from the top of a bunch, are much easier to find than lovage)

6 spring onions (scallions), top 5 mm (¼ in) and rooty bottoms discarded, finely sliced (green and white bits)

Find a good large bowl. Whisk together the cream, mayonnaise, vinegar and salt. Add the cabbage, herbs and spring onions and toss to coat, making sure the creamy dressing gets into every nook and cranny of every piece of cabbage.

Julienne the apples (not the cores) with the OXO Good Grips Julienne Peeler you must surely have bought by now! If you haven't bought the peeler, which is an error, you need to cut the apples into 2-mm (⅛-in)-thick slices, then cut those into 2-mm (⅛-in) sticks. However you deal with the apples, once you have, chuck 'em all in and mix 'em all about.

It's nice, but not essential, to leave this to sit for an hour or so, as the cabbage will soak up the dressing and soften some. Lovely.

Stored in an airtight container in the refrigerator this will last happily for about 3 days.

Let's get this straight: these can, and arguably should, always be bought in little jars or containers in almost any supermarket, corner shop, convenience store or deli that you might walk into. Buy them when you see them, they're sandwich gold. The best ones are Spanish and will hopefully be labelled Piquillo Peppers. If, however, you want to make them, despite being a little fiddly, they couldn't be easier to rustle up. As with all things seemingly simple, buying good peppers that actually taste of something, and using good oil, will ensure that these are supremely delicious as opposed to just nice.

If you only need these for a quick sarnie, rather than to make and keep, don't bother with the jar or garlic or olive oil mentioned below. Just burn your pepper(s), put them (hot) in a plastic bag or cling-filmed (plastic-wrapped) bowl to steam/sweat for 5 minutes, then whip the charred peel off and you're ready to go.

Makes about 400 g (14 oz), or enough for 4–6 sandwiches

4 classic red (bell) peppers or, even better, 6 longer pointy ones
3 garlic cloves, peeled and thinly sliced
100 ml (3½ fl oz/scant ½ cup) extra virgin olive oil (maybe more)

1 sterilised jar (page 253, optional)

Read the advice on sterilising jars (page 253) and get that done first.

The main thing you're doing here is removing the skin from the peppers. You do that by burning the hell out of them, sweating them, then peeling the blackened skin away. This leaves behind the nice sweet and slightly smoky flesh of the peppers and nothing else.

If your oven has a grill (broil) setting, preheat it to full blast and sit the peppers on a roasting tray right under it, turning them every 2–3 minutes until they are completely black and burned all over. If you don't have a grill, place them in and around your largest gas hob on full flame (seriously, you can also do this to make mad smoky aubergines), letting them blacken in direct contact with the flame, turning as needed.

If you don't have a gas cooker, you could burn them just above the coals on a barbecue, but I'd just abandon this and go back to the deli or supermarket and try to find some, you must have missed them.

Once completely blackened and still hot, place them in a Tupperware with a tight-fitting lid, or in a bowl sealed tightly with cling film (plastic wrap) or stuff them in a plastic bag, and leave for 10 minutes to steam and sweat. Once the peppers have softened and cooled down a bit, peel and rub away the black skins, which should be easy if you've burned them enough.. Cut the pepper in half and remove the stalk and seeds, leaving behind the soft, red flesh which you can cut into strips or sections, or leave in large pieces, depending on your preference.

Pack these into your sterilised jar mixed up with the sliced garlic and olive oil, making sure the peppers are completely covered with oil and making sure you don't put your fingers inside the jar. Tip more oil on top if necessary. Close the lid and let them marinate for a day. These will stay fresh in the refrigerator for a week or two at least (as long as they are covered with oil and as long as that jar was sterilised!).

Ned Halley's Breadcrumbs

Things of legend, like the man himself. He does croutons too, but that's for another book.

Preheat the oven to 140°C (275°F).If you kept these in an airtight jam jar, they would last for 10,000 years, or, according to our publisher's lawyers, about a week.

Slice whatever old, white bread you have into 1-cm (½-in) slices, then into 1-cm (½-in)-ish squares (including crusts). Put these on a flat baking tray and bang them in the oven until they're completely dried out, which I imagine will be about 40 minutes–1 hour. When completely devoid of any moisture, take them out and leave them to cool. Once cool, put them in a thick plastic bag and batter them with a rolling pan into crumbs. They all want to be small, but they don't all want to be powder. Sorry Japan, but these are as good as panko in my opinion, although Ned is my dad.

DEEP-FRIED MACARONI FOR A LASAGNA SANDWICH
AKA THE BLENDER DESTROYER

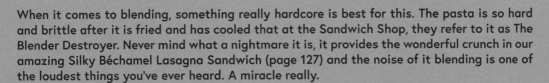

When it comes to blending, something really hardcore is best for this. The pasta is so hard and brittle after it is fried and has cooled that at the Sandwich Shop, they refer to it as The Blender Destroyer. Never mind what a nightmare it is, it provides the wonderful crunch in our amazing Silky Béchamel Lasagna Sandwich (page 127) and the noise of it blending is one of the loudest things you've ever heard. A miracle really.

Makes enough for about 4 sandwiches

100 g (3½ oz) macaroni or penne
1 litre (34 fl oz/4¼ cups) vegetable oil, for frying

Boil the pasta as per the packet instructions. Once cooked and drained, leave in the colander to steam dry for 10 minutes

Heat about 4 cm (1½ in) depth of oil in a high-sided saucepan and, once hot (about 180°C/350°F, or when a piece of bread dropped in sizzles almost immediately), carefully drop the pasta into the oil and fry until deep, golden brown and a little bubbly on the surface. This will take a while (up to 5 minutes sometimes). Remove carefully (using a spider (not that kind, ask the chatbot), or a slotted spoon) and drain on paper towels.

Once cold, bang it all in a blender and blitz until a coarse rough powder. Now sandwich as per the sandwich on page 127.

BEN'S REALLY NICE SPICED NUTS
AKA BEN'S NUTS

As the peeps down the nut factory are likely to say about their own output, these are the nut nut's, mutt's nuts.

Makes about 400 g (14 oz) or about 15 pudgey handfuls

400 g (14 oz) unsalted mixed nuts
20 g (¾ oz/1½ tablespoons) salted butter
1 tablespoon good oil, such as extra virgin olive oil or organic cold-pressed rapeseed (canola) oil
1 teaspoon fennel seeds
2 teaspoons Maldon (or other good flaky) sea salt
1 teaspoon freshly ground black pepper
2 teaspoons ground cumin
2 teaspoons ground coriander
½ teaspoon chilli powder

Preheat the oven to 180°C (350°F). Put the nuts in a single layer in a shallow roasting tin and roast for 10 minutes (or until golden), shaking occasionally. Set aside.

Meanwhile, pop the butter and oil in a small frying pan (skillet) and, when melted and frothing, add the fennel seeds, allow to fizzle for a second or two, then add the salt and remaining spices. Fry for 30 seconds until fragrant, tossing occasionally to ensure the spices don't burn. Once the spices are cooked and fragrant, pour over the nuts in the roasting tin and mix well before spreading out again into a single layer and allowing to cool completely.

Once cooled and stored in an airtight container, these fellas will keep merrily for a week, although suspicion tells me they won't hang about that long.

MASHED BLACK BEANS

These are made by getting good-quality black beans (without firming agent in them) from somewhere good like Brindisa, Belazu or Bold Bean Co or from an organic carton from the supermarket, heating them in a pan, in some of their juice and mash, mash, mashing them with a masher, until they are mostly smooth with a mix of some bigger chunks.

If they are very wet, depending on the amount of juice in the ones you bought, you can cook the mash in the pan a bit to evaporate some of the liquid. This simple thing is a wonderful way to add a warm, smooth, velvety richness to a sandwich without adding loads of flavour, and you can do it with any beans! Handy.

These were in the second Torta Ahogada I had in Guadalajara (page 90), but Ben's Refried Beans in the next recipe would also be AMAZING in there!

REFRIED BEANS

These are proof that whoever asked 'What's in a name?', wasn't wrong. You'd have thought these had already been fried and that you were now gonna fry them again, right? Wrong.

It seems that in England we translate 'frijoles refritos' a little too literally. My wife is Mexican, and I still don't quite get it. Here, we're gonna cook the bean mixture until dry and mashable, mash, mash, mash it and then allow it to cook a little more in the lard (shortening) or oil, which could be the refrying, but seems not to be. These work extraordinarily well in sandwiches, adding a wonderful flavour, and especially a glorious texture and richness. They are also great cooked, chilled, and then refried the following day to reheat them. So I guess, sometimes, they are refried after all...

Makes loads, almost 1 kg (2 lb 4 oz), which is enough for a meal for 4 and then for 4–6 sandwiches the following day

2 heaped tablespoons lard
   (shortening) or bacon dripping,
   if you're a baller), or vegetable oil
1 onion, finely chopped
1 garlic clove, grated
½ teaspoon dried oregano
2 x 400-g (14-oz) tins black beans,
   juice and all
½ teaspoon fine sea salt
1 teaspoon cider vinegar

Heat the lard or oil in a heavy-based pot over medium/low heat and add the onion. Cook for 6–8 minutes, stirring regularly, until the onion becomes soft. Add the garlic and oregano and cook for a further 2 minutes, stirring regularly so that it doesn't catch, before adding the black beans and their juice. Allow to come up to the boil, reduce the heat, then cook for 4–6 minutes until the mixture looks less watery.

Now, grab a masher or a good whisk and mash and bash the beans to a consistency you like the look of. Some go completely smooth, I leave a little texture. Continue to cook while doing this, adding a little extra lard or oil if you think it needs it and it's catching too much on the bottom. Give the beans a taste, adding the salt and vinegar as necessary. Once happy, turn off the heat and allow the beans to rest for a few minutes before serving. Or leave to cool, refrigerate, and fry hard in lard or oil the following day.

These will keep for a week in an airtight container in the refrigerator.

Boiled eggs

Sorry to do this, but because there are so many methods for boiling an egg, can I establish what I mean when I talk about a 10- or 7- (or any) minute boiled egg:

Bring a (small) pan of water to a full boil on a max heat, put the egg or eggs in with a spoon and, keeping the pan boiling at full blast, leave the eggs in there, bouncing about, for exactly the number of minutes you want the egg boiled. Then run the pan with the egg(s) in it under the cold tap (faucet) for 30 full seconds, until you can hold the egg(s) without stressing yourself at all. Tap, tap, tap, crunch the shells all over, peel and you're done.

Most of the time I like a hard-boiled egg, not a soft-boiled egg. When I say soft-boiled, I mean 7 minutes, which isn't soft enough for some people, but it is for me, and when I say hard-boiled, I mean 10 minutes, which is too much for some, but not for me.

211

HARRY MACKINTOSH'S SLOW-FRIED EGGS

A recipe for fried eggs? On my head be it, hahaha. Many years ago, Harry Mackintosh, the man who taught me to cook, made me one of these for breakfast, and served it in the best way ever, which was on top of a rare, ribeye steak, sitting on a heap of Fried Sloppy Onions (page 186), sitting on a piece of heavily buttered toast. He's a good man.

You want fresh eggs for this. Free range ones too at least, if not organic.

If you've ever wondered how to get a fried egg to look like a cartoon or emoji fried egg, this is how you do it.

Before you get started on one of these, please remember that instead of taking 15–20 minutes to make a fried egg, you can ALWAYS just fry one in your normal manner in about 20 seconds and use that instead! It's up to you. I think these are worth every second, you might not.

1 free-range egg per person
Vegetable oil (loads)

You only need one of these per person because they're rich. Fill an ideally non-stick, little frying pan (skillet) with vegetable oil so that it is at least 3 or 4 mm (⅛ in) deep. Put it on the hob, but don't turn it on yet. Crack your egg(s) in. The yolk should be above sea level, but the white should be below. Add more oil if necessary.

If your hob goes 1–9 like mine does, put it on 2. If you've got gas (hahaha), put the flame on really, really small. The idea is to cook the egg mad slowly. It should take at least 2 minutes for the white to begin to cook **at all**. And it should takes 15–20 minutes for the white to cook and firm completely, especially around the yolk, but still leave the yolk runny.

Doesn't it look brilliant! I love the texture of the white in these, so firm and so bouncy, in the most delicious of ways.

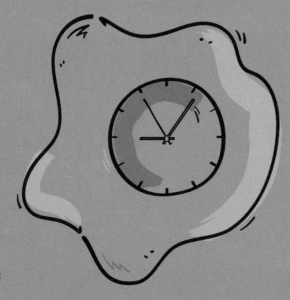

Should this recipe be in this section? Definitely not. But I nearly forgot it completely and we had to shoehorn it in at the last minute hahahahah!

In the wrong hands three of the scariest words in the English language are 'served with ratatouille.' Done right, it is wonderful and a total joy with roasted meats, steamed white fish and all kinds of things.

My friend Harry Mackintosh taught me to make it like this and despite being a lot of work, (which I tend to do about twice a year) everyone (including me) always loves it. Unlike the watery, mooshy, horrible stuff often called ratatouille, this is thick and rich and involves the deep frying of some of the vegetables, which we can all get behind I'm sure!

Makes enough to serve four as a side dish and have some leftover for sandwiches.

4 tablespoons extra virgin olive oil

3 onions, peeled, halved and thinly sliced

8 garlic cloves, peeled and finely chopped

1 teaspoon good quality dried thyme, or 1 tablespoon picked fresh thyme leaves

2 x 440 g (15½ oz) tins of tinned tomatoes

¼ teaspoon bicarbonate of soda (if you think putting bicarb in something like this is an abomination, don't use it)

2 litres of vegetable oil for deep frying

4 medium courgettes, topped and tailed and cut lengthways into long, thin strips

2 large emoji-esque aubergines, topped and tailed and cut lengthways into long, thin strips

4 roasted piquillo peppers from a nice posh jar (or 2 big, skinned, roasted peppers you've done yourself, page 203)

About 20 black olives (good ones, with stones), stones removed

1 tablespoon red wine vinegar (the best you have, white wine vinegar would do too, but not balsamic)

Salt and pepper

Put the olive oil in a big saucepan and get it on a medium heat. Once it's hot, add the onions, season with salt and pepper and cook until golden and beautiful (15 minutes?), stirring regularly. Add the garlic and thyme, stir together and cook until the garlic has lost its rawness (5 minutes?).

Put the tinned tomatoes into a bowl and moosh the tomatoes up with your hands. Squeeze them in your palm and force them through your fingers. Wash your hands and tip the tomatoes into the onions. Stir it all about and add the bicarb. Stir it again. The bicarb lightens things up and gives the impression you might have used fresh tomatoes.

Bring the tomatoes to the boil, lower the heat, and simmer (blip, blip) away stirring regularly for 15–20 minutes.

While this is happening, get another decent sized saucepan on the heat with the vegetable oil in it and bring it up to 180°C (350°F). You know the drill: if you have a temperature probe this is easy, if not, it is roughly the temperature at which a cube of white bread dropped in sizzles and goes golden in about 20 seconds. If it's quicker than that, watch out it's probably too hot, slower, it's not hot enough.

When the oil is at the right temperature, in batches of about 10 at a time, fry the courgette and aubergine slices until golden and put them on a wire rack with a baking tray underneath it to drain, or put them in a bowl lined with a good amount of kitchen roll.

Once the tomatoes' cooking time is up, take the pan off the heat. Using your hands break the olives open and remove the stones, if they break up it doesn't matter at all. Throw the olives (not the stones) into the tomato mix, followed by the aubergines and courgettes. Stir everything about until all has become one. Think of it as folding, not beating; you don't want to moosh your carefully fried slices.

Cut down the side of the red peppers, open them up and cut them lengthways into slithers. Cut those slithers in half to make shorter slithers. Mix them in with everything else. Add the vinegar, stir a final time and give it a try. Needs more salt and pepper? Go on then. Wants a bit more sharpness? Add a touch more vinegar. It's just about perfect? SANDWICH AWAY.

This'll keep in the refrigerator for a few days, just make sure you reheat it gently in a little pan with a splash of water and a lid and a regular stir.

SHOESTRING FRIES

These are the Sandwich Shop's most faithful crisp and have provided the crunch in our signature Ham, Egg 'n' Chips sandwich since day one baby! Before you go to the bother of making them like we do at the shop, you need to know that you can buy amazing Portuguese crisps on the internet called Batata Frita Palha, made by a brand called Dalimar, which are basically the same thing (there are Brazilian brands too). The English versions sold in supermarkets are rubbish in sandwiches and to be avoided completely. They are too wide, and mad dry because they are made of reconstituted potato, not whole pieces of potato.

Makes a lot

400 g (14 oz) potatoes, perhaps Maris Pipers or Roosters
2 litres (68 fl oz/2 quarts) rapeseed (canola) or sunflower oil, for frying
Salt (optional)

PLEASE tell me you've bought an Oxo Good Grips Julienne Peeler! If you haven't, find yourself four things: a container or large bowl, a source of running water, a sharp knife or mandoline, and some wound dressings if you're going with the mandoline option.

If you have bought the peeler, this is easy. Peel the potatoes with your regular peeler, then julienne them with the julienne one.

If you haven't bought the peeler, good luck. Peel the potatoes with a regular peeler then, slice or mandoline each one into 2 mm (1/16 in) thick slices. Then cut these slices into little sticks 2 mm (1/16 in) wide. The French call these allumettes (matchsticks) because they are the same dimensions as, you guessed it, matchsticks. .

However you arrived at your heap of potato matchsticks, submerge them in cold water and agitate them with your hands for a minute. Leave them to soak for at least 10 minutes before putting into a colander or sieve (fine mesh strainer) and leaving to drain and dry out. You want them to be in there drying for at least 30 minutes. Water and hot oil are not friends.

If you have a deep-fat fryer, heat it to 180°C (350°F), if you don't, you know the drill: heat the oil in a high-sided pan on a medium heat to 180°C (350°F). If you have a temperature probe, use it and monitor the oil; alternatively, place a cube of bread in the pan and when it is fizzing and brown within 20 seconds, you are likely at peak oil temperature for frying.

Drop the potato sticks into the hot oil in two batches, move them regularly with tongs or something and fry until they become golden brown shoestring fries. They will stick together a bit, but don't worry, you can crumble them apart later. Once golden and really crisp, remove with a spider (not that spider) or a slotted spoon, place on some paper towels and season with a little salt if you like. Repeat until you have a pile of perfectly crisp matchsticks. At the Sandwich Shop we don't salt them at all because the other bits of the sandwich are quite highly seasoned.

Stored in an airtight container, these are good for at least 2 weeks, although it's unlikely they will last that long.

A banana hotdog? Hahahaha.

1 tablespoon caster (superfine) sugar per banana

1 tablespoon water per banana

1 banana per person, peeled (ripeness is up to you and what you prefer)

1 teaspoon bourbon per banana (Woodford Reserve is particularly good, and very banana-y I always think, if you happen to have any)

10 g (½ oz/2 teaspoons) salted butter per banana

Pinch of salt

Add the sugar and water to a frying pan (skillet) and place on a medium heat. Swill the pan to combine everything but do not stir it, this might make the sugar crystallise and be less than delicious.

Watch this carefully as it all goes quite quickly, quite suddenly. For a while, you'll just be watching a clear bubbly liquid, but after a few minutes you'll see darkness creeping in from the edges, this is the pleasure we are chasing. Swill this around a bit, watch more darkness emerge and creep towards the middle of the pan. Once you have a lovely uniform copper colour to your bubbling sugar mix, add the bananas to the pan. Give these 20–30 seconds on one side, then the same on the flip side, being super careful when turning them as we are in the midst of a very hot caramel when making this and caramel BURNS, itself, and you. I like to use two spoons.

Once the bananas have started to colour/caramelise themselves on both sides, add the bourbon to the pan and let this spit and fizz and keep gently swilling the pan. It may ignite, which is fun, and fine, so don't panic, just stand back, let the alcohol burn off and the flames will subside very quickly.

Next, add the butter to the pan and swill this about. It will sizzle and melt and turn the sauce into a butterscotch-looking consistency. Add a pinch of salt, remove from the heat, roll the bananas around in the tasty goo, allow to cool slightly and then launch straight into the banana hotdog recipe on page 119.

There is no way you'll have anything left here, which is lucky, because it doesn't really keep.

But if there is any goo left in the pan, eat it with a spoon when it is cool enough not to burn the skin off the inside of your mouth. Welcome to heaven.

CONDIMENTS & SAUCES

A LOAD OF

MAYONNAISE

BACON FAT MAYO

ALIOLI

MEMBRILLO MAYO

LEMON AND BASIL AIOLI

'NDUJA MAYO/CHORIZO MAYO

MAYONNAISES

LIME PICKLE MAYO

PO' BOY MAYO

TARRAGON MAYO

MORUNOS MAYO

SAFFRON MAYO

BROWN BUTTER MAYO

MAYONNAISE (AND GARLIC MAYO)

Just as there is no need to make your own bread to make amazing sandwiches, there is similarly no need to make your own mayonnaise. There is nothing wrong with Hellmann's. But, if you do want to, this recipe is A ONE-POT WONDER and really rather good. All you need is a stick blender and the tall plastic pot it came with, or something similar. A Pyrex jug (pitcher) will do the job. This really is easy, go for your life, and check out the photos on the opposite page, which will hopefully help you along!

My dear friend Bebito taught me this, her mum's method, many years ago and I've never looked back – you go from raw ingredients to silky mayo in about 10 seconds! Perfect. And wang a garlic clove in as we'll discuss and you've made garlic mayo not mayo. Amazing!

Makes about 250 ml (8 fl oz/1 cup), or enough for 5–10 sandwiches

1 free-range egg
1 teaspoon Dijon mustard
Juice of ½ lemon
½ teaspoon salt
240 ml (7¾ fl oz/1 cup) good, neutral vegetable oil (not olive oil; it's too bitter)

For the Garlic Mayo:
1 garlic clove, peeled, finely chopped up and mooshed with a sprinkling of salt on it, with the side of a big knife, on a chopping board, until a nice uniform paste. If you want a REALLY quick garlic mayo, just mix this into Hellman's.

Put everything (including the garlic paste, if using) into your stick blender's tall pot in the following order: first the whole egg (not the shell hahaha), then everything that isn't oil, then the oil.

Put the stick blender in so that it is standing up straight, on the bottom of your vessel. Press the full speed button. You will see everything immediately start to become one. Slowly lift the blender head to the surface and go back down again. You will almost immediately have mayonnaise. If there are any bits that still look oily, give them a whizz with the blender. The whole thing should take about 10 seconds.

Stick your finger in, check the seasoning and adjust if necessary. Use on everything.

This will keep merrily for a few days in the refrigerator, in an airtight container.

BACON FAT MAYO

This is a personal favourite and the best thing EVER when making a BLT. I only use smoked streaky bacon to make a BLT, it gives off way more fat than back bacon and, I think, tastes much better. NEVER use cheap bacon. Only the supermarket's Finest. Once you've followed the method, you could bake the bacon until crisp, cool it, blend it and mix it into the mayo.

9 slices of smoked streaky bacon
1 batch of mayonnaise (page 220), or 3 heaped tablespoons store-bought (I like Hellmann's)
Big schploof of Tabasco sauce
Big schploof of malt vinegar (or cider or red or white wine vinegar)

Put the bacon in a cold frying pan (skillet). Over the course of 10–15 minutes, slowly increase the heat under the pan until loads of fat has rendered out of the bacon and the slices are browned but not crispy. Take the bacon out of the pan and tip all the bacon fat into the mayo. It'll look like there's way too much fat for the mayo. Bang in the Tabasco and vinegar and stir, stir, stir until everything becomes one again. Which it will.

1. Put everything in – egg first, oil last. Stand the blender up straight on the bottom.

2. Press go. Wiggle it about. With engine running, lift the blender to top, swinging it about.

3. Razz bits where there is still oil until everything is completely combined.

4. You've made mayo. In 10 seconds. Is there a Noble Prize for mayonnaise?

ALIOLI

We have covered garlic mayo already in the initial mayo recipe. This is different, this is the old-school, eggless, original oil and garlic sauce that a Spanish grandparent might get misty-eyed about. It's not mayo, but is often confused with one, which confusingly gives it a place here. If you want a quick alioli, grate a garlic clove into some Hellmann's and ride into the sunset. Otherwise, see below.

This old technique is barely used any more, but I suspect it would have been this sauce that one of the harbingers of deliciousness, Milli Taylor, had in the Serranito that she declared the best sandwich she'd ever eaten, so we thought we'd give you the recipe here. Fun, right? You'll need a pestle and mortar for this. If you don't have one, don't bother. A blender, etc, will probably turn the garlic bitter and make the sauce a bit rancid. Buy a pestle and mortar, they're more useful than you might have thought. I'm not taking the pestle, seriously.

Makes enough for 5–10 sandwiches depending on how liberal you are with its application

6 garlic cloves, peeled
¼ teaspoon fine sea salt
120 ml (4 fl oz/½ cup) really good extra virgin olive oil
Juice of ¼ lemon

Toss your peeled garlic cloves into your pestle and mortar with the salt. Give them a bash to open them up, then work in circular motions to smoosh and mash them until you have a nice sticky paste. Take your time here, it will make a huge difference to the finished sauce.

Once you have a completely smooth paste, slowly add the olive oil in an old-school-mayonnaise-making-style drizzle while continuing to work your pestle in circular motions.

Once all the oil is incorporated, add the lemon juice and swizzle it in with the pestle, after which you should have a decidedly creamy mayonnaise-like sauce, with no egg in it. Go forth and sandwich – try it on everything; you've got plenty.

This will last for about 2 days in the refrigerator in an airtight container before becoming far too lively by half.

OLLIE REYNOLDS' LEMON AND BASIL AIOLI

Here he is again: Ollie Reynolds. Fit as a butcher's dog. What a guy!

Makes about 350 g (12½ oz) or enough for 5–10 sandwiches depending on how bad ass you are

1 batch of mayonnaise (page 220), or 250 g (9 oz) store-bought (I like Hellmann's)
2 large garlic cloves
50 ml (1¾ fl oz/3½ tablespoons) extra virgin olive oil
Zest of 1 lemon, plus juice of ½
50 g (1¾ oz) basil leaves
10 ml (½ fl oz/2 teaspoons) apple cider vinegar
Pinch of sea salt

Put all the ingredients (apart from the mayonnaise) into an appropriate receptacle and blend with a stick blender until smooth.

Mix this into mayo, stirring and stirring until completely combined. Oi, oi Thiccston, we're coming for you (page 73).

This will keep nicely for a few days in the refrigerator in an airtight container.

MEMBRILLO MAYO

Membrillo is that quince paste stuff you get at Christmas with cheese round posh people's houses. It's great in a sandwich with leftover roast pork or chicken and it's lovely in any sandwich with pâté in it. It must have millions of uses, most of which I'm sure I haven't thought of. But I did think to blend it into mayo. Tweet me or X me, or whatever.

Makes enough for 5–10 sandwiches depending on what a mayo gangster you are

1 batch of mayonnaise (page 220) or 250 g (9 oz) store-bought mayonnaise (I like Hellmann's)
80 g (2¾ oz) membrillo
1 tablespoon extra virgin olive oil
1 teaspoon sherry vinegar (white wine vinegar will do)
Pinch of salt

Melt the membrillo in a saucepan over a medium heat with the salt, vinegar and oil. Once it's melted, bang the whole lot into the mayo and beat the hell out of it until completely combined. Is it tasty? Is it exactly what you need right now? Perfect. If not, tweaky-tweaky, a bit more vinegar, a bit more salt, a bit more membrillo if you fancy, it's your sauce after all.

This will keep happily for a few days in the refrigerator in an airtight container.

'NDUJA MAYO/CHORIZO MAYO

'Nduja like it? I do actually.

1 batch of mayonnaise (page 220), or 250 g (9 oz) store-bought mayonnaise (I like Hellmann's)
100 g (3½ oz) best 'nduja you can get your mitts on (OR 100 g (3½ oz) fresh, cooking chorizo sausage (sweet or spicy up to you) and a splash of olive oil)
Juice of ½ lemon

If you're making the mayo from scratch, get that done now. If you're using store-bought, bang it in a bowl. Heat the 'nduja gently in a small saucepan, on a low heat, for about 10 minutes until it is liquidy, then whisk it into the mayo to combine. Add the lemon juice and you're done.

To make chorizo mayo instead, you're doing basically the same thing but with fresh cooking chorizo. Take the chorizo out of its skin if it will let you, discard the skin and chop it up into tiny bits; if it won't let you, just chop it up anyway. Cook the bits in a splash of olive oil very gently, in a small saucepan, for a long time (10 minutes?). Press them with the back of a spoon to break them up and get all the gorgeous orange fat to come out of it and (eventually) turn the tiny bits of meat into chewy little bits of awesomeness. Whisk the whole lot, while hot, into your mayo until completely combined.

This will keep for a few days in the refrigerator in an airtight container.

LIME-PICKLE (AND GRAVY?) MAYO

Congratulations on embarking on one of the great sandwiches. I often find Mixed Pickle even better than Lime Pickle for making this, but it's harder to come by, so I won't bang on about it. Feel free to skip the gravy/cooking juices/liquid and just whizz up some pickle and mix it into mayo! Try dunking chips into it, or bhajis, or quite frankly anything, put your finger in there.

Makes enough for 5–10 sandwiches depending on how cool you are

1 batch of mayonnaise (page 220), or 250 g (9 oz) store-bought (I like Hellmann's)
4 heaped tablespoons (your favourite) lime pickle (some might want even more)
6 tablespoons cooking juices from the Goat Tikka Masala Braise on page 160, heated up in a pan (optional)

Use a stick blender to blend the lime pickle (and hot gravy/cooking juices, if using) together until smooth. If it is too dry to blend properly without the gravy, add some vegetable oil. Put the mayo in a bowl and whisk the blended pickle mixture in until completely combined.

This will keep hunky dory for a few days in the refrigerator in an airtight container.

TARRAGON MAYO

This is great with any soft herb – basil, chervil, coriander (cilantro), parsley, etc. Just the leaves though – no stalks!

Makes enough for 5–10 sandwiches depending on how much you like mayonnaise

1 batch of mayonnaise (page 220), or 250 g (9 oz) store-bought (I like Hellmann's)
50 g (2 oz) fresh tarragon, leaves picked
2 teaspoons capers, washed and finely chopped
1 tablespoon tarragon vinegar (if you have it, white wine vinegar if not)
3 tablespoons extra virgin olive oil
Big pinch of salt
1 teaspoon of Dijon mustard (optional)

If you're making the mayo from scratch, get that done now. In a separate bowl or container, blend (for a full 20 seconds), the fresh tarragon with the capers, vinegar and olive oil. If you've had enough blending for some reason, you could just hand chop the tarragon leaves and capers as finely as you can manage.

Bang the mayo and remaining ingredients, into a small bowl and whisk everything together. If your mayo feels too thick with all the gear mixed in, thin it out with a teaspoon of water.

This will keep very well for at least 2 days in the refrigerator in an airtight container.

PO' BOY MAYO

Louisiana, and New Orleans more specifically, is home to a few great sarnies including the mighty Muffuletta and Turkey and The Wolf's Mason Hereford's various entries to the canon. It is the Po' Boy though that floats my boat the most. Barring an occasional braised beef and gravy version, the Po' Boy tends to involve seafood, and as if that wasn't enough, that seafood tends to be dredged/breaded and deep fried...

However different the fishy/meaty elements may be, some things are always about when the Po' Boy's in town. There's always baguette shaped bread, mayonnaise, American mustard, shredded lettuce, pickles and hot sauce (and sometimes melted butter). So, why don't we bring a few of those things together and make a Po'Boy mayo unmistakably reminiscent of Big Mac sauce...

Makes enough for plenty of sandwiches, depending on your mayonnaise politics

1 batch of mayonnaise (page 220) or 250 g (9 oz) store-bought mayo (I like Hellmann's)

2 big dill pickles, coarsely grated

1 teaspoon or tablespoon Louisiana hot sauce of your choosing, depending how spicy you are (I am always spicy, and I always choose Tabasco, but you could go Crystal *bien sur*)

1 tablespoon American mustard (I like French's)

Bang everything in a bowl, mix and mix and mix until combined and adjust with more of anything if the fancy takes you. I'll leave the melted butter to you.

This will keep very well for at least 2 days in the refrigerator in an airtight container.

MORUNOS MAYO

If you mix up everything here with about 75 ml (2½ fl oz/5 tablespoons) extra virgin olive oil, and leave out the mayo, you have one of the great barbecue meat marinades. Just sayin'.

Makes loads

1 batch of mayonnaise (page 220), or 250 g (9 oz) store-bought mayonnaise (I like Hellmann's)

1 teaspoon sweet smoked paprika

1 teaspoon ground cumin

½ teaspoon ground coriander

2 garlic cloves, finely grated, sprinkled with salt and mooshed into a moosh with the side of a big knife on your chopping board

Juice of ½ lemon

If you're making the mayo from scratch, get that done now, if you're using store-bought, bang it in a bowl and whisk everything else in.

This will keep very well for at least 2 days in the refrigerator in an airtight container.

SAFFRON MAYO

Some people think this is a bit much; I love it! Try making this first with half the saffron to see if it floats your boat.

Makes enough for 5–10 sandwiches depending on your heart health

5 ml boiling water
0.25 g saffron
1 batch of mayonnaise (page 220), or 250 g (9 oz) store-bought (I like Hellmann's)
Juice of ¼ lemon
½ garlic clove, finely grated, sprinkled with salt and mooshed into a moosh with the side of a big knife on your chopping board

In a small bowl, pour the boiling water over the saffron, stir and leave to steep for 15 minutes to release the saffron's full colour and flavour.

If you're making the mayo from scratch, get that done now with the garlic in. If you're using store-bought, bang it in a small bowl and whisk in the lemon juice and garlic. Once the saffron's had its 15 minutes, tip it and all the water into the mixing bowl and whisk until combined.

This will keep extremely well for a few days in the refrigerator in an airtight container.

REALLY NAUGHTY BROWN BUTTER MAYO

Gosh this is a naughty thing to do. Life's a joy sometimes. The best bánh mì I ever had, had mayo in it that was so buttery it blew my tiny mind. I couldn't figure out if there was actually butter in it and was unable to enquire further. This is the closest I've got to recreating the flavour and it's really rich and lovely and useful in anything that likes mayonnaise and a certain ethereal buttery richness, which most things do. I've used it in the Bánh Mì on page 85 because I had it in a bánh mì, but I bet you can come up with loads of other things to do with it. Tweet me, or X me or whatever.

Makes enough for 5–10 sandwiches depending on what your doctor's told you

1 batch of mayonnaise (page 220), or 250 g (9 oz) store-bought (I like Hellmann's)
100 g (3½ oz/7 tablespoons) salted butter
Some lemon juice (optional)

Put the mayo in a bowl and ready a whisk.

Melt the butter in a little saucepan on a medium heat. Swill it regularly, round and round. Keep it on the heat until it has foamed, stopped foaming and started going brown. It wants to go as brown as grandma's sherry and be full of little toasty brown bits. I hasten to add that it wants to be brown, not black. If it starts to smoke it has burned and should be thrown away. This is brown butter, not burned, black butter.

Once the butter is nice and dark brown, tip it all into the mayonnaise and whisk and whisk and whisk until it is completely combined. Depending on your tastes, you might want a squeeze of lemon to balance the richness, otherwise, bánh mì away.

This will keep spot on for a few days in the refrigerator in an airtight container.

Ideally, you'll be having this punchy little number alongside garlic mayo and croutons because you're making bouillabaisse, from a book written by someone much more serious than me. If you are, a little of that bouillabaisse would be a great (loosening) addition to this, fishy mayo-ish sauce. I suspect you're not making bouillabaisse though, and there isn't a recipe for it in this book, so just wang it in any fish (finger?) sandwich and see how it goes.

Makes enough for 2–4 sandwiches depending on *joie de vivre* levels

1 thick slice of good white bread, crusts removed and cut into little cubes
0.2 g saffron
2 garlic cloves, finely grated, sprinkled with salt and mooshed into a moosh with the side of a big knife on your chopping board
1 long red chilli, cut into chunks (not too spicy)
Pinch of salt
4 anchovy fillets
1 free-range egg yolk
1 teaspoon red wine vinegar
¼ teaspoon cayenne pepper
100 ml (3½ fl oz/scant ½ cup) olive oil
Juice of ½ lemon

Soak the bread and the saffron strands in enough water from a recently boiled kettle to completely wet the bread and mash it all together with a fork. Allow to cool. If you have made bouillabaisse, use that instead of water.

A French cook might make this in a pestle and mortar, but use a food processor if you have one, it's easier. Put the garlic, chilli, salt, anchovy fillets and completely soaked saffrony bread moosh in the food processor and blitz (or pound) to a paste. You could do this with a stick blender too. Add the egg yolk, vinegar and cayenne pepper, and blitz again until completely combined.

Now, as if making a mayonnaise, slowly drizzle in the oil, blending the sauce as you do so. As the sauce thickens, add a squeeze of lemon juice or two and then return to drizzling in the oil. (Once all of the oil is incorporated, you might want to thin it out a little with some warm water.) Once you're happy with the consistency, give the rouille a taste, adding more lemon, salt or cayenne pepper as you think it needs it. Once you're happy, I'm happy, which makes us all happy. What a day!

This will keep for 2 days in the refrigerator in an airtight container.

COCONUT CHUTNEY

This straddles sweet and savoury, in a slightly weird way. It's odd, but I like it and it's really nice slathered in things involving grilled meat or loads of spices and chowed down.

Makes about 150 ml (5 fl oz/ scant ⅔ cup) or enough for 4 sandwiches

100 g (3½ oz) coconut flesh, grated (or use desiccated/shredded if you have to, but you'll need more water)
30 g (1 oz/¼ cup) salted, roasted peanuts
2 green bird's eye chillies, halved (seeds removed if you're that way inclined)
1 garlic clove, peeled
½ teaspoon ground cumin
Small pinch of fine sea salt
Juice of 1 lime

If you have bucolic notions of hand-muddled chutneys made in a pestle and mortar, you do you, but I like to get a wriggle on when I'm hungry, so it's a blender for me.

Put everything in the blender with 50 ml (3½ tablespoons) cold water and blitz. Keep blitzing. Blitz until you have a smooth paste. Stop blitzing and give it a taste. It should be rich and earthy and spicy and slightly sour, and coconutty. Adjust the lime and salt to your taste. Decant to a jar or bottle and store somewhere cold but within easy reach, like the refrigerator, where it will keep for a week happily. You might want this with the Kati Roll on page 108 or with all manner of things. Go for your life.

TAMARIND CHUTNEY

This sour little legend is as good in sausage sandwiches as curried prawns. Give it a go! Ideally, we'd be doing this with dried tamarind fruit and jaggery, soaking the tamarind in boiling water, blitzing it, cooking it out with the jaggery and spices, then cooling it and using it. Finding dried tamarind and jaggery is not easy though (unless you shop on Sous Chef – just sayin'). Instead, you can reverse engineer the flavour by using tamarind paste, available in many posh supermarkets, and dates, like we've done here, like the bloggers we are.

Makes about 200 ml (7 fl oz/scant 1 cup), which should serve you well for a little while

10 dates, stoned and roughly chopped
100 g (3½ oz) tamarind paste
¼ teaspoon salt
100 ml (3½ fl oz/scant ½ cup) hot water
¼ teaspoon ground coriander
½ teaspoon ground cumin
¼ teaspoon ground ginger
½ teaspoon chilli powder

Using a blender (or stick blender), blitz the dates together with the tamarind paste, half the salt and the hot water. You should have a loose, pouring consistency, so add more water if needed. Once you have the consistency that you're after, add the spices and blitz to combine. Have a little taste – it should be sweet and sour at the same time. Add the rest of the salt if you think it needs it.

This will keep merrily for 2 weeks in the refrigerator in an airtight container.

MEERA SODHA'S CORIANDER CHUTNEY

This will be in every book I ever write and in every refrigerator I ever own. We use it at the Sandwich Shop for tons of things! It's as good with a chicken wing as it is with steak, on grilled (broiled) fish or with roast potatoes. It also as happy mixed into thick yoghurt or mayo as it is on its own. Amazing.

It's got a nice ping from the chillies, and really the only switch from Meera's original recipe is using lime instead of lemon and a touch less sugar. At the Sandwich Shop we also switch the green chillies for pickled jalapeños sometimes, just for the lols.

I always have a jar in the back of the refrigerator to swipe a cheeky carrot, cucumber, cold roast potato or just about anything through when the fancy takes me.

Makes about 250 g (9 oz) or enough for 5–10 sandwiches depending on how much you like it

100 g (3½ oz/large bunch) coriander (cilantro), roughly chopped (stalks and all)
100 g (3½ oz/¾ cup) plain, unroasted peanuts
Juice of 2 limes
2 small green chillies (seeds and all), roughly chopped
½ teaspoon salt
½ teaspoon ground turmeric
2 tablespoons soft light brown sugar
50 ml (2 fl oz) good vegetable oil, such as organic, cold-pressed rapeseed (canola) oil

Pop everything into a blender and blitz until it's got a pesto-like consistency. I often end up adding a tablespoon or two of cold water just to get it to where I like it consistency-wise.

It will keep for up to 5 days in a jar in the refrigerator, not that it tends to last that long.

HONEY MUSTARD

I think this stuff is amazing even if it is often derided in America as a bit 'basic'. Who cares, dunk a chicken nugget (or Select) in that and tell me it's not awesome!

I'd like to pretend this was something cleverer, but what you're doing is mixing honey and mustard in a ratio that you think pleasing. I like 2 parts Dijon mustard to 1 part runny honey.

PICO DE GALLO

Is it a condiment or sauce? Not really, but it's here anyway, hahaha. My mother-in-law (who, like her daughter, my wife, is also called Magali, and is also Mexican) says that the only thing fish and chips (or as she calls it, fish and fries) is missing, is Pico de Gallo – Magali, this one's for you. Fresh, zingy and pleasingly simple, this goes with practically anything, anywhere, at any time, but particularly well, somewhat unexpectedly to most of the UK, WITH FISH AND FRIES!

This recipe makes quite a big batch, which is no bad thing. See if you can find something it doesn't go with. Tweet me, or X me or whatever.

Makes enough for 4 sandwiches, or enough for loads and loads of fish and fries

1 onion, finely diced
Juice of 1 or 2 limes, probably 2, but start with 1 (it's hard to predict the juiciness of your limes)
¼ teaspoon fine sea salt
2 big tomatoes, cored and finely chopped
2 jalapeños (fresh if you if you can get them (seeds removed) or a few heaped tablespoons of pickled slices from a jar), finely chopped
Handful of coriander (cilantro), finely chopped (stalks and all)

Pop the onion into a bowl with the lime juice and salt and let it sit for 30 minutes. Add everything else. Stir it up. Let it sit for 10 minutes or so. Adjust the lime juice and salt to your taste. I'd keep this for 2 days tops.

What a banger. Some people insist that chimichurri should be made with dried, not fresh herbs, because that's what the gauchos do, or did, or something, but Francis Mallmann makes his with fresh herbs, which I think is nicer, so what you gonna do... Slam loads of it in a baguette with a load of chopped-up rare steak or a massive sausage is what I guess Francis would do, and coincidentally.... see page 71.

Makes enough for 4 sandwiches, or enough for plenty of errant dunking/smearing

Large bunch of flat-leaf parsley, leaves picked and finely shredded

½ big bunch of fresh oregano, leaves picked and slightly less finely shredded

4 spring onions (scallions), top 5 mm (¼ in) and rooty bottoms discarded, halved lengthways and very finely sliced (green and white bits)

4 garlic cloves, grated

½ teaspoon chilli (hot pepper) flakes

100 ml (3½ fl oz/scant ½ cup) red wine vinegar

Juice of 1 lemon

250 ml (8 fl oz/1 cup) extra virgin olive oil

¼ teaspoon salt

It's a knife not a blender for this baby! Sorry. Once you have chopped everything up, combine all the ingredients in a bowl. Stir well. Done.

This works on almost everything it touches and is one of my favourite recipes in this whole book. As with all sauces containing garlic and chilli flakes, the flavour will build and develop as it sits. It is delicious almost immediately but leave it in the refrigerator overnight and it might just be even better in the morning. If you like that kind of thing in the morning.

I'd keep this for 2 days tops.

SALSA VERDE/GREEN SAUCE

Sometimes I think Fergus Henderson's right, and that even though it may be a bit of work, it's a sharp knife or nothing for Green Sauce. Chopping it allows the elements to retain their individuality, which is nice.

Then at other times, I love my green sauce blended, because all those separate elements become one, in a rather delicious manner. Tricky.

If you don't have a really sharp knife, and the desire to use it, go blended every time, but if you do have the knife, and the urge to use it, go chopped and see how the dust settles.

Confused? Me too. What I am trying to say, is that even with the same ingredients, you have two different sauces here. Some days one is better, some days the other. Life's awkward innit, but fun all the same. See what you prefer.

Makes enough for 4 sandwiches, or enough for high-level dunking

4 garlic cloves, very finely chopped
6 anchovy fillets, equally finely chopped
1 heaped tablespoon capers, drained, rinsed and finely chopped (if salted, soaked in water for 10 minutes, drained and finely chopped)
1 tablespoon Dijon mustard
1 tablespoon red wine vinegar
Juice of 1 lemon
Large bunch of flat-leaf parsley, stalks and all, leaves picked and finely chopped
½ large bunch of dill, finely chopped (stalks and all, apart from the really thick stalks below the first fronds)
½ large bunch of mint, leaves picked and finely chopped, stalks discarded
250 ml (8 fl oz/scant 1 cup) good extra virgin olive oil (or maybe less if you're chopping not blending)
Salt

If you're blending, whack the whole lot in a blender and blend it. If you're chopping, chop it all, and add the oil at the end, stirring it in until it's oily and nice but not oily and runny. You want a loose-ish texture. It shouldn't look oily, but it shouldn't look dry either. What a fine example of recipe writing this is. Sorry.

This stuff's sandwich credentials are a path well-trod, but it's amazing with any meat or fish really, stirred into some beans, or whisked up in a salad dressing! Crack on and see what happens. Creo en la magia.

Oh, yes! I once met a guy who loved making salsa verde for dunking raw vegetables in for his lunch. He always blended his and found that sometimes it was too runny and didn't stick to his veg well enough. His solution was to blend a fully boiled potato into the sauce, which I have done again recently. Man's a legend and clearly a top-level dunking connoisseur, and an admirer of a nice smooth salsa verde, I'll tell you that.

I'd keep this for 2 days tops.

It's like a red salsa verde, right? Not really, no. But it is very good. The salsa rossa spectrum goes from roughly chopped to finely pulsed and in some places, it is even a cooked sauce. I like it to have a bit of texture and be quite arresting and vinegary, so it cuts through stuff and livens things up. As with all salsas, play around with it, find a flavour and texture that suits you.

Makes enough for 4 sandwiches, or enough for plenty of drizzling and slathering

100 ml (3½ fl oz/scant ½ cup) extra virgin olive oil

1 teaspoon crushed fennel seeds

2 garlic cloves, sliced wafer thin

400 g (14 oz) good ripe tomatoes, cored, finely chopped, juice retained if possible

2 roasted red (bell) peppers, skinned and finely chopped (page 203), or use the ones from those posh jars

1/2/3 long red chilli(es) – up to you, halved, deseeded and finely chopped

3 tablespoons red wine vinegar

½ teaspoon salt

10–12 grinds of black pepper

Place a saucepan on a low heat and add the oil. Give it a couple of minutes to warm, then add the crushed fennel seeds and garlic, let them gently cook in the oil and, when the garlic starts to colour at the edges and go sticky, add the chopped tomatoes, peppers and chilli. Toss this about in the hot garlicky oil and let it all warm through so that the flavours get to know one another. Add the vinegar, salt and pepper and remove from the heat.

If you want you can blend this to a smooth sauce, or you can leave it on the heat and keep cooking it slowly for 10 minutes or so until more intense. That's a different vibe though.

Stick a finger in. Does it want more oil? More vinegar? More salt? More chilli? Or is it perfect, just as it is?

You can serve this as is, still warm, or let it cool and use it at room temperature. It is really good with any white fish that's been boiled, grilled (broiled), steamed, fried, roasted, barbecued or… is there anything else? It's really good with all cooked fish.

I'd keep this for 2 days tops.

SALSA FRESCA

This is for the torta ahogada on page 91 but that is not to say that's its only use! It's so nice that it must be handy in many other sarnies and for many other things that need a little pick-me-up. You could also have it for lunch, on toast, in the garden, in the summer, with a bottle of Sancerre. Just sayin'...

   A food processor, rather than a blender, is ideal here because you don't want it chunky exactly, but you don't want it liquid smooth either, do you know what I mean?

Makes enough for 4 sandwiches

4 big, fat, ripe tomatoes
½ teaspoon ground cumin
1 red onion, chopped
2 garlic cloves
2 tablespoons organic
   (cold-pressed if possible)
   rapeseed (canola) oil
   or extra virgin olive oil
½ teaspoon salt
½ teaspoon sugar
Juice of 1 lime

Razz the whole lot in the food processor so some of the texture remains. Your work here is done.

   The reason there is no chilli in this is that you add chopped fresh habanero to the salsa yourself when you have the sandwich.

   Keep for 2 days tops.

234

SALSA CASERA

This one is for the second torta ahogada on page 91. Unlike the zingy salsa fresca in the other one, this is cooked, sweeter, smoother and a good deal richer. You might recognise the name of this one as you can buy tins of the stuff from good shops stocking Mexican produce. In the UK it's often from that brand La Costena, which I know is everywhere in the US too. Anyway, here's how you can make your own!

Makes enough for 4 sandwiches

12 very special dried yahualica chillies (use chilli de árbol if you can't get these)

1 small (or ½ large) red onion

2 garlic cloves, smashed

1 teaspoon good, dried oregano (or epazote if you can find it)

1 teaspoon ground cumin

125 ml (4 fl oz/½ cup) white wine vinegar

75 ml (5 tablespoons) organic (cold-pressed if possible) rapeseed (canola) oil or extra virgin olive oil

½ teaspoon fine sea salt

The only tricky bit of this recipe is heating the dried chillies correctly, don't burn them, but they do need to be exposed to heat. Get a dry frying pan (skillet) on a medium heat and when hot put the chillies in. Toast for 2 minutes, turning and pressing regularly from side to side until they noticeably soften and their scent starts to fill the air. That's it. Remove from the heat, cut the stalks off the tops, squeeze most of the seeds out, and throw the peppers in a blender.

Next, add the onion, garlic, oregano, cumin, vinegar and 50 ml (3½ tablespoons) of water to the blender and blitz to a smooth paste. Give it a full minute of blending; this wants to be smooth. You might need a splash more water to help everything along. Once smooth, pour the sauce into a bowl through a sieve (fine mesh strainer) to get any little bits out. Use a spatula to moosh everything you can through the sieve.

Finally, add the oil to the frying pan and return it to the heat. When the oil is hot, add the strained salsa to the pan. It will sizzle and whine, which is exactly what you want as this effectively scalds the salsa and helps give it a distinctive taste. It will settle to a simmer, and once it does, add the salt, give it a good stir and leave it to bubble away for 5 minutes or so until slightly thickened and darkened. Remove from the heat, and sandwich.

The main choice with a cooked salsa torta ahogada is whether to have the sauce hot or not (temperature wise). Have both and see what you prefer.

I'd keep this for 2 days tops.

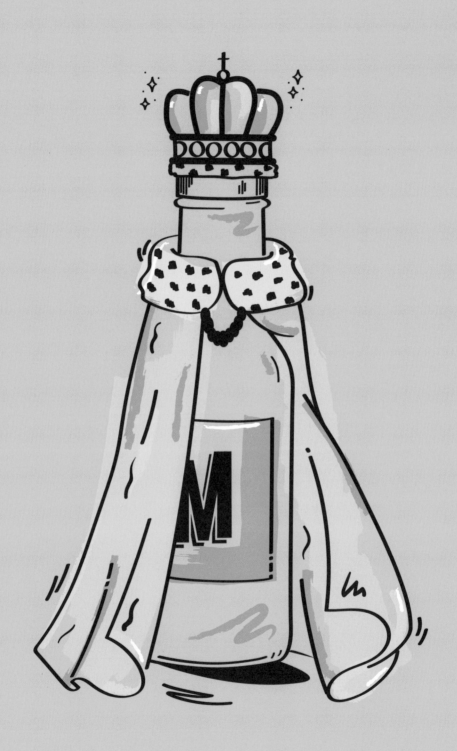

CORONATION SAUCE

This is destined for the Coronation Fried Chicken Sandwich on page 81, but equally, if you have some leftover poached (or roast) chicken, you're in luck.

Makes enough for 2 sandwiches

2 heaped tablespoons store-bought
 mayonnaise (I like Hellmann's)
2 heaped tablespoons
 full-fat Greek yoghurt
1 tablespoon mild madras
 curry powder
1 teaspoon red wine vinegar
Salt and pepper

Mix all the ingredients together. As always, give it a taste. Bit flat, up the curry powder and vinegar. Lacking depth, bit more salt and pepper. Too rich, maybe a drop of lemon juice or again a splash more vinegar. How easy is that?! And so much better than all those fancy ones. And none of that almonds and raisins rubbish – it's not a chocolate bar, it's a chicken sauce, what were they thinking?

This will keep for 3–4 days, at least.

AMBA

I cannot hear the name without thinking of bugs encased in beautiful goo and Jurassic Park and my Dad for whom it was the PERFECT movie, because it involves not only a car chase AND dinosaurs, but A CAR CHASE INVOLVING A DINOSAUR. Between me and you, I have occasionally used mango chutney with lime juice in it instead of amba when making a Sabich (page 56) at home, but that would doubtless make my friend Itamar want to kill me (if my uselessness hasn't already!?) and it's not really in the spirit of writing a genuinely good cookbook is it? In one of their many brilliant cookbooks (Honey & Co. at Home) legends Sarit Packer and Itamar Srulovich have a wonderful recipe for amba and the spice mix it is based on, which I have mostly amalgamated for this recipe. Big love Honeys. This sauce really brings a Sabich to life and must have a thousand other uses too. Because of its similarity to piccalilli it'd certainly be lovely in a ham, egg 'n' chips sandwich! Make some, whack it on stuff, see what you think.

Makes enough for 4–6 Sabich

1 teaspoon ground turmeric
1 teaspoon fenugreek seeds
1 teaspoon mustard seeds
1 teaspoon amchoor powder
1/2 teaspoon cayenne pepper
The flesh of 2 ripe mangoes
4 tablespoons extra virgin olive oil
½ onion, very finely diced
½ teaspoon fine sea salt
2 garlic cloves, grated
Zest and juice of 1 juicy, unwaxed
 lemon (use 2 if you can't get
 amchoor powder, but it isn't
 the same obvs)

All the dry ingredients (including the salt) need crushing together into a powder. Use a pestle and mortar, spice grinder or anything you can think of to get them there.

Blend the mango flesh until smooth.

Put the oil in a saucepan and put it on a medium heat. Once hot, add the onion and garlic and cook for 5–6 minutes, stirring regularly, until soft and nice. Add the spices and cook for a few minutes, stirring regularly. Sling in the blitzed mango pulp and bring it all up to the boil, whip it off the heat, add the lemon zest and juice, stir thoroughly and allow to cool before whacking in an airtight jar.

Kept in the refrigerator, this should keep for a week.

PIRI PIRI SAUCE

The piri piri chillies that give this addictive sauce its name are quite similar to the little firecracker bird's eye chillies often found in Southeast Asian cookery. If you want to ensure prime authenticity, you can buy fresh and dried piri piri chillies online, but it might be easier/cheaper to buy those bird's eye ones. This sauce somewhere between to the piri piri oil that you'll commonly find in Portugal and the piri piri sauce that you'll find at your local Nando's.

Makes enough for about 6 sandwiches, or enough for plenty of drizzling and dunking

8–10 red bird's eye chillies, green tops removed
1 roasted, skinned red (bell) pepper (page 203), or 1 from those nice jars
4 garlic cloves, peeled
150 ml (5 fl oz/scant ⅔ cup) extra virgin olive oil
Juice of 1 lemon
½ teaspoon fine sea salt

Pop all the ingredients in a blender and blitz to a smooth sauce. If you want it faultlessly smooth, pass it through a sieve (fine mesh strainer). I don't mind a bit of texture but see how you go.

This'll keep for a week at least, but it will separate and need the hell shaking out of it to bring it back together.

BLACK OLIVE TAPENADE

Tap, tap, tapenade. I really recommend trying this with green olives too. It's a different vibe, more treble, less bass, but still wonderful. If you can, use those posh Gordal ones. Lovely!

Makes enough for 4 sandwiches

2 garlic cloves, grated
1 tablespoon capers (drained if in liquid and rinsed if in salt, then drained)
Zest of 1 unwaxed lemon and maybe some juice
½ teaspoon chilli (hot pepper) flakes
Small bunch of parsley, leaves picked, and stalks finely chopped
4 sprigs of thyme, leaves picked
200 g (7 oz) black olives with stones, stones removed (don't buy those pitted black olives)
100 ml (3½ fl oz/scant ½ cup) extra virgin olive oil, plus extra if desired

Dust off your food processor. Into the bowl of said machine, add the garlic, capers, lemon zest, chilli flakes and parsley stalks. Blitz until they are a sticky mess, scraping everything down in the bowl whenever necessary, and then add the parsley leaves and thyme. Blitz again.

Add the olives to the mixer along with half the olive oil. Blitz again in short pulses so as to retain some texture to the sauce. Taste it.

You can add some lemon juice at this point if you want a little sharpness, but otherwise I suspect you will be feeling pretty smug. If you want your sauce to be a little looser, add the other half of the oil and give it another little blend.

This is very useful in sandwiches when mixed with yoghurt or mayo to temper it a bit and an absolute classic with leftover lamb. I had a Turkish girlfriend once and the first time I ever stayed at her parents' house they (and I) all had tapenade on toast for breakfast and I just loved it!

This will keep a few days I reckon.

TZATZIKI

Tzatziki loves nearly all roasted or barbecued things and is an excellent accompaniment to far too many things for me to list here. Try it out for yourself, I dare you.

Round mine and Magali's dear friends Nick and Talia's house for Sunday lunch once, Nick casually said he'd roasted a chicken, which he had, but he served it unexpectedly with tomatoey, braised green beans, potatoes cooked in the chicken tray and tzatziki, and it was just AMAZING!

Makes enough for 4 – it could be 4 sandwiches, or on the side of a meal for 4

1 large cucumber, peeled, cut in half lengthways and seeds removed with a spoon
2 big garlic cloves, grated
½ teaspoon salt
2 tablespoons extra virgin olive oil
450 g (1 lb) full-fat, thick yoghurt
1 tablespoon red wine vinegar

In the sink, grate the cucumber into a sieve (fine mesh strainer) or colander, on the coarse side of a box grater and leave it to sit for 20 minutes.

In a nice bowl, put the grated garlic, oil, salt, yoghurt and vinegar. Mix this about and leave to stand while you wait for your cucumber to be ready.

Once 20 minutes is up, take the cucumber in your hands and squeeze and squeeze it. Water will come out. Nice. Mix the cucumber into the yoghurt and you're done. Try it. Add more salt and/or vinegar if you think it needs it.

You could strain the yoghurt for this, but part of the joy is that this is easy, so I won't make you do that. But you could if you want. Ask the chatbot.

I'd say this'll last 2 days kept in the refrigerator (3–4 tops).

CACIK

Without wanting to incite anything, cacik and tzatziki are quite similar. The devil's in the detail.

Makes enough for 4, could be 4 sandwiches, or on the side of a meal for 4

1 large cucumber, peeled, cut in half lengthways and seeds removed with a spoon
½ teaspoon salt
450 g (1 lb) full-fat, thick yoghurt
2 garlic cloves, grated
30 ml (2 tablespoons) extra virgin olive oil
Juice of ½ lemon
2 teaspoons dried mint

In the sink, grate the cucumber into a sieve (fine mesh strainer) or colander, on the coarse side of a box grater.

Squeeze the cucumber to remove as much water as possible and then bang it in a bowl with all the remaining ingredients and mix the hell out of it. Taste it. Adjust salt and lemon to your taste.

At the Sandwich Shop we often make this with 50/50 cucumbers and dill pickles, all grated and sat in a sieve. It is SO good.

This'll keep, in the refrigerator, for 2 days definitely, 3 days almost certainly.

HORSERADISH SAUCE

I like Colman's horseradish sauce from a jar loads, but I like this even more and it can blow your socks off if you're not careful; whether you've got 'em on or not, watch out.

Makes enough for 4 sandwiches, plus some

40 g (1½ oz) fresh horseradish, peeled and finely grated

150 ml (5 fl oz/scant ⅔ cup) really posh crème fraîche (I like Crème d'Isigny)

¼ teaspoon salt

Juice of ¼ lemon

½–1 teaspoon caster (superfine) sugar, depending on your preference (optional – but Simon Hopkinson does it, just sayin')

Mix all the ingredients together and you're good to go. If I've got some of this in the refrigerator, there's little I won't have it with – pizza, fish and chips, anything. It's great with Rachel Roddy's boiled meat (page 170), or in the boiled meat sandwich (page 106), or in most sandwiches to be honest.

This'll keep the best part of a week in a little Tupperware in the refrigerator.

GREEN GODDESS SAUCE

We've got Alice Waters' *Chez Panisse Vegetables* book to thank for this one! It's a banging sauce and goes miraculously well with nearly anything it touches – for breakfast, in a sandwich with a few poached eggs like they do at the Allpress Espresso Roastery? Yes, please. I find basil in blended herb sauces makes everything taste like pesto so I have left that out.

Makes enough for 4 sandwiches, easily

1 shallot, very finely diced

1 garlic clove, very finely chopped

3 tablespoons white wine vinegar

Juice of 1 lemon

½ avocado

2 nice anchovies (those Cantabrian ones are great), finely chopped

120 ml (4 fl oz/½ cup) extra virgin olive oil

100 ml (3½ fl oz/½ cup) double (heavy) cream

50 g (1¾ oz) flat leaf parsley, leaves picked and finely chopped

50 g (1¾ oz) tarragon, leaves picked and finely chopped

50 g (1¾ oz) coriander (cilantro), leaves picked and finely chopped

Salt and pepper

Put the shallot and garlic in a bowl and let them sit in the vinegar and lemon juice for 20 minutes like you're making pico de gallo (page 230) in a rush. After 20 minutes put the avocado and anchovies in there and mash, mash, mash everything together with a fork or the end of a whisk.

Next, whisk in the olive oil and then the cream a bit at a time, like you're making mayo, until completely combined.

Now, all you've got left to do is bang the herbs in, give it some salt and pepper, stir it all up and laugh all the way to the flavour bank. Good, innit?!

This one's not a keeper, it's got fresh cream in it you see. Tomorrow it'll be fine, but the day after that you wanna chuck it straight out.

ANOTHER VINAIGRETTE

Thanks to Ben, I know the greatest vinaigrette of all time is 1 part lemon juice, 3 parts olive oil and some salt, but sometimes you want something a bit clingier. In that scenario, this is a certified banger.

Makes about 100 ml (3½ fl oz/ scant ½ cup), which would dress a whole salad for 4–6 people

4 tablespoons olive oil
1½ tablespoons lemon juice
1½ teaspoons Dijon mustard
½ garlic clove, grated
¼ teaspoon salt
Little squeeze of runny honey if you're that way inclined (optional)

I like to bang this all in a lidded jar and shake it to wake it. You can razz it up in a blender too or whisk it all together in a little bowl, it's your call.

Once suitably emulsified, taste it and adjust the acid, saltiness and sweetness according to your palate.

You can bang a teaspoon of mayo in here too if you want it really clingy, which can be extremely pleasing when staring down the barrel of a salad for lunch or some plain, boiled green beans you don't know what to do with.

Why would you keep this? If you did, give it a few days and sling it out.

BALSAMIC REDUCTION

A 90s throwback that deserves its place in your sandwiching arsenal, just in case the drizzle comes back or something...

1 bottle of cheap balsamic vinegar (likely 200–250 ml/ 7–8 fl oz/scant 1 cup–1 cup)
1 teaspoon caster (superfine) sugar per 50 ml vinegar

Pop both the vinegar and sugar into a pan and swirl to combine. Place on a medium heat and bring to a simmer. Reduce the heat to low and simmer for 10–20 minutes or until reduced by about two-thirds. Remove from the heat and leave to completely cool. It will continue to thicken as it cools, which is cool. Once cool, pop it in a bottle or airtight container and drizzle it on stuff.

As this is vinegar and sugar, it will keep until the sun dies and all life on earth ceases to exist, but for the benefit of our publisher's legal team, let's say this will keep unrefrigerated for 2 weeks in an airtight container.

TOUM

This garlic sauce is very addictive indeed, and it leaves you an unwelcome conversational partner, breathwise, for a good while after consumption. Another plus is that it's very easy to make.

Essentially it is a close cousin to alioli, or is it aioli, well, whichever one is just garlic and oil and salt and lemon juice, and it shares more than a similarity to entry level skordalia, but that's for another day, and clearly, another book.

Makes enough for 4 sandwiches, or enough for plenty of drizzling and dunking

1 whole head of garlic, cloves
   separated, peeled and halved
1 teaspoon fine sea salt
Juice of 1 lemon
300 ml (10 fl oz/1¼ cups) extra
   virgin olive oil

Add the garlic cloves and salt to a food processor and blitz until a complete smoosh. Stop occasionally and scrape down the sides to make sure everything is completely blitzed. Add half the lemon juice and continue to blitz. Add the remaining lemon juice and blitz until the smoosh starts to look white and vaguely fluffy.

Now we're into mayonnaise technique territory. With the food processor running, very slowly (at first), drizzle the oil into the sauce. Go nice and slow. Once you've added half the oil, add a tablespoon or two of very cold water just to loosen the sauce a bit. Return to the oil and drizzle quicker until everything is incorporated. If your sauce is still quite thick, add a little more water, perhaps a tablespoon or two, and mix until you have the consistency of runny mayonnaise. This and grilled meat in a sandwich? Ooofff...

This'll keep 3 full days in the refrigerator, I reckon.

ZHOUG

Zhoug is a fiery and puckering herby little number with a spicy punch you want to watch out for, especially as you never really know how hot a chilli is until you've banged it in something. Consequently, you could use less than asked for below.

Makes enough for 4 sandwiches, if not more

1 teaspoon fine sea salt
1 teaspoon cumin seeds, ground
½ teaspoon coriander seeds, ground
2 garlic cloves, roughly chopped
4 green chillies (I like the long ones
   with a bit of a kick), chopped
Juice of ½ lemon
Small bunch of flat leaf parsley
   (stalks and all)
Small bunch of coriander (cilantro)
   (stalks and all)
100 ml (3½ fl oz/scant ½ cup) extra
   virgin olive oil

Some argue you get a superior flavour from using a pestle and mortar here, but I can never be bothered. Just use a food processor or a blender.

Start by adding the salt, cumin and coriander seeds, garlic and green chillies to the food processor and blitzing. Add the lemon juice and blitz again. Then add the herbs and oil and pulse until you have a nice rough herby sauce. I like a bit of texture to my zhoug, but if you want a smoother sauce, continue to pulse until you have something you like the look of.

This'll keep for 2 days in the refrigerator.

MEXICO'S SALSA VERDE

One of the finest salsas to ever lubricate a lengua (tongue). The Mexicans have done it again. My wife Magali and I made Mexican pizzas at our friend Ethan's pizza restaurant with this as a base instead of tomato sauce and they were AMAZING! It is sour, fresh, refreshing, tingly, spicy and basically everything that is nice in the world that isn't a dessert or act of kindness. It works great with anything fatty, roasted, barbecued or braised and is an integral part of one of the great breakfasts: chilaquiles. Seeing as you've sourced a tin of tomatillos, we're using it all here, so this makes a large amount, but that is no bad thing, unless you only need a little bit of course, then it's a total nightmare.

Makes enough for about 20 sandwiches, or enough for endless drizzling and dunking

1 tin (about 750 g/1 lb 10 oz) tomatillos, drained
  (El Mexicano whole tomatillos are available online and are pretty good)
1 onion, chopped
3 fresh jalapeños or green chillies (seeds and all)
50 g (2 oz) coriander (cilantro), washed (stalks and all)
Juice of 1 lime (you might need more, so keep another couple up your sleeve or arsenal)
½ teaspoon salt

Sling all the ingredients in the blender and whizzzzzzzzzzz. Does it need more lime?

  Starts to lose its fun vibe after 2 days in the refrigerator. But technically keeps about a week.

243

THE SANDWICH SHOP'S ATTEMPT AT GÖKYÜZÜ'S CHILLI SAUCE

This is the chill sauce we use in the An Ode to An Adana sandwich at the Sandwich Shop and that is on the Ode to Adana Hotdog on page 53.

It is magnificent alongside anything grilled (broiled), barbecued or rich and fatty, especially when paired with a big blob of cacik (page 239).

Makes enough for 8 sandwiches, or enough for plenty of drizzling and dunking, get some friends round

400 g (14 oz) proper nice, dark red, ripe and nearly squidgy tomatoes
100 g (3½ oz) roasted red peppers (page 203), or posh ones from a jar
1 onion, chopped
6 tablespoons extra virgin olive oil (or use the oil from the pepper jar if you like)
150 g (5½ oz) pickled guindillas (those pickled, crunchy, green chillies in a jar)
1–2 tablespoons guindilla pickle juice from the jar (maybe more, keep it all)
4 garlic cloves, chopped
1 tablespoon pul biber
1 tablespoon caster (superfine) sugar
1 teaspoon fine sea salt

Add all the ingredients to a blender, blitz it all up, taste it, adjust it as you please with more pickle juice, salt or sugar, eat it all over stuff.

This'll keep for 5 days in the refrigerator.

BARBECUE SAUCE

Hello barbecue sauce. What are you saying?

Makes enough for 5 or even 10 sandwiches

2 tablespoons vegetable oil
1 small onion, grated
1 garlic clove, grated
2 tablespoons tomato purée (paste)
200 g (7 oz/scant 1 cup) tomato ketchup
2 tablespoons Dijon mustard
75 g (2½ oz/⅓ cup) soft light brown sugar
120 ml (4 fl oz/½ cup) cider vinegar
1 teaspoon salt
1 teaspoon freshly ground black pepper
1 teaspoon ground cumin
1 teaspoon sweet smoked paprika

Heat the oil in a large pan on a medium–low heat. Add the onion and garlic and cook for 10–12 minutes until caramelised and really gooey. Add the tomato purée and cook that out for 2 minutes to remove the rawness, then add all of the remaining ingredients, stir to completely combine and dissolve all the sugar, then simmer really gently for 10(ish) minutes (might take 20) on a low heat until you have a thick, sticky sauce. You could blend it and strain it to make it smooth, but I suspect it would be messy, and really sticky.

This keeps for a week in the refrigerator.

TALEGGIO BÉCHAMEL

This is from the lasagna sandwich (page 127), and it is naughty. I once melted loads of 'nduja into it too to make lasagna with and it was REALLY NAUGHTY! This would be amazing with scamorza too.

Makes enough for 4 sandwiches

50 g (1¾ oz/3½ teaspoons) butter
50 g (1¾ oz/6 tablespoons) plain (all-purpose) flour
500 ml (17 fl oz/generous 2 cups) milk
1 teaspoon fine sea salt
10–12 grinds of black pepper
¼ nutmeg, grated
200 g (7 oz) Taleggio, cubed

Melt the butter in a saucepan on a medium heat. Once frothing, add the flour and stir to a paste. Cook for 5 minutes until brown and biscuity, stirring loads. Start adding the milk and it'll turn to a dough. Then, as you add more and more milk, a big glug at a time, whisk and whisk it in until combined and smoothed every time – by the time the milk runs out ta-da, you've got béchamel.

You can now gently simmer it until it thickens to how you want it, which I think isn't as thick as some make it. Especially when you're about to put cheese in it. Add the salt and pepper and nutmeg, then the Taleggio and whisk until all the cheese is melted. Then you're off.

If this goes cold it'll go firm and look a bit weird, but trust me, it's still great and you can still smear it on top of the bolognese for a lasagna sandwich and grill (broil) it to melt it and be extremely happy with the results.

This keeps for 5 days in the refrigerator.

TARAMASALATA OR COD'S ROE
(IF YOU'VE EVER WORKED IN A TRENDY LONDON RESTAURANT)

That neon pink gear in supermarkets has its place, arguably in the Bánh Mì Sandwich on page 85 for example, but the proper stuff, made from scratch, is reminiscent of all good Greek holidays, and even more delicious. Here's how to get there, without buying a plane ticket!

Makes enough for 4–6 sandwiches, or plenty to use as a dip like you're back in Tinos, smoking hashish with Marcos

80 g (2¾ oz) good white bread, crusts cut off and cubed
1 whole, fresh cod's roe (about 200 g/7 oz), cut in half and all the roe scooped out and the skin discarded
Juice of 1 lemon
½ garlic clove, grated
100 ml (3½ fl oz/scant ½ cup) extra virgin olive oil

Before anything else, pop the bread in a bowl with a few tablespoons of water and mix it about and mash it with a fork a bit. Leave that to one side to soften while you pop the roe, lemon juice and garlic into a blender. The bread should now be a soft pulp, squeeze any excess water out and pop the moosh into the blender too. Blend.

With the blender still running, add the oil in a steady stream, much like mayo, and once it's all combined, you'll have a very good tarama/cod's roe ready for your Bánh Mì Sandwich (or some radishes with their leaves left on, or anything else you like).

This harissa right here is Tunisian harissa. Tunisia is where harissa is from. The word itself comes from 'harasa', to pound, to break into pieces, you might say, to harass. You can buy very, very good harissa. The rose harissa from Belazu Fine Foods is still one of the most addictive concoctions you can put in your mouth, especially mixed into yoghurt and dunked with roast potatoes. I keep a large commercial-size bucket of the stuff in my refrigerator at all times. If you have a harissa you feel equally strongly about, keep that in stock and use it liberally, mixed into mayo or yoghurt, or spread on any available breaded surface, you'll find more and more excuses to use it. If you don't have a favourite brand and would like to make some yourself, there is no pounding below, but certainly some harassing from a blender.

Makes loads, almost 750 g (1 lb 10 oz), although you'll get through this quicker than you might imagine, I imagine!

150 ml (5 fl oz/scant ⅔ cup) extra virgin olive oil, plus extra to finish
2 teaspoons cumin seeds
1 teaspoon caraway seeds
3 garlic cloves, grated
200 g (7 oz) tomato purée (paste)
300 g (10½ oz) pul biber or Aleppo chilli flakes
1 tablespoon fine sea salt
1 tablespoon red wine vinegar

Heat a pan on a medium heat and add the oil. Once hot and starting to shimmer, add the cumin and caraway seeds and allow to sizzle for 30 seconds or so (but not to burn) before adding the garlic, allowing that to sizzle and to turn a little golden. Then add the tomato purée and cook it out for 1–2 minutes, stirring constantly.

Remove from the heat and add the chilli flakes, salt and vinegar. Leave to cool for a minute before adding 300 ml (10 fl oz/1¼ cups) water and stirring to combine. Return to the heat, bring to a simmer and leave blip, blip, blipping away on a low heat for 15–20 minutes, stirring occasionally, until the harissa has reduced to a loose paste and become one homogenous thing.

Leave to cool before checking the seasoning and adding more salt or vinegar as you think right.

Store in sterilised jars (page 253) with a layer of oil on top to seal the sauce. Kept in the refrigerator you'll easily get a month out of this, although I suspect you'll have snaffled it all before then.

PICCALILLI

This is the piccalilli recipe from the first sandwich book, but I wanted to put it in again, because when teamed up with some ham hock meat (page 158), one of Harry Mackintosh's Slow Fried Eggs (page 212), some shoestring fries (page 214) and some mayonnaise with malt vinegar in it, you can recreate the Sandwich Shop's signature Ham, Egg 'n' Chips Sarnie! Woo Hoo! You could always divide everything by 2, 3 or 4 and make a smaller amount. Or even 5 or 6.

---

200 g (7 oz) cauliflower or Romanesco cauliflower, leaves and all, cut into pea-sized chunks

200 g (7 oz) broccoli, cut into pea-sized chunks

200 g (7 oz) fine green beans, chopped into short lengths

200 g (7 oz) carrots, peeled and grated

200 g (7 oz) shallots, peeled and finely chopped

100 g (3½ oz) fennel, cut into pea-sized chunks

4 red chillies, halved, deseeded and finely chopped

50 g (1⅓ oz) salt

1 teaspoon cumin seeds

1 teaspoon coriander seeds

15 g (½ oz) yellow mustard seeds

10 g (½ oz) ground turmeric

10 g (½ oz) English mustard powder

20 g (¾ oz/3 tablespoons) cornflour (cornstarch)

600 ml (20 fl oz/2½ cups) white wine vinegar

2 apples, grated

2 mangoes, peeled, stoned and roughly chopped

150 g (5½ oz/¾ cup) caster (superfine) sugar

3 garlic cloves, crushed

2 tablespoons dried oregano

4 bay leaves

3 x 750 ml (25 fl oz) sterilised Kilner (Mason) jars (page 253)

This recipe needs a little planning. You could cut up all the veg and whack it in a bowl in the refrigerator the day before because it is a mammoth task. Whether you chopped it yesterday or not, sprinkle the cut veg with the salt and use your hands to combine well. Cover with a tea towel (dish towel) or cling film (plastic wrap) and leave for 6–8 hours or overnight. When you are ready to make the piccalilli, drain the resulting liquid from the bowl, and bang the veg in a colander and wash it well under cold running water and let it drip dry or 10 minutes or so.

Meanwhile, in a spice grinder or using a pestle and mortar, add the cumin seeds, coriander seeds and mustard seeds and crush to a powder. Next add the turmeric, mustard powder and cornflour and grind together. Finally, add 2 tablespoons of the vinegar and mix into a loose paste.

Place a saucepan large enough to hold all your vegetables over a high heat and add the apple, mango, sugar, garlic, oregano, bay and remaining vinegar to the pan. Bring to the boil, stirring the mix occasionally to ensure that the fruit and sugar break down and dissolve. Once boiling, add the spice paste to the liquid and stir until it has completely combined. Add all the vegetables.

Cook for 15 minutes on a low heat, stirring gently but regularly, until the vegetables have just softened and started to release some juice. Spoon into sterilised jars (page 253) and leave to cool. Once cool, make mini cartouches (there's a video of how to do this on the @lunchluncheon YouTube channel, or you could ask the chatbot) and press them onto the top of the veg inside the jars and store in the refrigerator for 3–4 weeks before using. The wait will be worth it; trust us. And you'll have enough to give EVERYONE some for Christmas!

PICKLES

IMPORTANT: How to sterilise your jars

To get started, buy an at least 1 litre (34 fl oz/4¼ cups) Kilner (Mason) jar just for pickling. I am a foolish rogue, and at home often pickle things in Tupperware that I have handwashed, and experience no unwanted bacterial side-effects at all, but I hope you understand, I cannot recommend that you do that. I must advise you to only use glass, and to sanitise properly, every time. It just isn't responsible/safe not to.

To sanitise a Kilner (Mason) jar, preheat the oven to 180°C (350°F). Separate the lid, the jar, the metal ring thing and the rubber ring and wash them all thoroughly in hot soapy water. Dry them with a clean dish towel. Keeping them all separate, put the jar (standing the right way up), lid and metal ring thing (NOT the rubber ring), on a baking tray and bang them in the preheated oven for 10 full minutes. Carefully take the tray out of the oven and leave everything to cool completely. Put the jar back together without touching the inside. Congratulations, you have sterilised.

If you have a dishwasher, this is the errant sanitiser's simpler friend. Run your jars, lids and bits (again all separated) through the machine on a hot cycle, allow them to dry naturally and once reassembled (without touching the insides of the jar), you are ready to go.

If you're good and properly sanitise your jars prior to pickling, your little goodies will last until well after Elon Musk has settled the moon, or Mars or whatever it is he's doing.

The last thing to point out is fingers. NEVER put your fingers in the pickle jar. Always get your goodies out with a clean fork or tongs or something, not your digits. Fingers in the jar is how gatecrashers get into the pickle party, and they always end up ruining things.

Here's the Sanitising To Do List one more time, so you can tick it off:

☐ Preheat the oven to 180°C (350°F)

☐ Wash jar, lid and the rubber ring in hot soapy water

☐ Dry with a clean tea towel (dish towel)

☐ Put jar, metal thing and lid (not rubber ring) in the oven for 10 minutes

☐ Take out, let cool and reassemble without touching inside the jar.

☐ Use a clean fork to remove pickles, NEVER put your fingers in the pickle jar! **253**

PICKLING LIQUOR INTRODUCTION AND MY GO-TO PICKLING LIQUOR

Read the section on sterilising on the previous page before reading this. I'll see you back here in a minute.

The pickling liquor recipe below will pickle nearly anything. It is so simple; some might call it too simple. There's no dried this or dried that, because when not done right, those things tend to either do nothing or distract from the main act, end up bitter or just get stuck in your teeth.

This section of the book is intended as a method and inspiration, as much as a list of specific things to do. Go wild, use dried this and dried that if you so wish, pickle the s**t out of it. Most firm vegetables (and some fruits) pickle very well – experiment. On the train to Pickletown you may find something that doesn't take to it, but they are few and far between. It's normally worth trying again but leaving the bits bigger, or indeed, cutting them up smaller. Size makes a huge difference – the bigger/thicker and denser something is, the longer it takes to pickle. And if your garlic goes blue, it's weird but edible, not botulism, ask the chatbot about it.

The only things to really remember are that you should a) use a sanitised jar (page 253) and b) make sure the things you are pickling are submerged in the liquid. If they're floaty, light things and drifting to the surface, cut a small circle of greaseproof paper (baking parchment) the same size or a little larger than the inside of your jar and using tongs or a fork or something, press it down onto the surface of the liquid. Ta-da, problem solved.

The recipe below is a classic 3:2:1 pickle liquor. It's what we use for everything at the Sandwich Shop and is the only time I can think of where the potential vagaries of the American cup system work better than the metric system. Because it's very high in vinegar and sugar, it pickles things quickly (small things in a matter of 4–5 hours), which is invariably useful in the constant panic that is running a restaurant.

When it comes to the precise amount of liquid needed to fill a jar/cover your pickles, this is not an exact science because I can't be sure how small or large you've cut your veg or how small or large your vessel of choice is. If you do start with a 1 litre (34 fl oz/4¼ cups) jar though, one batch of this liquor will have you covered for sure. One big English cucumber chopped into chunks and put in a 1 litre (34 fl oz/4¼ cups) Kilner (Mason) jar, will need 600–700 ml (20–24 fl oz/2½–scant 3 cups) liquid to easily cover everything, and the recipe below makes a litre. Dreamy.

For 1 batch

3 cups (750 ml/25 fl oz) white wine or cider vinegar
2 cups (460 g/1 lb) caster (superfine) sugar
1 cup (250 ml/8 fl oz) water

Put all the ingredients into a saucepan (along with any dried aromatics you might have decided to go rogue and use – whole dried chillies, coriander seeds, mustard seeds, celery seeds, ground turmeric etc etc) and bring the liquid to just below the boil, stirring until all the sugar is dissolved. Take the pan off the heat and leave the liquor to cool completely, before tipping it into the jar over the things you are pickling.

If you are using undried things in your pickles (for example: slices of ginger, chopped shallots or fresh herbs – generally dill is best, but tarragon can be nice too), add them to the pickle jar before the cooled liquor goes in.

If you are pickling lots of things (or less things) and need to use jars bigger or smaller than 1 litre (34 fl oz/4¼ cups), as long as you keep the ratios the same, you can double or halve (etc) the liquor recipe to your heart's content.

Please read the page on sterilising jars (page 253) and the pickling liquor recipe (page 254) BEFORE going about this recipe.

Mirepoix (carrot, onion and celery) is the foundation of flavour in vast swathes of French cookery and every bit as ubiquitous in much Italian and Spanish cooking, where it is called soffritto/sofrito respectively. In Cajun cookery (where it is often referred to as the Holy Trinity) the same function is performed by onion, celery and green (bell) peppers, which would also make a great pickle.

These are from the Sandwich Shop's Lasagna Sandwich so probably have the wrong name, but that's how it's worked out somehow.

Should fill a 1 litre (34 fl oz/4¼ cup) Kilner (Mason) jar, which is enough for loads of lasagne sandwiches

250 g (9 oz) each of carrot, onion and celery
1 batch of Pickling Liquor (page 254), cooled

Make sure your liquor has completely cooled.

While it cools, peel the onions and carrots and trim the top and bottom from the celery stalks. Cut everything into very small chunks of as even a size as you can manage.

Put all the veg into a 1.5-litre (51-fl oz/6¼-cup) Kilner (Mason) sterilised jar (page 253) and top up with the cooled liquid until everything is completely submerged, pressing a round of greaseproof paper (baking parchment) onto the top of the liquid with a fork, if necessary, to keep things below sea level. These want a day before being used.

This will keep for months in the refrigerator as long as it stays submerged and you never put your grubby little fingers anywhere near the inside of the jar.

PICKLED JALAPEÑOS
(OR ANY CHILLI YOU LIKE, REALLY)

Please read the page on sterilising jars (page 253) and the pickling liquor recipe (page 254) BEFORE going about this recipe.

These little firecrackers will run a spicy rumba across your lengua while puckering you up with one hand and sating your greedy little need for sweetness with the other. Long story short, they're like bottling spicy crack.

You could use any chilli here and slice them up or even leave them whole (pricked right through with a skewer a few times) depending on how spicy you like things and what you want to use them for. Those nice long, pale green Turkish chillies work wonderfully when pickled this way and left whole (pricked right through with a skewer a few times).

Should fill a 1-litre (34-fl oz/ 4¼-cup) Kilner (Mason) jar

350 g (12 oz) fresh jalapeños, destemmed and sliced quite thickly (5 mm/¼ in)
1 batch of Pickling Liquor (page 254), still warm

With this one, you're putting the liquor into the sterilised jar and over the chillies while it's still warm (not hot, but warm – you get me? Leave it for 10–15 minutes after you turn the heat off), which makes for a slightly softer chilli, which I think is nice, but you may disagree. If you do and you want to keep all that crunch, let the liquor cool completely before chucking it in the jar.

Once you've tipped the warm (or not) liquid over the chillies, make sure they're completely submerged, pressing a round of greaseproof paper (baking parchment) onto the top of the liquid with a fork, if necessary, to keep things below sea level. Seal the jar up while the liquor is still warm, let it cool completely, then bang it in the refrigerator.

It is best to wait 48 hours for these. They'll keep for at least a month in the refrigerator, as long as they stay submerged and you never put your fingers in.

Please read the page on sterilising jars (page 253) and the pickling liquor recipe (page 254) BEFORE going about this recipe.

These certainly are an addiction and a crucial component of one of my favourite sandwiches: Meatloaf, Pommes Purée and Pickled Carrots (page 104). I eat them straight from the jar (got out with tongs or a fork!) like some people might eat popcorn or crisps.

If you're making these for the Bánh Mì on page 85, substitute half the weight of carrots for peeled and julienned mooli/daikon. You can julienne and pickle loads of things. You could add julienne cucumber to the carrot and daikon. You could julienne beetroot (and turn all your pickles purple) or kohlrabi, turnips (so farty), the possibilities are endless.

I really hope you've bought an OXO Good Grips Julienne Peeler by now or making these is gonna be a NIGHTMARE. If you've got the julienne peeler, it's easy. If you haven't, just pickle them in long thin strips done with a regular veg peeler (and the same thing with the mooli/daikon if you're using that), otherwise you'll be there all bloody day.

Should fill a 1 litre (34 fl oz/ 4¼ cup) Kilner (Mason) jar

700 g (1 lb 9 oz) carrots, julienned
1 batch of Pickling Liquor
 (page 254), cooled

Pack your sterilised jar with the carrots (and mooli/daikon) without touching the inside and pour in the cooled pickling liquor until everything is completely covered, pressing a cut round of greaseproof paper (baking parchment) down onto the surface of the liquid with a fork or something if things are poking their heads above the liquid.

Seal the jar, put it somewhere cool and dark, like the refrigerator. These will be pretty tasty after 3 hours or so, but if you can bear to wait give them a day if you can. Remember, mooli/daikon is from the Brassica family and, like radishes, gets a little pongy when pickled. Not kimchi or sauerkraut pongy, but a little sexy pong nonetheless.

These will keep for a month in the refrigerator as long as they stay submerged and you never put your mucky little fingers anywhere near the inside of the jar.

PICKLED CUCUMBERS

Please read the page on sterilising jars (page 253) and the intro/pickling liquor recipe (page 254) BEFORE going about this recipe.

So many of the sandwiches in this book require and/or would love the crunch and piquancy of a pickled cucumber that it would be criminal not to give you a recipe, and as long as you've got some time on your hands, these are super fun. The sliced bigger cucumbers will pickle quicker than the whole mini ones.

Should fill a 1 litre (34 fl oz/ 4¼ cups) Kilner (Mason) jar

650 g (1 lb 7 oz) tiny cucumbers about the length of a middle finger (you might need to visit a proper greengrocer for these, but the supermarkets do sometimes sell them)

OR

650 g (1 lb 7 oz) big (normal) cucumber, cut into 5 mm (¼ in) thick rounds (not those tough-skinned, knobbly cucumbers you guys in America get though, the nice thin-skinned ones we get in England that HEB etc normally sell as 'English Cucumbers')

1 batch of Pickling Liquor (page 254), cooled

Put the cucumbers in your sterilised 1-litre (34-fl oz/4¼-cup) Kilner (Mason) jar. Don't touch the inside of the jar. If the cucumbers don't fit in the jar, either make another jar, or eat the extras with your lunch or as a tasty snack. Fill the jar with the cooled pickling liquor.

The cucumbers need to be completely submerged by the liquid, so, if necessary, press a cut round of greaseproof paper (baking parchment) onto the surface of the liquid with a fork or some tongs or something.

With the rubber ring on the lid, close it up and pop the jar somewhere dark and cool, like the refrigerator, for 24 hours (a week for whole little cucumbers). These will keep for months as long as they stay submerged and you never put your naughty little pickle-snaffling fingers into the jar.

TINKERINGS:

My friend Lorcan Spiteri makes the best burger I've ever had at Studio Kitchen in London, and he makes classic dill pickles to go in it. He always uses those smaller, really crunchy, thin-skinned cucumbers and cuts them into nice fat rounds. These are when a pickle does want things added to it: add 1 heaped teaspoon of ground turmeric and 1 teaspoon of yellow mustard seeds to the liquor before you heat it up and stuff half a bunch of dill into the jar with the cucumber slices before pouring the cooled liquid in. Done.

These should arguably have been in a different section because this is really a salad, not a pickle, but it's too late now innit?! One of the easiest ways to knock this up is to have a ready supply of chilli oil (with bits, always). Lao Gan Ma is probably the world's best-known brand, but maybe you have another favourite? Maybe you read Fuchsia Dunlop's cookbooks or have the *Xi'an Famous Foods* book and make your own like a boss, who knows.

Makes enough for 4 people to have as an accompaniment

This version is for if you DON'T have and can't get Lao Gan Ma Crispy Chilli in Oil (or another brand, or some you've made):

2 large, whole (English) cucumbers

4 tablespoons rice wine vinegar

2 tablespoons light soy sauce

½ teaspoon sesame oil

3 tablespoons tahini (remember to always stir the hell out of the jar)

½ teaspoon chilli (hot pepper) flakes

2 garlic cloves, grated

½ teaspoon salt

½ teaspoon sugar

Some coriander (cilantro), if you have it, finely chopped

This version is for if you DO have Lao Gan Ma Crisp Chilli in Oil (or another brand, or some you've made):

2 large, whole (English) cucumbers

3 tablespoons oil from the Crispy Chilli Jar

1 heaped tablespoon of the bits from the Crispy Chilli jar

1 tablespoons light soy sauce

2 garlic cloves, grated

½ teaspoon salt

½ teaspoon caster (superfine) sugar

2 tablespoons rice wine vinegar (use black Chinkiang vinegar if you have it, use white wine vinegar if you have to)

1 tablespoon malt vinegar

1 teaspoon sesame oil

½ teaspoon crushed Sichuan peppercorns (a pestle and mortar will be handy here) (if you can get them)

Whichever version you are making, give your cucumbers a wash, put them on your chopping board then whack them, one at a time, from top to bottom, with something heavy like a rolling pin. Rotate the cucumber 90 degrees and whack it up and down again. You don't want to crush them completely but hit them until they crack open and split and break. Once they've cracked and split, top and tail them and cut them into quarters lengthways and cut those into 3 cm (1¼ in) chunks on a diagonal (apparently this is called 'a lozenge'). The great thing about these is that the smacking makes the insides all jaggedy and really good at soaking up the sauce.

Thoroughly whisk all the ingredients other than the cucumbers in a large bowl. Stick your finger in. Does it need more vinegar, is it salty/spicy/garlicky enough, etc? Adjust it to your taste. It should be punchy. Throw the cucumbers in, mix everything about and get cracking.

These are great served with any roasted/grilled meat dishes especially with rice there to soak up that sauce and are an unexpected treat in all kinds of sandwiches. Experiment! Try them in a bun with the Red Braised Pork on page 159 and some plain, boiled rice – isn't the rice brilliant in a sandwich?!

At home, I often steam a variety of veg and dress it with the second dressing as an accompaniment to many dinners involving grilled or roasted meat and as I said, often rice. I steam radishes, little turnips, baby gem lettuce quarters, celery, tons of stuff. I always use the second dressing because I always have chilli oil (Fuchsia Dunlop's recipe in *The Food of Sichuan* is great, as is the much more complicated version in Jason Wang's cookbook *Xi'an Famous Foods*).

I find these don't keep well at all. Something about the saltiness/acidity of the dressing pulls too much water out of the cucumbers and they stop being nice. Eat all these in one sitting.

As I said in the first Sandwich Book, these are simple to make, and stupidly useful in sandwiches.

Makes enough for 4 sandwiches

1 large red onion, peeled and finely
  sliced
Juice of 1 lime
¼ teaspoon salt
1 teaspoon nigella seeds (optional)

Put the sliced onion in a Tupperware with the lime juice and salt and massage them all together. Squeeze, squeeze, squeeze. Lid on, and shake, shake, shake. That's it. The longer you leave them in the refrigerator (3–4 days) and the more regularly you shake the hell out of the tub (5 times a day?), the more insanely lurid pink and lip-puckering they'll become, which is a good thing. I have been known to keep these at home in the refrigerator for weeks and they sometimes start to fizz and ferment, which is fun, and delicious. They are also great (but no way near AS great) and WAY less pink if you don't touch them again after making them.

If your lime is a bit hard, give it a good firm roll on your chopping board under the ball of your hand before cutting it, you'll get oodles more juice from it that way.

If you want to make these even livelier, add a sliced red chilli and you can always switch the lime for lemon.

Using the method above (and with loads of violent shaking – every ten minutes?), the onions will be tasty and usable after 2 hours if you're in a rush.

Just before you eat these, you can mix the nigella seeds through them. Only do it just before consumption though, otherwise they'll swell and lose the pleasing smokey pop/crunch thing they have going on.

BIBLIOGRAPHY

A Good Bake by Melissa Weller (Knopf, 2020)

Alpine Cookery by Meredith Erickson
(Ten Speed Press, 2019)

Appetites Cookbook by Anthony Bourdain
(Bloomsbury Publishing, 2016)

BAO by Erchen Chang, Shing Tat Chung and
Wai Ting Chung (Phaidon Press, 2023)

Bistro Cooking by Patricia Wells (Kyle Books, 2010)

Bread by Jeffrey Hamelman (John Wiley & Sons, 2004)

Charcuterie by Michael Ruhlman and Brian Polcyn
(W. W. Norton & Company, 2005)

Charcuterie and French Pork Cookery by Jane Grigson
(Michael Joseph, 1967)

Chez Panisse Vegetables Cookbook by Alice Waters
(William Morrow Cookbooks, 2004)

Chez Panisse Café Cookbook by Alice Waters
(William Morrow Cookbooks, 2004)

Chez Panisse Menu Cookbook by Alice Waters
(Random House, 1995)

Classic Food of China by Yan-Kit So (Papermac, 1994)

Cookin' With Coolio by Coolio (Simon Schuster, 2009)

Eat Me by Kenny Shopsin (Knopf, 2008)

Eating at Hotel Il Pellicano by Will Self
(Violette Editions, 2013)

Feast by Anissa Helou (Ecco, 2018)

Five Quarters by Rachel Roddy (Headline, 2015)

Fog City Diner Cookbook by Cindy Pawlcyn
(Ten Speed Press, 1993)

Food of Life by Najmieh Batmanglij
(Mage Publishers, 2011)

Franklin Barbecue by Aaron Franklin and Jordan Mackay
(Ten Speed Press, 2015)

French Regional Cooking by Anne Willan
(Hutchinson, 1983)

From Julia's Kitchen by Julia Child (Alfred A. Knopf, 1975)

Grand Livre de Cuisine by Alain Ducasse
(Ducasse Books, 2009)

Grill Smoke BBQ by Ben Tish (Quadrille Publishing, 2016)

Heston Blumenthal at Home by Heston Blumenthal
(Bloomsbury, 2011)

Honey & Co at Home by Sarit Packer and
Itamar Srulovich (Pavilion Books, 2018)

Honey From a Weed by Patience Gray
(Prospect Books, 2001)

Hunan by Mr Y. S. Peng and Qin Xie
(Preface Publishing, 2014)

India Cookbook by Pushpesh Pant (Phaidon Press, 2010)

Is This A Cookbook? by Heston Blumenthal
(Bloomsbury Publishing, 2022)

Jane Grigson's Vegetable Book by Jane Grigson
(Penguin, 1998)

Japanese Cookery by Shizuo Tsuji (Kodansha Amer, 2012)

Jeremiah Tower's New American Cookbook by
Jeremiah Tower (Harper Collins, 1986)

Julia and Jacques Cooking at Home by Julia Child
and Jacques Pepin (Alfred A. Knopf, 1999)

La Grotta Ices by Kitty Travers (Square Peg, 2018)

La Mère Brazier by Eugénie Brazier (Modern Books, 2016)

La Tante Claire by Pierre Koffmann (Headline, 1994)

Le Gavroche Cookbook by Michel Roux Jr (Cassell, 2001)

Leaves of the Walnut Tree by Anne and Franco Taruschio
(Pavilion, 1995)

Lisboeta by Nuno Mendes (Bloomsbury Publishing, 2017)

Made in India by Meera Sodha (Fig Tree, 2014)

Mallmann on Fire by Francis Mallmann (Artisan, 2014)

McDonald's Behind the Arches by John F. Love
(Bantam Books, 1995)

Meat by Anthony Puharich and Libby Travers
(Murdoch Books, 2018)

Mediterranean Seafood by Alan Davidson
(Prospect Books, 2012)

Memories of Gascony by Pierre Koffmann
(Mitchell Beazley, 2012)

Mexico The Cookbook by Margarita Carrillo Arronte
(Phaidon Press, 2014)

Modern Cookery for Private Families by Eliza Acton
(Quadrille Publishing, 2011)

Modernist Cuisine by Nathan Myhrvold and Maxime Bilet
(The Cooking Lab, 2012)

Mosquito Supperclub by Melissa M Martin
(Artisan, 2020)

My Mexico City Kitchen by Gabriela Cámara
(Vintage, 2019)

Nancy Silverton's Breads From La Brea Bakery
by Nancy Silverton (Villard Books, 1996)

New Classic Cuisine by The Roux Brothers
(Little Brown, 1989)

North Atlantic Seafood by Alan Davidson
(Prospect Books, 2003)

Nose to Tail Eating by Fergus Henderson
(Bloomsbury Publishing, 2004)

Of Cabbages and Kimchi by James Read (Penguin, 2023)

On Food and Cooking by Harold McGee
(Scribner Book, 2004)

Pig Curing and Cookery by Ambrose Heath
(Faber and Faber, 1952)

Pitt Cue Co by Tom Adams, Simon Anderson,
Jamie Berger and Richard Turner (Mitchell Beazley, 2013)

Plenty by Yotam Ottolenghi (Ebury Press, 2010)

Pork and Sons by Stephane Reynaud
(Phaidon Press, 2007)

Portugal The Cookbook by Leandro Carreira
(Phaidon Press, 2022)

Prashad (Cooking with Indian Masters)
by J. Inder Singh Kalra (Allied Publishers, 1986)

Prune by Gabrielle Hamilton (Random House, 2014)

Real Cajun by Donald Link
(Clarkson Potter Publishers, 2009)

Revolutionary Chinese Cookbook by Fuchsia Dunlop
(Ebury Press, 2006)

Road Food by Jane and Michael Stern (Perennial, 1992)

Roast Chicken and Other Stories by Simon Hopkinson
(Ebury Press, 1999)

Sandwich by Bee Wilson (Reaktion Books, 2010)

Secrets of the Red Lantern by Pauline Nguyen
(Murdoch Books, 2007)

Seven Fires by Francis Mallmann (Workman Publishing,
2013)

Short and Sweet by Dan Lepard (Fourth Estate, 2011)

Summer Collection by Delia Smith (BBC Worldwide, 1994)

Tacopedia by Déborah Holtz and Juan Carlos Mena
(Phaidon Press, 2015)

Tartine Bread by Chad Robertson (Chronicle Books, 2010)

The Art of Fermentation by Sandor Katz
(Chelsea Green Publishing, 2013)

The Book of Jewish Food by Claudia Roden
(Penguin, 1999)

The Book of Schmaltz by Michael Ruhlman
(Little, Brown, 2013)

The Bread Book by Linda Collister and Anthony Blake
(Sedgewood, 1994)

The Carved Angel Cookbook by Joyce Mullineux
and Sophie Grigson (Grafton, 1992)

The Chinese Kitchen by Deh-Ta Hsiung
(Kyle Cathie, 2010)

The Clatter of Forks and Spoons by Richard Corrigan
(Fourth Estate, 2008)

The Complete Bocuse by Paul Bocuse (Flammarion, 2010)

The Complete Nose to Tail by Fergus Henderson
and Justin Piers Gellatly (Bloomsbury Publishing, 2012)

The Complete Robuchon by Joel Robuchon
(Grub Street Publishing, 2008)

The Constance Spry Cookbook by Constance Spry
and Rosemary Hume (Grub Street Publishing, 2011)

The Cook's Companion by Stephanie Alexander
(Viking, 2005)

The Curious Cook by Harold McGee
(John Wiley & Sons, 1992)

The Dooky Chase Cookbook by Leah Chase
(Pelican Publishing, 1990)

The Essential Cuisines of Mexico by Diana Kennedy
(Crown Publications, 2000)

The Essentials of Classic Italian Cookery by Marcella
Hazan (Boxtree, 2011)

The Family Meal by Ferran Adrià (Phaidon Press, 2011)

The Fifth Floor by Henry Harris (Fourth Estate, 1998)

The Food Lab by Kenji Lopez-Alt
(W. W. Norton & Company, 2015)

The Food of Sichuan by Fuchsia Dunlop
(Bloomsbury Publishing, 2019)

The Food of Vietnam by Luke Nguyen
(Quadrille Publishing, 2013)

The Futurist Cookbook by F. T. Marinetti (Penguin, 2014)

The German Cookbook by Alfons Schuhbeck
(Phaidon Press, 2018)

The Mile End Cookbook by Noah and Ray Bernamoff
(Clarkson Potter, 2012)

The Nordic Cookbook by Magnus Nilsson
(Phaidon Press, 2015)

The New Best Recipe by America's Test Kitchen
(Cook's Illustrated, 2004)

The Oxford Companion to Food by Alan Davidson
(Oxford University Press, 2006)

The Oxford Companion to Italian Food by Gillian Riley
(Oxford University Press, 2009)

The Prawn Cocktail Years by Simon Hopkinson
and Lindsey Bareham (Michael Joseph, 2006)

The Quality Chophouse by William Lander,
Daniel Morgenthau and Shaun Searley
(Quadrille Publishing, 2019)

The Red Rooster Cookbook by Marcus Samuelsson
(Harvest Publications, 2016)

The Sopranos Family Cookbook by Artie Bucco
(Little, Brown & Company, 2002)

The Turkish Cookbook by Musa Dagdeviren
(Phaidon Press, 2019)

The Mughal Feast by Salma Yusuf Husain
(Roli's Books, 2021)

The Weekend Cook by Angela Hartnett
(Bloomsbury Absolute, 2022)

The Whole Chicken by Carl Clarke (Hardie Grant, 2020)

The Zuni Café Cookbook by Judy Rodgers
(W. W. Norton & Company, 2003)

Today's Special by Anthony Demetre (Quadrille
Publishing, 2008)

Traditional Portuguese Cooking by Maria de Lourdes
Modesto (Verbo, Editorial, 2001)

Vefa's Kitchen by Vefa Alexiadou (Phaidon Press, 2009)

Week in Week Out by Simon Hopkinson
(Quadrille Publishing, 2007)

Xi'an Famous Foods by Jason Wang (Abrams, 2020)

I still cannot believe we get to write these ourselves hahaha!

Max Halley is fitter than Brad Pitt, better hung than a
Manet exhibition and the world's number 3 classical pianist.

Ben Benton is a cook, writer and restaurant consultant.

MAX'S ACKNOWLEDGEMENTS

Ben Benton, YOU ARE AMAZING!!!!

Agostino Carrea, for making this book, the cover and everything else as good, funny, magical and downright bloody beautiful as can be. Despite all our best efforts to the contrary.

Eila Purvis, for letting Ago work his magic, having a vision of the project as a whole and for being a joy to work with.

Eve Marleau, without whom no one would be holding this book at all, and without whom Ago would never have got to make it this good.

Robert Billington and Jack Storer, for the brilliant, BRILLIANT photographs and making the entire shoot such a fun, generous, creative and welcoming environment to work in.

Alexander Breeze, for the boundless brilliance, refined good taste and for showing all the members of the Magic Circle what 'magic touch' really means.

Coco and Cecil, welcome to the world; the next one's for you.

Ned, Sheila and Lydia, as always, for being the best of the best.

My godchildren Arthur Betts and Zephyr Hodgkinson Bridle YOU ARE BOTH BRILLIANT AND I LOVE YOU BOTH VERY MUCH!!!

Socorro, Magali and Pedro, thanks for having me. *No puedo esperar a verlos de nuevo, estar juntos y verlos con Coco.*

Marcus and Sandra Clapham, Jessica Ramirez and Claudia Reading, for making our wedding day so special (and for the washing machine)!

James Pamphlion and Tom Mcsweeney, welcome to the fam. The Sandwich Shop is dead. LONG LIVE THE SANDWICH SHOP.

Cam Fraser, for being utterly, relentlessly brilliant and one the true freaking greats.

Dre Stylianou, for being utterly reliable, charming and always knowing how we do things.

Harry, Rosie, Sophia, Seth, Reuben and all the Sarnie Shop legends!!!!

Will McSweeney, for everything and all that's to come.

Simon Thomas, Matthew King, George Constantinou, Chris Barrett, Salvo Russo, Ioannis Grammenos, Madjid Chaouche, Mike Haydon and all at the Hippodrome Casino.

Tony the Butcher for being a SUPERSTAR!!!

Woffy and all at Tabasco for being generous, fun and extremely supportive.

Mark Sadler/Forces Creative, for being the best of the best.

Ethan and Millie. Nuff said. Ethan, you know all you do and all you have done. Thank you mate. Your kindness and generosity know no bounds.

Jordan Davids, Tommy Tullis, Toby Wilson and the pubs fam, for everything.

Faye and Itamar, 'Ocelots Forever', even though it's been too long.

Sarah Moakes, for being consistently kind and lovely despite the permanent nightmares.

Simon Allenby, for keeping the wolf from the door.

Gav Singleton, for always being ready and dotting all the 'I's and 't's.

Josiah Newbolt, for the brilliant films we've made together, and all the lols obvs, and all the more to come!

Simon Rimmer, Tim Lovejoy, Paddy Ruddy, Maddie Coombe, Charlie Critchfield, Grainne Hallinan and all the Sunday Brunch Fam, for continued generous support and welcoming me in!!! Thanks for everything guys.

Ben Canning and Liam Askarian, for everything, often.

Julian Ornelas, for being the coolest cat ever. Mexico Magico.

Isaac Lee-Kronick, for making the best music ever and being an utter joy.

Neil Gill, Jamie Green, Ben Falk, Michael Chalmers and James Bridle, for never-ending friendship and always being there, even if I'm not.

Alex Gkikas for new-found friendship, coffee and sauce.

Emy, Mahfuz and Polat and all the guys at Emy's, you are the best neighbours ever.

Josh and Pippa, for putting up with all the drunk phone calls. Now I mention it, that's a long list...

Mr Merry, Kat, Elsie, Arthur and George, I hope y'all live forever. Vegas Baby!

Owen Barratt, for the Sausage Parties and all the dinners, lols, walks and sausages just generally really. So, so, so much luck with Owen's Sausages and Hams.

Fin and Lorcan Spiteri, for everything you do and have done. Thanks boys.

Johnnie The Window-Cleaner, for always being about and using our phone to entertainingly call the MOST insalubrious people on the planet.

Joe Beeching, for getting shit done and lessons in green.

Michael Hill, Finlay Renwick, Junyin Gibson and all at Drake's for taking a punt and making something rather fun. And for the gorgeous suits OBVS.

Charlie Teasdale, for being a badass.

Ed Cumming, for always being willing to listen to stupid ideas.

Lisa Markwell, for being a total legend and always taking an interest.

Wong Kei, for 30 years of lunches.

Poppy and all at Fernet Brangca, for being generous and amazing.

La Colombe d'Or, for being the best place in the world.

BEN'S ACKNOWLEDGEMENTS

To Eila and Marleau, for having the patience of saints.

To Ago, for having the patience of a saint.

To Dr Billington, for having the patience of a saint.

To Harriet, for having the patience of a saint.

To Max, for absolutely everything else.

INDEX

269

Published in 2024 by Hardie Grant Books,
an imprint of Hardie Grant Publishing

Hardie Grant Books (London)
5th & 6th Floors
52–54 Southwark Street
London SE1 1UN

Hardie Grant Books (Melbourne)
Building 1, 658 Church Street
Richmond, Victoria 3121

hardiegrantbooks.com

Text © Max Halley and Ben Benton
Photography © Robert Billington
Photograph on page 9 © Magali Halley
Illustrations © Agostino Carrea

British Library Cataloguing-in-Publication Data. A catalogue
record for this book is available from the British Library.

Max's World of Sandwiches
ISBN: 978-1-78488-600-4

10 9 8 7 6 5 4 3 2 1

Publishing Director: Kajal Mistry
Commissioning Editor: Eve Marleau
Senior Editor: Eila Purvis
Design and illustrations: Agostino Carrea
Copy-editor: Vicky Orchard
Proofreader: Gillian Haslam
Photographer: Robert Billington
Food Stylists: Max Halley, Ben Benton and Robert Billington
Prop Stylist: Alexander Breeze
Production Controller: Sabeena Atchia

Colour reproduction by p2d
Printed and bound in China by Leo Paper Products Ltd